THE ACTOR'S CHEKHOV

Nikos Psacharopoulos and the
Company of the Williamstown Theatre Festival,
on the plays of Anton Chekhov

THE ACTOR'S CHEKHOV

Nikos Psacharopoulos and the
Company of the Williamstown Theatre Festival,
on the plays of Anton Chekhov

Written and Edited by Jean Hackett

SK
A Smith and Kraus Book

A Smith and Kraus Book
Published by Smith and Kraus, Inc.

COVER AND TEXT DESIGN BY JULIA HILL
Manufactured in the United States of America

First Edition: March 1993
10 9 8 7 6 5 4 3 2 1

The publisher kindly thanks the Williamstown Theatre Festival for the use of the photos in this book.

Library of Congress Cataloging-in-Publication Data
Hackett, Jean.
    The actor's Chekhov : Nikos Psacharopoulos and the company of the
    Williamstown Theatre Festival, on the plays of Anton Chekhov, 1962-
    1987 / edited and written by Jean Hackett. --1st ed. p. cm.
    "A Smith and Kraus Book."
    ISBN 1-880399-27-x : $23.95 (hard cover). -- ISBN 1-880399-05-9 :
    $14.95 (pbk.)
    1. Chekhov, Anton Pavlovich, 1860-1904--Stage History-Massachusetts.
    2. Chekhov, Anton Pavlovich, 1860-1904--Dramatic production.
    3. Actors--United States--Interviews. 4. Acting, I. Psacharopoulos,
    Nikos, d. 1989. II. Williamstown Theatre Festival (Massachusetts)
    III. Title.
    PG3458.Z9S836   1993
    792.9'5--dc20   93-19960
                                                    CIP

Acknowledgments

I'm very grateful and moved by the actors interviewed here, who gave so generously of their time, energy and talent to this project. I thank Peter Hunt and the Williamstown Theatre Festival for more than access to archive material, but that too. Former WTF Artistic Associate Bonnie Monte also helped me find and put the pieces together, as did WTF Board member Irwin Shainman. Steve Lawson, WTF's man for all seasons, guided me the entire way, with his unerringly good editorial taste and with his usual genius for detail and accuracy.

Marisa Smith and Eric Kraus supported me, challenged me, and most importantly understood what I was trying to do, sometimes even more than I did. I can't imagine a more rewarding author/publisher relationship. As well, I'm lucky to have for an agent someone with the values and integrity of Susan Schulman.

And I thank some wonderful friends - Barry Creyton for offering his clear thinking as well as his laser printer; my New York friends Betsy Aidem and Carrie Nye who read portions of the manuscript and offered invaluable suggestions; and my L.A. friends Rhonda Aldrige and Laura Wernette, who shared my day-to-day struggle as a first time writer. My family was also involved: my sister Joyce who often did an extremely helpful first edit of the interviews, my sister Julie often gave me the benefit of her insight; and my parents (who Nikos also called "family") cared and enthused and encouraged. And I thank Carol Lubetsky, who helped me find my work again.

Nikos, directing

for Nikos

TABLE OF CONTENTS

Foreword

Williamstown Theater Festival is in the heart of the Berkshire Mountains in western Massachusetts. There is an energy in the bones of WTF that is unlike any other theater in the world. Presiding over it from 1956 until his death in 1988 was a remarkable original, a man named Nikos Psacharopoulos.

Williamstown has always loomed for me as some sort of grail, some sort of initiating holy place you had to pass through to be officially in the theater.

I had gone to Yale School of Drama from 1960 to 1963 and studied directing with Nikos. Nikos would always talk about one's work being 'plas-teek' or 'not plasteek' enough. Was he instructing us in explosives by talking about the bomb ingredient 'plastique' that terrorists used? He proclaimed it with such authority one could never be sure of what it was that Nikos was actually saying. It was like studying with the I Ching. The carrot at the end of Nikos' directing class was an invitation to come work for the summer at WTF, which of course never came for me because I couldn't direct my way out of any kind of bag. Besides I was a playwright and Nikos' theater did not specialize in doing new plays. It was an actor's theater.

However, in 1973 I was doing a new play called *"Rich and Famous"* at the Academy Festival Theater in Lake Forest, Illinois with Ron Leibman, Linda Lavin and Charles Kimbrough directed by Mel Shapiro when we got a call from WTF. Would we be interested in playing "Rich and Famous" at Williamstown? We all jumped at the chance.

Williamstown that summer of 1973 was everything I had imagined. It seemed to be the capitol of my favorite state: inspired chaos. I loved the enthusiasm of the apprentices and I wrote parts for them into the play. (One of them grew up to be the brilliant George C. Wolfe.) Nikos saw *"Rich and Famous"* and gave me notes about my play, but I still couldn't understand anything he said.

The show before ours was "Private Lives" with John Cunningham and a late and lamented actress, Virginia Vestoff. I kept going to see it as often as possible because it showed a whole new way of doing Noel Coward: muscular and musical and hilarious. Years later, when we were casting "Six Degrees of Separation" at Lincoln Center, I remembered the spontaneous elegance and wit of John Cunningham's Williamstown performance and happily cast him.

In 1987 I worked again at Williamstown on a new play called "*Moon Over Miami*". The dream cast (a Williamstown specialty) included Nathan Lane, Lewis J. Stadlen, Julie Hagerty, Glenne Headley, Laurel Cronin, Max Wright and James Belushi. Nathan at one point in our insane summer of rewriting and rehearsal, screamed out in frustration and mad glee (again, a Williamstown specialty): "This is the weirdest play I have been in!" (Again, not the first time those words have been uttered at WTF.) Jerry Zaks who came to see the play saw Nathan for the first time and years later would cast him in "*Guys and Dolls*".

Williamstown is a place where actors shine in a way that they've never shone before. For example, Jon Robin Baitz went to Williamstown, saw Ron Rifkin for the first time and wrote "*Substance of Fire*" for him. But what happened with John Cunningham or Ron Rifkin or Nathan Lane is not guaranteed. Williamstown is a place where actors have been known to go out for a cigarette and call in hours later that they were back in New York. Williamstown is a place where a troupe of actors have assembled for the first day of rehearsal to learn that Nikos had forgotten to hire a director. But at its best - and a person, a place must only be judged by its best - Williamstown is a place where actors who are brilliant find a way to extend themselves even further. Maria Tucci and James Naughton giving definitive performances in "*Night of the Iguana*" and "*The Rose Tattoo*". Forever Christopher Walken will be my idea of Vershinin and then there was Frank Langella's Cyrano. And Stockard Channing in "*The Homecoming*".

In December 1992, Stockard Channing had scored a tremendous personal success in "*Six Degrees of Separation*" in London. She and I went to see Harold Pinter who was appearing in his play, "*No Man's Land*". After the performance in a restaurant nearby, Pinter learned that she had played Ruth at Williamstown. "Oh yes, the theater run by that Greek chap." Stockard said to the great playwright, "I always said if I met you I would tell you what Nikos said to me during that production. At first I couldn't get the part to do what I wanted. Nikos said to me 'Be Be Be.' Well, I couldn't figure out what that meant. Be be be? A few nights into the run, I was cutting through a forest to get to the theater and I ran into Nikos who was in no way surprised to see me in a forest. He said to me, as if he bumped into each other on 57th street, that he'd been thinking about my performance and why I was still wrestling with it.

'I know how to help you. You know what is written on the tombstone of the Greek poet Kazantsakis?' 'I didn't,' I said. I think this is what Nikos said. I think I heard him say, " 'I have no hope. I have no fear. I am free.' Run to the theater. Now you can play the part." "And somehow, as I went through the forest, I knew that he had given me a gift and I went to the theater and played the part and everything was all right."

Pinter repeated the inscription. "I have no hope. I have no fear. I am free." He turned to his wife. "My god, she's right."

That's probably a pretty good crystallization as any of the Williamstown philosophy. Let's leave Nikos in that Berkshire forest waiting for unsuspecting actors making a short cut to the theater so he can drop the right sentence into their souls and help them become more than they ever dared and move more directly into the intention of the text and realize the way the playwright felt at the moment of writing. That is the only measure of success. Yes, that is the way the writer meant it.

Williamstown is the place created by Nikos where there is truly not enough time for anything. All you can do is leap in and risk drowning. And hopefully find new ways to swim, new ways to reach the shore. That sense of Nikos-inspired free fall is the tissue binding together all the interviews of this book. "Have no hope. Have no fear. Be free." Is that indeed what is inscribed on Kazantsakis' grave? Let's say it is. It is the essence of acting to risk living in the moment. And the moment and the risk are to Williamstown Theatre Festival what Wagner is to Bayreuth.

John Guare
January, 1993

INTRODUCTION
by Jean Hackett

"The artist must always work, must always think ahead, otherwise it is impossible to live," Anton Chekhov said toward the end of his life. In the months before Nikos Psacharopoulos' death, in early January, 1989, he was doing just that – thinking ahead to the 35th anniversary season of the theater he founded in 1955, the Williamstown Theatre Festival, while working on moving his production of *Sweet Bird of Youth* from Toronto to New York. He was in the middle of his winter teaching schedule at Yale and Circle in the Square. And he was anticipating the coming April, when he planned to be married for the first time.

Moments before Chekhov died, at a German spa, he asked his wife for a glass of champagne. A moment later he murmured that he was dying ("ich sterbe"). Then he drank remarking that he "hadn't drunk champagne in ages." To anyone familiar with Chekhov's work, this inconsequential comment in the midst of a moment of great consequence was hardly uncharacteristic. The unexpectedness of Nikos' death – also while vacationing at a remote resort – was equally characteristic, especially in the myriad of unfinished things left in its wake.

Nikos shaped his professional life around surprises and contradictions, assiduously avoided being pinned down or "setting" anything, liked nothing more than changing plans at the last minute and virtually never announced anything he intended to do in advance. As a director, he had no use for a "finished" product: by the time any play he'd worked on hit the stage he'd already detached from it, let it go without a backward glance and mentally was far onto the next. As a teacher, too, the only acting work that interested him was – a word he used over and over – "unfinished," work with rough edges, without polish, work driven by an inner necessity so great it could never be fully accomplished. The work he valued most happened unexpectedly – as he often said, "in spite of yourself, not because of yourself."

This book began out of one of the things left unfinished. The

i

original idea was a book on Nikos teaching acting – a project I convinced him to embark on in 1987. His legacy as a teacher was far-reaching: for 35 years he taught at Yale University; for 19 years at Circle in the Square Theater School; for 14 years he ran his own advanced class for professional actors, and along the way did teaching stints at NYU, Columbia, Amherst, Williams and others...as well as 33 years of training apprentices at the WTF. Nonetheless he had never evolved, nor wanted to evolve, a "Nikos Psacharopoulos" theory of acting. "Teaching acting is like being a doctor," he'd say. "No two diagnoses are alike."

I persuaded him, however, to begin tape-recording his class sessions. Having studied acting with him for seven years (as an undergraduate at NYU, then in his workshop for professional actors), I felt confident that culling the best representative critiques from many hours of tapes would yield an exciting curriculum on his diverse but specific approach. His ambivalence about teaching acting on paper, however, probably accounted for only fifteen class sessions having been recorded over a two-year period – not nearly enough for what I had in mind.

Nine months after his death, I received a call from the publishers Smith and Kraus in Newbury, Vermont. A few years before, Nikos had done an interview that served as an introduction for a book they'd packaged – *The Actor's Book of Movie Monologues*. Now they were planning a book for actors containing scenes and monologues from Chekhov. Marisa Smith knew of the extensive work Nikos had done on the Chekhov plays over the years at Williamstown, and she wondered if I had in my possession any material of his that might serve as an introduction for it. Nikos had never written anything on Chekhov, but I hoped to find something by searching the class tapes.

For the most part, Nikos let his students work in class on whatever scenes they wanted; there might easily have been no critiques on Chekhov scenes. But I was lucky. I found three critiques of individual scenes from Chekhov's plays – two from *Uncle Vanya*; one from *Ivanov*. (Interestingly enough, the two major Chekhovs Nikos never chose to direct.) The tapes also had bits and pieces about acting Chekhov in the critiques on scenes by other playwrights. Finally, on the last tape I listened to, I found an extensive critique of the entire second act of *Uncle Vanya*. I offered to edit an introduction drawn from this. Marisa and her husband, Eric Kraus, then asked me to choose representative Chekhov scenes and monologues from the plays and write brief introductory passages. I also decided to interview two or three actors who'd worked at Williamstown with Nikos on Chekhov's plays.

But as I immersed myself in piecing it all together, I began to feel that a book of scenes essentially for the uninitiated didn't match up with Nikos' lifetime of work on the plays. At the same time, it became difficult to pick which two or three actors to interview for the book. The Williamstown Theatre Festival did a Chekhov play at least every other year between 1962 and 1988, mostly directed by Nikos, (the others by homegrown Festival directors Austin Pendleton, Tom Brennan and Jeff Bleckner, with John Madden – *Ivanov* – the one exception) with actors who "grew up" professionally with WTF and returned regularly. A *company* came together at Williamstown to do Chekhov over and over again; choosing any two or three names out of the whole seemed arbitrary. And, as an actress, my own interest ran much more toward exploring process than disseminating scenes and monologues.

Gradually the book changed form. The number of interviews kept expanding – really, the actors themselves led me to each other, asking if I'd talked to this one or that one, insisting that I must. Like following clues on a treasure hunt, I went from actor to actor, not really knowing what I was looking for, or where I would end up. Not even, really, knowing what I was doing. I certainly had no expectations about what would emerge collectively and no agenda for each individual interview – except to bring up subjects which fascinated me: topics that I personally was keen to encounter about acting Chekhov and Nikos' approach.

Eventually, Marisa, Eric and I shelved the idea of a resource book for beginning actors. After transcribing the class tapes I went through archive material and discovered some of Nikos' rehearsal notes, jotted in the backs of scripts and on rehearsal schedules. Along the way I found interviews Nikos had done on directing Chekhov and I pieced together notes that I and other students had taken in his classes. And I kept talking to actors. I ended up with eighteen interviews to balance what I decided to call "The Acting Notebook" – a compendium of critiques, notes and interviews by Nikos on acting Chekhov. All put together, the result, I think, is a journal of a phenomenon that took place over a twenty-five year span at the WTF – a phenomenon forged by a long-term commitment between a group of artists and a director to the plays of Anton Chekhov.

* * * * * * * * * * * * * * *
"I think if people do not understand plays, those plays

are not presented in an exciting enough way. When people say of a play they've seen, 'it is wonderful, it is great, they don't worry about who wrote it or if it is Theater of the Absurd or Modern or Experimental or this or that. It is a piece of experience communicated in human terms. When we started doing Chekhov, people thought it was very experimental. Now Chekhov has become a commercial rite in Williamstown. We don't do it any more as a 'Work of Art,' although it is a brilliant work of art. Chekhov has finally made it."

Nikos Psacharopoulos

In his foreword to a collection of Chekhov plays translated by Robert Corrigan, Harold Clurman begins by admitting: "An historian might well exclaim today, 'To think that *The Sea Gull* was once considered an unintelligible play, and that even Stanislavsky failed at first to appreciate it.' But I am not at all certain that I did on my initial encounter with the play – and that was so much later than Stanislavsky!" Much later than either Stanislavsky or Clurman, the problem with appreciating Chekhov continues.

Reading *The Sea Gull*, *The Three Sisters* and *The Cherry Orchard* as a young acting student mystified and bored me. There seemed nothing to hold onto – no suspense, no plot, no way to find the "event" in any particular scene, or the objectives and obstacles for the characters. Even more confusing, on the title page of *The Cherry Orchard*, Chekhov describes it as "A Comedy"! But I found nothing but a grey wash of sadness and loss – and very few punch lines. My tepid college introduction to Chekhov, (defining the plays as "centrifugal" rather than "centripetal") only confused me more. Nor was it any help seeing productions of Chekhov on stage. In my junior year, a well-known American actress in a major revival of *The Three Sisters* suggested in *The New York Times* that the play "inspires rather than entertains." The few productions I saw (including that one) proved to do neither. Slow-moving and meandering, these pastiches of seemingly inconsequential conversation only inspired a sinking sensation of moroseness. I couldn't fathom at all why great actors saw working on Chekhov as the realm of the sublime.

Then, one sweltering summer afternoon in 1978 – my first season as a member of WTF's non-Equity acting company – I saw a tape of WTF's latest production of *The Sea Gull*. It was directed by Nikos and featured Blythe Danner as Nina, Lee Grant as Arkadina,

Frank Langella as Treplev and Kevin McCarthy as Trigorin. Olympia Dukakis, Louis Zorich, Marian Mercer and William Swetland were also in the cast. The production itself had been staged the summer of 1974; the taped version I saw was made for PBS' "Great Performances" series – very nearly a reinactment of the stage version, albeit opened up to take in the Massachusetts-cum-Russian countryside. That afternoon, at a makeshift screening for Festival company members, thirty of us budding-actor-types gathered around a single TV screen and watched what the *L.A. Times* had called "probably the best production of *The Sea Gull* that you'll see anywhere." What I remember most is – I got it.

My head got it, my heart got it; my detached thought process turned into emotional involvement. I recognized myself and people I knew in Nina, Arkadina, Trepleff, Trigorin; I felt in them and the play all my own longings, my own secrets, my own despair. If the essence of falling in love is recognition, then that too. The chord was struck.

That summer I went back to all the Chekhov plays again. Suddenly I seemed to have the knack for reading them – seeing that version of *The Sea Gull* made Chekhov's world accessible to me. I began to understand where the humor was, where the fun could be in playing these characters, and how intimately the plays reflected my own inner life and aspects of my friends and family. And from seeing that particular *Sea Gull* I also discovered what two decades of Williamstown theatergoers and artists had come to know as well: that something extraordinary was happening in the synthesis of Chekhov and director Nikos Psacharopoulos.

*   *   *   *   *   *   *   *   *   *   *   *   *   *   *   *   *

"I think what Tyrone Guthrie says is right, every play should be seen again every five or ten years. When Picasso did 'Guernica,' he certainly did a hundred and twenty-six versions before he decided which version he wanted to do. And I think since there are different actors, it's especially fun seeing what new people bring in. What is really exciting is that my own attitude toward the play changes. For instance, the first time I did 'The Sea Gull,' I took it very, very seriously because I was quite young at the time. Then, when I did it again, I think I found much more of the humor in the material.

"What really happens is that you work, as Durer said,

from the most infinite variety to the utmost simplicity. When you are fairly young, you try to clutter everything. Eventually you try to find out what is essential, what is important.

"And you don't have to talk and talk about it. You can be brilliant in five minutes and you can take a lifetime to be dull. You must pin down the one line in a sketch that you have to use for a hundred lines, the one line in a scene, the one trait in a character. You have to reach the moment in your life where you find out what it's all about, and I don't think you can search for inspiration with a vengeance. Either you're inspired or you're not."

Nikos Psacharopoulos

Increasingly during Nikos' 33-year tenure as artistic director of the Festival, certainly, by the late seventies, WTF's identity was enmeshed with a commitment to "great" plays. Shakespeare aside, this meant a focus on productions of Euripides, Sophocles, Moliere, Brecht, Ibsen, Shaw, Tennessee Williams and, especially, Anton Chekhov. Between 1962 and 1977, WTF had done three productions of *The Three Sisters*, three of *The Sea Gull*, two of *The Cherry Orchard*, two of *Uncle Vanya*, and one of *Platonov*. Another *Three Sisters*, another *Cherry Orchard*, another *Vanya* and an *Ivanov* were to come in the eighties.

Not only did Nikos go back to these plays over and over, he made them part of the indigenous culture. Chekhov became a household word to Festival audiences and the announcement of any one of his plays virtually guaranteed a sold-out run, even before the casts were announced. But it didn't hurt matters that the casts included such actors as Tom Atkins, Louis Beachner, Tom Brennan, Kate Burton, Stephen Collins, John Cunningham, Blythe Danner, Daniel Davis, Colleen Dewhurst, Olympia Dukakis, Joyce Ebert, Peter Evans, John Glover, Lee Grant, William Hansen, John Heard, Edward Herrmann, Celeste Holm, Ken Howard, Amy Irving, Richard Kavanaugh, Laurie Kennedy, Frank Langella, Roberta Maxwell, George Morfogen, Carrie Nye, Austin Pendleton, Anne Pitoniak, Christopher Reeve, Laila Robins, William Swetland, Maria Tucci, Richard Venture, Christopher Walken, Dianne Wiest, Louis Zorich and others. "There's an old Greek proverb," Nikos was fond of saying. "If the monastery is good... there'll be plenty of monks."

What evolved over the years between Nikos, these actors (and some designers like Will Steven Armstrong, Santo Loquasto, John Conklin, Danya Ramicova, and Jess Goldstein) was a collective vision and an intrinsically American technique for doing Chekhov's plays. It grew out of trial and error, it grew out of Nikos' (and the actors') innate sensibility, and it matured in a robust and unique environment – the Williamstown Theatre Festival.

* * * * * * * * * * * * * * * *

"We wanted good theater, so we had to train a company, but more important, we had to train an audience. Other theaters worry what audiences like. We are trying to create our own audiences. And obviously the fact that we play to standing room means that they accept the kind of work we do... The challenge is a challenge to ourselves. It's the quality of the work that interests us. We're constantly trying to find plays that no one thinks will work and make them work. We try to go to actors who have not done a specific part – a serious actor doing a comic part or the other way around. We try to stretch the actors, designers, directors. It's really a training place, a training ground for brilliant professionals."

Nikos Psacharopoulos

In the spring of 1978, Nikos asked me and several other members of my class at Circle in the Square – along with some of his students from Yale and elsewhere – to become members of the Festival's non-Equity acting company. I spent the next four summers completing the most invaluable part of my acting training.

By the early eighties, working at Williamstown had become a milestone for the "serious" actor, one of the few recognizable markers for legitimacy as an theater artist. So much so that actors who'd already made major names for themselves in film or television eagerly waived salary, billing and leading roles in order to be part of the company. WTF's commitment to this "family" of actors ran the gamut from giving seasoned professionals the outlet of working on an ever-increasing range of challenging roles, to nurturing and training a succession of generations of emerging talent. "There has to be an organic way for people to find talent and nurture talent rather than *use* talent," Nikos said in an interview in 1986. "In New York and L.A. people use talent. Here we try to discover potential talent and develop it."

Being a member of the non-Equity or non-professional company wasn't a pure acting job. It also meant making poster runs, working in the box office and cooking strike breakfasts in the middle of the night for the hundred or so apprentices and interns doing their round-the-clock shift of striking the set of the last show while putting up the set for the next. We also produced and directed and acted in our own projects (presented, usually, in a field or a gym around midnight). And, with luck, we played small and even not-so-small parts on the Main Stage.

My first role in 1978 – in which I had the thrill of crossing the stage twice – was that of the second upstairs maid in *Idiot's Delight*. Other nameless roles during my four non-Equity summers included a passenger departing for the netherworld in *Camino Real*, the orange girl in *Cyrano de Bergerac*, the charwoman in *The Front Page* and a party guest in the third act of *The Cherry Orchard*. And I also got the chance to play some wonderful roles: in *Summerfolk*, *Whose Life Is It Anyway?*, *The Greeks*, *Arturo Ui* and *Room Service*. But, for all of us 'non-Eqs,' most important was the chance to take part in an increasingly rare rite of passage – watching up close, day after day, great actors in the nuts and bolts process of plying their craft. And, by doing so, developing the values and techniques that would inform our work throughout our professional lives.

For a young actress still in college, the atmosphere couldn't have been more heady or exhilarating. Williamstown every summer had become a sort of exuberant Noah's Ark for every possible species of theater artist – the best acclaimed actors; the best unsung actors; kids not much past their first high school play; garden variety celebrities; award winning designers and directors; the cream of emerging talent from the country's foremost acting schools; teachers and technicians and playwrights and cabaret performers – in a melting pot so egalitarian that it was just as easy to see famous actors in the audience for an apprentice scene night as it was to see them in a Chekhov play on the Main Stage.

Nikos' penchant for the unexpected meant that no one ever really knew on a day-to-day basis what was happening next at WTF; he'd long since stopped setting the schedule of plays for the season in advance. Actors, plays, even opening night dates were up in the air all summer long, and every hour of every day brought new grist for the rumor mill about who and how and what would be going on next. Nothing was beyond the pale: actors shooting into town incognito on the red-eye to audition for a play going into rehearsal that afternoon, plays rehearsing without directors, directors rehearsing with casts of only apprentice stand-ins, apprentice stand-ins bumped up on two days notice to leading roles.

The Second Company (eventually The Other Stage) cloned the chaos and the rest of Festival lifestyle was just as zany, its diurnal and nocturnal eccentricities inspired mostly by a zeal for creativity. A normal day at the Festival included set building, acting classes, dance classes, costume calls, cabaret rehearsals, Sunday Special event rehearsals, project rehearsals, Second Company and Main Stage rehearsals, all leading up to the evening's performance. After which, equity actors and apprentices performed at local restaurants in the cabaret, a musical revue that changed every two weeks. After *that*, at maybe one in the morning, on to the "Zoo"- the floating company speakeasy that unofficially operated from various basements on the Williams College campus. Maybe, just *maybe*, by that time the rehearsal schedule for the next day had gone up on the call board, so various groups then traipsed back through the mountain mist to the theater to find out if their call had been posted for the morning – which by this time couldn't have been more than two or three hours away. As Nikos was famous for telling the latest crop of apprentices at the beginning of every season, "This is not a summer camp."

The frenetic, rife-with-possibility climate was part of the lure of the place; so was the beauty of the area itself – the historic Williams College campus enlivened by the rush of fragile New England summer; the town with only two streets (named "Spring" and "Water") shadowed by the serene Berkshires. But most of all, at that time, there was an aura around the Festival emanating from some of the most sophisticated and resonant acting work going on in American theater. The edge at Williamstown – what made it important for both actors and audiences – was its propensity for the eruption of moments of breathtaking acting.

Human moments – I think of George Morfogen's inanely comic seriousness while making a speech to the armoire in *The Cherry Orchard* – where you recognized your own absurdity with a jolt and then laughed at yourself in that recognition. Romantic moments – Frank Langella's third act aria to Roxanne in *Cyrano de Bergerac* – that enveloped a spellbound audience in an almost palpable euphoria. Primitive, raw moments – Roberta Maxwell as Electra in *The Greeks* shouting to the world and to the gods that her brother Orestes lived. And emotional moments of such power and depth that you gasped before the tears came – Carrie Nye's disintegration as Blanche under the naked light bulb in *A Streetcar Named Desire*; Joe

Morton's final blind departure into the light in *The Legend of Oedipus*; Blythe Danner as Masha hurling herself shamelessly across the stage at Vershinin in the fourth act of *Three Sisters*, wrapping her legs around his waist and wrenching us all to our own most intimate, private place of heartbreak and loss.

Productions weren't flawless. Mounting a major play once every two weeks took its toll: casts were sometimes uneven and often under-rehearsed. Nonetheless there was that constant: an abundance of great *moments* on stage. Where suddenly, unexpectedly, the passive experience of watching from the audience became charged with a jolt of visceral connection – moments at the heart of why one goes to see theater or chooses to make a career in it. The charm of the area itself, the glittery fallout from celebrities in the audience and on stage, the festivity of opening nights with hundreds of bottles of champagne being popped open on the front lawn – these were peripheral. The main event, the thing Nikos most often achieved, was the consistent offering of great acting moments.

Nowhere were these moments more in evidence than in the Chekhovs. They sprang from Nikos' inborn sense of the life in the plays and from a process grounded in the company's shared history...with each other, with Nikos, and with Chekhov's writing.

* * * * * * * * * * * * * * * * * *

"The real question is how well the actor has learned to give himself permission to use the acting equipment – his emotional world, his voice, his body and his attitude. I think actors torture themselves too much by confusing acting and the acting instrument with decisions. I'm not saying people should not think, but I just believe that you often don't really know with a great painting or sculpture what the exact thought is, because the piece of art has to be stronger than the artist. Again, I'm not saying that actors should not think. All I'm saying is that if thought made us great artists, we'd all be Picassos.

"You've got to be able to play the instrument first, before you are an artist. If you play that instrument in a certain kind of way, then, of course, you become a different kind of artist. But the point is, you can't just say that because you think, because your thoughts are great and your perception of the material is great, you're an artist. You're not. It is the emotional and the physical response that is important,

*which obviously is based on an intellectual world. Most of
the people I work with are really very bright. That's not what
I'm talking about. I think acting is like the great Saint Joan
line, 'I hear my voices first and I find reasons for them
afterwards.' "*

When I began the interviews with the actors included here, I
expected detailed discussions and analyses about ways to approach
roles and recountings of specific direction Nikos gave in rehearsals.
Some of this did happen, but to a large degree the interviews moved
quickly out of the tangible and concrete into more elusive areas.
Nikos' work on Chekhov seems not to have been based on a
philosophy he'd constructed; he did not have *ideas* about Chekhov
so much as he had *feelings* and – to quote Austin Pendleton – an
actor was encouraged to "live in the world of Nikos' feeling" about
each particular play. In the interviews, actors began talking about
"breakthroughs" and "releases," about using parts of themselves
which they had not known how – or had the courage – to use before.
Somehow the melding of Chekhov and Nikos pushed them to the
terra incognita of that which is most challenging, disturbing and
mysterious in the acting process. They seemed to find not a process
of accretion but of "messing things up," and the breakthroughs they
came to – reaching and realizing those great acting "moments" –
had to do almost entirely with forgetting ideas about the play and
connecting on a gut level to the inner journey of the characters, in
tandem with venturing to places within themselves both risky and
deeply authentic.

This territory isn't a place that lends itself easily to words.
Blythe Danner gropingly describes it as connecting to "a place in the
body where inspiration comes from, emanating from where we were
born." For Stephen Collins it meant edging up against the
"maladjusted" within himself; for Kate Burton and Roberta Maxwell
and John Glover, it involved a complete giving up of control of the
notion of shaping the performance, abandoning themselves to the
unsettling realm of "not-knowing" what they were doing on stage.
Christopher Walken and Olympia Dukakis champion the surrender
to "chaos" but acknowledge with the others the dangers of such
extremes of letting-go, and the imperative of having a "safe space"
in order to do so.

By the time WTF did its most realized productions of Chekhov,
that metaphorical safe space had been created. Enough trust seems to
have evolved between Nikos and his actors that they came to the
rehearsal room ready and willing to make available all aspects of

themselves – silliness, sexuality, embarrassment as well as confidence, aggression as well as vulnerability, the bad child as well as the good – in order to fulfill the requirements of the play. Nikos not only pursued and "provoked" the unreasonable, the inappropriate, the primitive, the foolish and the out-of-control; he accepted it and embraced it. In turn, his actors risked the emotional free-falls and the uncensored behavior rampant in his productions of Chekhov.

The 1976 production of *The Three Sisters* seems to be this at its zenith – Olympia, Blythe, Austin, John Glover all speak of reaching extraordinary levels of freedom in their work, of feeling "permission" to explore on the most intimate level the cacophony of pain, hunger, longing, shame and even ecstasy integral to the "score" of the play. As Ms. Danner puts it, "the demons were unleashed." It seems that within Nikos' often inarticulate and highly contradictory process, artifice and defensive exteriors were stripped away – in order for emotional truth to break through spontaneously and gloriously in the foreground.

* * * * * * * * * * * * * * *

"A lot of people talk about 'becoming a character,' but I wonder if character simply exists or if character is something you do. If somebody has six things to do, why do they worry about being a character? It's the six things that they do that becomes the character. It's like all theatrical terms. Anytime somebody translates one form into another, you're in trouble. It's like food critics trying to find an accurate word to describe a meal, which is difficult, because it's a taste. This constant need to define the art world with words is very problematic. I never know what people mean. I only know what I see and what I hear. And that's why I think you can't really write a textbook about acting. The easiest way of showing something about acting is to use a videotape. With a tape you see what is really happening."
Nikos Psacharopoulos

I knew it would be tough translating Nikos' spoken word to the printed page. Those who worked or studied with him knew that it always took a few weeks just to get a handle on his Greek accented, highly iconoclastic use of English. Strangely enough, I think that was one of the things that made him a great teacher – he strung words together in ways that no English-speaking person would conceive. Which perhaps made it possible for those working with him to hear and perceive what he said in unconventional ways, too, with more immediacy. Most actors never minded getting line readings from Nikos because you never actually got the exact line. He would say it with a series of little sounds, or absolutely backwards, or another line entirely. So you got a sort of rhythmic, intuitive sense of how the line should go and at the same time there was no way at all, literally, to repeat his reading.

For the sake of this book, however, my intention was to clean up, re-word and edit the series of little sounds so that they could be received in a more concise, logical way. But, daunted by the task of translating Nikos' creative process into coherent language, I eventually abandoned my compulsion to organize and clarify, tie up loose ends and present a nicely wrapped package. Rather than wording the inarticulate, I've tried to embrace it, both in transcribing Nikos' tapes and in my interviews with the actors. To remain true to the feeling-tone, I've tried to preserve the groping for the words and some of the roundabout ways Nikos used in getting to the point. Rather than eliminate sections where Nikos uses only a tone of voice and inflection for translating Chekhov's world to his students, I've tried to instead give a description of that tone of voice and inflection.

I also left repetitions – both in Nikos' critiques and from interview to interview. When I first studied acting – not that this has changed! – I found I often needed to hear something over and over again until it "clicked." (As Nikos was fond of quoting: "Drop by drop, knowledge comes to the unwilling.") The repetitions, I hope, also serve to highlight certain consistent trends that Nikos and the company found in their work together.

But perhaps videotapes or audio tapes would've done the job better. It's just not possible to capture on the page the physical gestures, the accent, the garbled sounds, the humor that came from Nikos' highly unselfconscious attempts to communicate his meaning.

For example, in his long critique of the second act of *Uncle Vanya*, there's an almost operatic section where Nikos, encouraging the student actress to play with more abandon, acts out her character's heightened emotional state at the end of the act. As Nikos makes up his inimitable version of the lines, there are sounds in the background of movement, of things being randomly thrown in the air and falling to the floor. As the event builds, the class bursts into laughter. Nikos hits the crescendo of the scene in a way that's both emotional and funny, and the class responds with more laughter and applause. When it dies down there is a long silence. Nikos says, "You see?" There is another silence.

Finally it becomes clear that the actress playing Yelena has begun to cry. Nikos says softly, "You see, now you are crying, that's what the scene is all about." And then he goes on, just as passionately, with the rest of the critique. Without a description of what happened, the words alone sound like a direction to the actress to "cry" at the end of the scene. Actually, a non-verbal communication took place that allowed the actress, on a gut level, to get what the "life" of the scene was about. A breakthrough.

* * * * * * * * * * * * * * * * *

"For a class I like to see somebody who is 'working,' who's making the audition a process rather than a result. That shows me what the person is rather than what they can do. It's just like doing scales – emotional scales – the way a singer would come and sing a few notes; I don't really worry about the melody, I don't really worry about the interpretation of the play. Now, there are some directors who love to have an interpretation, saving them from really having to make this kind of judgment. Unfortunately, too many times directors love to have choices made by actors, because then they don't have to make choices. I basically believe I can make any choice I want to for an actor; I just want actors to do them well."

Nikos Psacharopoulos

As well as his student and an actress with his company, I was also Nikos' companion for the last ten years of his life. No doubt my personal feelings have impinged on my objectivity here – and, at the same time, I hope that I didn't let my need for objectivity overshadow what a privilege and joy it was to know him, learn from him and love him.

Not only did I come to the project with *that* bias, the actors I interviewed here are either people I've worked with, or friends, or both. Some, like Kate Burton and Laila Robins, are my contemporaries; some, like Austin Pendleton and Tom Brennan, were my directors and teachers; others, like Carrie Nye and Blythe Danner and Olympia Dukakis, I held on various pedestals during my early years at Williamstown and became friends with as time went on. And even with those actors I am less well-acquainted with, such as Christopher Walken and Lee Grant, there's the shared bond of love for Nikos that I know enhances my already considerable regard for their talent. With all of this, I still hope the book is more than just a family album. Although it would be inaccurate if it weren't partially that – the operative word throughout the years for Williamstown and Nikos and the actors has long been "family."

C. S. Lewis suggests that the death of a family member actually opens us up to a greater level of intimacy with that person than before – we claim our connection with them in a new way, we incorporate them more deeply as part of our own selves. And so it is, I believe, with Nikos' WTF family. It became joyously clear, as I proceeded that his talent and energetic vision had not disappeared with his passing but had come to reside within the members of the family. Reading the interviews all together, it's apparent that they are "related" to each other – not as individual melodies but as different instrumental lines in the same symphony, with themes and variations that echo, expand on, rework and riff from one piece to the next; with a shared vocabulary and point of reference to which only family members have access.

* * * * * * * * * * * * * * *

"We are all faced with the same problems when we are doing a play. The solutions we give to those problems are different. The moments we emphasize are different and the points that we make are different because of our backgrounds, what we are like and our scope of understanding. What we see is the result of what we are or of what we are becoming."

Nikos Psacharopoulos

Nikos Constantin Athanasios Psacharopoulos VII came to the United States from his native Greece in 1947, when he was 18 years old, to study at Oberlin College. He grew up in Athens during the Nazi occupation and spent his teenage years staging anti-German skits and revues in narrow side streets and makeshift performance spaces. Nikos picked Oberlin College because it gave him a full scholarship, but his parents, who had lost most of their money during the war, couldn't afford to pay the boat passage to America. In Nikos' last year in high school, a Greek shipping magnate who knew the family wrote a note offering Nikos a position with his company and a lucrative salary. Nikos wrote a scathingly idealistic

Nikos and family right before he left for America in 1947.

letter back, declining that life in favor of life as an artist. The man who offered him the job was so impressed that he offered to pay Nikos' passage to America.

When he left Greece for America, his entire family accompanied his departure. As the ship sailed, his mother, who had been full of nothing but cheerful optimism, suddenly hurled herself into a tug boat anchored below, unreasonably trying to follow her son. This image shows up many years later in Nikos' direction of Masha's physical response to Vershinin's departure in the fourth act of *The Three Sisters*.

Nikos arrived in Ohio in 1947, with no winter coat, very little English and a few dollars in change. By day he took classes and washed dishes in one of Oberlin's dining halls; by night he worked in a laundry and read plays. His long-time friend, actor/director Tom Brennan, who went to school with him, remembers Nikos stating early on that he had already read "seven hundred plays." "I was appalled," Tom said. "I think maybe I'd read two."

Very quickly, Nikos took over the student drama group, "The Mummers," and began directing original works by fellow classmates John Kander and Jim Goldman. One summer he was dating a girl from Mansfield, Ohio, whose family was friendly with a wealthy townsman who owned the Studebaker dealership. This man, whose daughter aspired to be an actress, offered to raise the money for a summer theater that Nikos would run, starring, of course, his daughter. At the beginning of that summer, though, when Nikos and his Oberlin entourage arrived in Mansfield ready to go to work, evidently the money hadn't been found. "Didn't you get my telegram?" asked the man, stricken. "It was as if Nikos didn't even hear him," Tom Brennan said. "He started pulling out sketches of the costumes for *Antigone*. 'Look at zee folds of thees dress,' Nikos said. 'Your daughter ess going to be waandenful!' He talked about the schedule of shows for the season. The man tried to interrupt but Nikos wouldn't let him. Finally the Studebaker dealer threw up his hands. Ten minutes later, we walked out of there with a summer theater."

Nikos went on to the Yale School of Drama, graduating in 1954 with a master's degree in directing, his thesis a production of Ibsen's *Peer Gynt*. He became a member of the faculty at Yale and directed the "Dramat" productions of *La Ronde, A View from the Bridge, Love in Buffalo* (Yale's first musical) and Kazantzakis' *He Who Must Die* (with a set so vast and complex that the daunted crew painted in large letters on the back of the flats, "Greek Go Home.")

In the summer of 1955, Nikos received an offer to be the associate director of a fledgling summer theater on the campus of Williams College. The following summer he became Executive Director. Between 1956 and 1988, Nikos directed 96 of WTF's 265 Main Stage productions. Besides WTF, Nikos directed on and off-Broadway, for the New York City Opera, the New York Pro Musica, the American Shakespeare Festival, the Long Wharf Theater, the Pasadena Playhouse and Circle in the Square, all work very close to his heart. But his home and family clearly was the Williamstown Theatre Festival.

* * * * * * * * * * * * * * * * *

"In terms of humanity, I think 'Three Sisters' is marvelous. I understand the family in 'Cherry Orchard' much more; it is closer to the Greek. I always have friends I remember with 'Three Sisters'; I have relatives I remember with 'The Cherry Orchard.' "

Nikos Psacharopoulos

Nikos' knowledge and instincts about Chekhov grew with his work over the years, but his early life and upbringing were equally influential in preparing him for Chekhov. In the year after his death, I received this translation of a letter Nikos wrote to his life-long friend, Chris Nikolauopoulos, on August 1, 1945. It is an account of a voyage Nikos made at 17 years old, after the end of the Nazi occupation of Greece, to his paternal home on the island of Siphnos.

It is a simple letter, full of details of everyday life and connection to the past – with an unmistakable sense of new beginning arising from the ashes of his country's years of war, ruin and oppression.

To me, in other words, it is full of those things we have come to call "Chekhovian"... and prescient of the joyful and important collaboration to come.

My dear Christopher,

From the old "mansion" of the Psacharopoulos' family, this first day of August 1945 in Siphnos, the isle of tranquility clad in white...

I am in the midst of one of the greatest adventures of my life

– our small caique sailed from Faliro Bay on Thursday. At 2 o'clock in the morning we lay anchor at Cape Sounion near the old temple of Poseidon. The moon was full and I slept on a mattress of pebbles and seaweed. It was still dark when we sailed again out to the open sea. The Aegean was angry with big waves and a howling wind. But it was a great experience, I was hardly affected! A few hours later we found haven in the leeward side of a cape on the island of Seriphos to wait out the storm. We spent the night in an abandoned shack with a big tin can for a pillow! In the morning I walked down to the small port and had a wonderful, if primitive, breakfast – goat's milk, pears and homebaked bread.

The rest of the voyage to Siphnos was marvelous! The water had calmed down and all the passengers (who were fewer than the crew!) came back to life with singing, cries of delight and much laughter, making the time pass unnoticed till we made it to Kameres, the port of Siphnos. If you think that there is anything on wheels other than carts on this island, you are wrong! Nothing! An old, sympathetic donkey carried me to my ancestral home high up on a hill at Artemon several kilometers to the interior. It had been so long since I had seen it last! It was such a great feeling to unhinge the iron bars from their rusty locks on the gate and to open once again the faded green shutters and the cracked window panes to let the sun bathe the old familiar rooms...

In the next few days I organized myself – cleaning up and preparing a bedroom, bathroom, living room and a study. Today is Wednesday and I am sitting at my ancient desk writing to you. It's true that I have already missed you all! But, if I could help it, I would never leave this lovely island sitting in the middle of my beloved Aegean...tomorrow morning, I will be off for an excursion to my favorite spot – Chrysopigi – where I will spend two or three days worshipping Apollo, who hardly misses a day passing over Siphnos with his golden chariot casting his rays like arrows from his bow. (Don't worry, I will take care of my health. I won't stay too long under the hot sun!)

I have read your letter many times – and Yannis' letter, too.

*They are the only notes of Athenian life here. My goodness!
Such outbursts of bright humour! Yannis' description of the
incident on the street with Father and your reference, Chris,
to Eugene O' Neill was just great!*

*Nothing much really 'happens' here on this peaceful island
– no incidents, no episodes to write about! Except of course
for a wasp that had the audacity to sting me and within a
few minutes the whole village knew about it!*

*Time to seal this letter. I almost forgot to mention: last night
I found (guess what?) jasmines – yes, jasmines – and put
them in little makeshift vases (water glasses, really) all over
my desk and my bedroom. You can imagine my joy! All I
need now is a few cans of paint to make the walls come to
life.*

*Please write again, many letters! You and Yannis, too. You
can write together if it's easier! I greet you all with many
kisses and love.*

Nikos
August 1, 1945

THE ACTOR'S CHEKHOV

Nikos Psacharopoulos and the
Company of the Williamstown Theatre Festival,
on the plays of Anton Chekhov

Part One

THE INTERVIEWS

"He who desires nothing
hopes for nothing
and is afraid of nothing
cannot be an artist."

Chekhov (Letters)

Laurie Kennedy (Irina), Austin Pendleton (Tusenbach) in "The Three Sisters," 1976

"...It's interesting that sometimes we can see the world completely upside down, but if we're really convinced about it we can make anybody believe it. And then the excessive things that actors do appear to be a necessity rather than decorative or theatrical.

"I think the trick of it is finding the scale of an emotional world that becomes once removed from the norm. And then, once you're in that world, everything goes. Then anything is okay. When we did 'Uncle Vanya' in Williamstown with Austin he decided as Vanya to sit on the floor during one of the monologues. And the first time he tried it, it didn't work. But the second time it did work, because he just stayed on the floor forever. He started crawling on the floor and hitting the floor. And some other actor would not get away with playing on the floor like a kid and hitting the floor, but his conviction about the emotional necessity of being that kinetic, which was fascinating, made it work.

"It's interesting because in dancers we certainly believe it. We believe it in people who are quite bold, who tell the story with movement, who tell the story with the dance. I remember seeing Carmen DeLavalade do a poem with movement, and every time she talked about the stars, from what she did with her hands you had a feeling there were two million stars blinking! It was excessive! It was not exactly subtle. But because it was based on a great conviction, it worked. It's like some of the people we see in the street, right? We see a lot of people in the street who do some very strange things, and we really believe that more than we do on stage! If we put it on stage somebody says, 'What is that?!'

"It's that same sort of thing we love Austin for. He really did some excessive acting with Vanya, but because he was so undone and so desperate and so committed, it never seemed extraneous or theatrical. If anybody else did those kind of mannerisms you'd say, 'Forget it!' But because he really believes in it, you say, 'Oh, that's wonderful!' It is a matter of the scale of intensity of your acting being in relation to the scale of your perception of your problem in the scene. If your perception of your problem is big, you can get away with murder up there."

Nikos Psacharopoulos

1

AN APPETITE FOR JOY
Interview with Austin Pendleton

Mr. Pendleton began his long association with WTF in 1957 as a charter member of the apprentice workshop, and went on to act, direct and become an associate director with the Festival. In 1969, his first Chekhov role with WTF was Trofimov in *The Cherry Orchard*. In 1972, he directed a production of *Uncle Vanya*; in 1976, he played Tusenbach in *The Three Sisters*; in 1980, he played Trofimov again, and, in 1984, he took the title role in *Uncle Vanya*. Austin and I talked on an October morning over breakfast at a Greek diner in New York City.

JEAN Let's talk a little about your experience of doing Chekhov at Williamstown, with Nikos.

AUSTIN Well, first of all, the big take that I felt that Nikos had on Chekhov was how passionate those characters are. There had been a cliche for many years, certainly in America, that the whole secret to Chekhov was in the subtext, in what you were not saying. It was an approach to the word "subtext" that was extreme: that in Chekhov, if you were saying one thing, you absolutely meant another. Well, Nikos put all that to rest. He said that what they say is *exactly* what they mean and this is a direct expression of the passionate feelings that the characters have. Nikos had a feeling about Chekhov that was almost – joyous, he himself felt joyous about it, but also that the characters were joyous, almost no matter how much pain they were in. That there was a tremendous appetite for pursuing what they wanted which gave their lives a sort of heightened charge and energy that other people didn't have. And that was perhaps the main way that, in 1980, Nikos and Colleen Dewhurst fell afoul of each other in *The Cherry Orchard* – because she saw the other view of Chekhov; she had come up to Williamstown hoping and expecting to do that. I think she had never played any Chekhov, and she was pre-conditioned for a certain kind of life in the play. And he wanted this passionate woman who just hurled herself at things and went after

2

things with a tremendous appetite. I don't know if he ever used the word "joy" but that was certainly what his approach generated.

I don't think I ever was more thrilled being in a production of a play than the production of *The Three Sisters* that Nikos directed in 1976, with Olympia Dukakis, Blythe Danner and Laurie Kennedy in the title roles. I think it's the best production of a play I've ever been in. I just don't think it ever gets any better than that. Nikos had defined his approach to Chekhov to its absolute peak, and he also had a cast where there was in no person any resistance at all to how he saw it. It was hard for some of the people, it was hard for Blythe initially, but she got it. And I think it was probably one of the best things she's ever done, a breakthrough for her. There was such a tremendous energy and joy in that rehearsal room.

JEAN Tell me a little more about the rehearsal process.

AUSTIN Well, the play before *Three Sisters* was *Our Town* with Geraldine Fitzgerald as the Stage Manager, and it was so successful they decided to extend it a second week. All of a sudden we had this extra week of rehearsal for *Three Sisters*. So, every morning, we had a run-through in the Ex, the room downstairs from the theater where Nikos liked to rehearse all his plays. And Nikos would invite all kinds of people to come and watch these rehearsals, it was like an extra week of performances. And then, after the run-through, we would rehearse for the rest of the day. Like being in previews. And I remember I couldn't wait, every morning, to get there and do it! I also think that until about two or three years ago, it was the best work I'd ever done. I made a breakthrough about two or three years ago in my acting, I sort of went underground here in New York as an actor and my acting started to take on some new release and some new colors, but that performance of *Three Sisters* anticipated that by a number of years, and it's the only performance that really did. In fact, a few months after our *Three Sisters* I played Tusenbach again at the Brooklyn Academy of Music with an all star cast, and I had a great success of it, but I wasn't as good as I had been in Williamstown. I mean, I was still good, but the fact that I was as good as I was in it had to do with having done it for Nikos.

JEAN How was the BAM production different?

AUSTIN Well, it wasn't terrible. But it was the kind of Chekhov that Nikos fought all the time. It had Rosemary Harris and Barnard Hughes and Ellen Burstyn and Tovah Feldshah, some very talented people, all who were working very, very hard. The director was the Englishman, Frank Dunlop, a very good director, but I don't think he really trusted that the play worked. He was always trying to give it an energy, just sort of trying to apply an energy to it. I always thought that Nikos *found* the energy in the plays. He didn't arbitrarily move them along. Nikos' productions of Chekhov always did move along but they moved along because of the choices that he found for the characters, not because they were just being moved along – you know what I mean? He directed Chekhov as if Chekhov were – and I think Chekhov is – the most active of playwrights. Which of course is not what people think. And the only time he got in trouble was when somebody would resist that, like when Colleen resisted that. Although even with that, that was a very interesting production, and Colleen was pretty good in it. I mean somehow, something happened through all the arguments. Nikos was unhappy with that production, but he shouldn't have been.

JEAN Why was Ms. Dewhurst so unhappy? What did she want to play?

AUSTIN She wanted to lie there in a hammock and be indolent, she wanted to recline and be passive to what was happening. And it's not idiotic to look at the role that way. It's not even unintelligent to look at the role that way. But there is another way to look at it and that was the way that Nikos looked at it. I think probably if you analyzed it intellectually, Colleen was looking at being haunted by the paralysis of the role. That this woman, Ravevskaya, was just going to allow her home to be sold because she would rather be in Paris with her lover. And she kind of knew that she was paralyzed and didn't know what to do about it. And the text supports that; that's not stupid.

But I think that Nikos had more the feeling that the woman was hurling herself at life. She wants the orchard but she wants Paris and she wants them both absolutely passionately. And she hurls herself into every situation, hoping that it would all resolve itself. And that, of course, is very, very different from what Colleen wanted to play;

4

it contributes a whole different kind of dynamic. And Colleen, who was, of course, a wonderful actress, developed a kind of inner life that had to do with what she wanted and, in the meantime, Nikos kept wanting other choices, which were at variance with the inner life that Colleen was developing.

JEAN Who played Ranevskaya the first time you did it at WTF?

AUSTIN Olympia Dukakis. And, you know, they fought also. I mean, Olympia, having worked with Nikos a lot, was more able to embrace what he wanted, but she felt pushed around in it in a way that she did not in *Three Sisters*.

The first time we did *Cherry Orchard* together, Olympia couldn't come in until the second week – those were in the days that we only rehearsed for two weeks – because she was acting in Central Park in New York. So we rehearsed the first week with some apprentice reading her role. When she finally arrived – it was a Sunday evening and I remember she came in and she knew all the lines. We were doing the first act where Ranevskaya comes in and sees the nursery, sees her home again for the first time in years and all burners were going for Olympia. I mean, she was weeping, she was joyous, she was so full as Ranevskaya. It was her first rehearsal and she was doing all of it. And I looked over at Nikos, at his face, and I saw that he was very excited and happy. She went through the whole scene and they were both crying and laughing and at the end they embraced, and then he said, "Okay, now dear, here's what we do." And he took the whole performance apart! And I think that was a setback between them.

JEAN It must have been fascinating to play the same scenes with both Olympia and Colleen.

AUSTIN In the summer of 1980, I directed *Candida* with Blythe at Williamstown, and, the day after it opened, an apprentice drove me up to New Hampshire to Harold de Felice's theater and I started to direct Olympia in *The Cherry Orchard*. And while I was there I got a call from Nikos saying that he had decided at the end of the season to do *The Cherry Orchard*, that Colleen was going to play Lyuba Ravenskaya and would I play Trofimov. And I thought, "I can't do

5

that, I just directed this play." But then I thought, you know, not to do *The Cherry Orchard* with Nikos and with Colleen Dewhurst, I mean, this is stupid! I also thought it would be a wonderful exercise for me as an actor – to be in rehearsal and totally forget what I had just directed. *The Cherry Orchard* opened in New Hampshire and I drove back and began rehearsing with Nikos. I would rehearse all day with Nikos and then I would drive to New Hampshire, a two-hour drive, and watch my show. And I got into kind of a zen thing – I mean, I had just directed it. And the very moments that I had found a certain way, Nikos was doing a whole other way, and I had to just go with it. And it was exciting because I loved what he was doing.

JEAN Trofimov in *The Cherry Orchard* and Tusenbach in *Three Sisters* are similar as characters. Although Trofimov isn't as emotionally connected –

AUSTIN Well, Trofimov is kind of stupid, let's face it. He's certainly emotionally stupid and I think he's even intellectually stupid.

JEAN Yes, he seems to live in a world of ideas about life, rather than life itself.

AUSTIN What redeems him is that, however foolishly, he does live in the world of ideas, but he lives in it very passionately and committedly. All his energies go into that. But he's nowhere near as in touch with himself as Tusenbach or Constantine or Vanya or any of the other ones I've played. Or Vershinin, I suppose, although I've never played that. Trofimov is deeply in touch with not being in touch! I don't know of another character exactly like that. There is a joy and a passion and an electricity about his every waking moment that he manages to achieve without being in touch with large areas of himself. Only a genius would write a character like that, because that's not supposed to happen in reality, although we know so many people of whom it's true, particularly in our profession, but in any profession, I'm sure. It was Nikos who saw all that in it. It's a much more frustrating role to play because he never really communicates as a person to anybody else. Tusenbach does only that. Treplev, as screwed up as he is, communicates, and Vanya certainly does. But

Trofimov never really talks to anyone else in terms of who that other person is. That's the whole point of him. That's why he falls down the stairs. It's a physicalization of where he is, he doesn't see where the stairs are. need 2 read TCO clearly!

And you never really believe he's in love with Anya. He's in love with the *idea* of love, the idea of them being the young couple of the revolution. But he's not in love with *her*. Tusenbach *is* in love with Irina; Treplev *is* in love with Nina. Even Vanya is truly hung up on Yelena – I don't know if it's exactly "in love," but it's *her* he has feeling about, not some idea. When you get to the end of an evening of playing Trofimov – and I've done it twice – you don't have that feeling of *completion* you have with any of the other roles. Because Trofimov zings through life without ever looking to the right or to the left.

JEAN But playing Tusenbach in *Three Sisters* was different. You mentioned that with that role, you came to a real breakthrough in your work. What was that all about?

AUSTIN Well, first of all – this was something I always thought Nikos was wonderful at with people he knew and loved and who loved him. When we did *Three Sisters* – that was a summer – it was the most painful summer, I think, of my life, so far! Emotionally speaking, I was an open wound walking around up there. Some very painful things in my life that summer. And of course Tusenbach is a character who is in perpetual pain.

And Nikos... [He pauses for a moment.] Now let me try to find exactly the words for this, because it's a very exact, specific thing. Nikos, as I intuited at the time, knew everything, internally, that was going on with me. I intuited this, but then I much later found out, indirectly, that in fact he actually did know. But he never said a word about it. He just created a rehearsal atmosphere where you knew he wanted everything from you. He wanted you to bring in everything that was going on and he wanted it working in that rehearsal room. So, first of all, I came in with all this – woundedness – it was all with me, in the rehearsal room. And then Nikos immediately put me on to how active Tusenbach is. And what I saw – I say I "saw," but it wasn't really an intellectual process. The realization happened somewhere in the body, although I don't know where, but it

7

happened. But what I saw was that Tusenbach was a person who converted his pain, he converted all of his great pain into – an appetite for joy.

I saw that. I saw that, very early on, from the things that Nikos was guiding me to. And, as I said, on top of everything else, I knew that Nikos knew what was going on with me personally, although he never said a word about it. He had that with people he liked and trusted, and he had a way of communicating a sense of knowledge about them. He would never ever say anything, never presume, really, to talk about your life with you, but you knew he knew. And you knew that you were not only being given permission to bring it in to rehearsal, but you were being urged to. And through all of this, through all the spoken and unspoken things between us, he got me into the perception that Tusenbach turns his pain into an appetite for joy. And, well, that's the character.

JEAN And wouldn't you say that's the play, too?

AUSTIN Exactly. Once that alignment took place, I was incapable of not being in the moment in that play. At any given moment, I was incapable of not being really released, and I acted as I had never acted before and as I did not act again for maybe twelve or thirteen years. I mean, I acted well other times, but not like that. I know it for a fact. For one thing everybody said so, but they didn't have to. I knew it. I don't know if that would have happened with another director.

JEAN Blythe said something similar about a breakthrough in her work at that time. Part of it for her was feeling permission to use all of herself. She said she no longer felt like she had to be appropriate, no longer had to be the "good girl" in rehearsal.

AUSTIN In that play in particular he made her into a very bad girl. He got her mad – but creatively, excitingly mad, not mad at him or the process, but mad, just mad, angry! And he wouldn't settle for anything else, and she just – day by day you could see her embracing and moving toward it more and more. And it was the best Masha I've ever seen.

my scene ✓

JEAN Probably one of the most moving scenes in the play is the Act IV scene between Tusenbach and Irina. Irina's agreed, finally, to marry Tusenbach, but right before the wedding he's challenged to a duel by Solyony. In this Act IV scene between them, he's going off to fight the duel, but Irina doesn't even know about it! What's going on in this scene? Does Tusenbach know he's going to die?

AUSTIN Oh yes.

JEAN Here's his speech from the end of that scene, right before he goes off to the duel. Would you read it out loud and then tell me what comes up for you?

AUSTIN (as Tusenbach)
> "It happens sometimes that little things, foolish trifles, suddenly and for no apparent reason become very important. You laugh at them as you have always done. You try to dismiss them as things that don't matter and yet you go on and feel that you have no power to stop. Oh, let's not talk about it any more. I feel so fine right now. It's as if I were seeing the firs and oaks and birches for the first time – they seem to be looking at me, questioning, waiting. What beautiful trees they are, and how beautiful life should be near them ... I must go. It's time. Look at that tree over there. It's all dried up and dead but it still waves in the wind with the others. I can't help thinking that if I die I shall still be part of life one way or another. Good-by, dearest. The papers you gave me are on my desk under the calender." *

JEAN Is the trap to let it become too sentimental or poetic?

AUSTIN Yes. But those traps were so implicitly avoided in the way that Nikos approached the scene, they never even came up, we didn't even know that the traps were there. It was like walking past a burning building, and after you passed it, it would collapse but you never even knew. I remember that Nikos would encourage here that Tusenbach have a kind of lust for communication; it was like a form of making love, I guess. I'm not sure he used that phrase but

Reprinted by permission of the Nikos Psacharopoulos estate.

9

whatever he did say resulted in that. And making love is not a sentimental act. *Talking* about making love is sentimental, but making love is not. And for me it was like Tusenbach was making love to Irina in this last scene, which he had been looking forward to doing for years, and now he knew he was never going to do. So he was doing it another way, with words.

JEAN Which makes it very active.

AUSTIN As I remember, by the time Nikos and I got to that scene in the fourth act, we were so much in sync, we hardly ever talked about it. He would say things like, 'don't take a moment there,' or 'take a moment there.' He had so put me on a track for the first three acts that he almost didn't have to say anything by the time we got to that scene. The choices and feelings emerged from his concept of how to approach the role.

JEAN I was very moved by what you said before about turning great pain into an appetite for joy. If *Three Sisters* is about anything, I think it's that.

AUSTIN Also *Three Sisters*, probably more than any play I know, is about the simple heroism of getting through the day. Not plodding through the day, but really, *really* getting through the day. And Nikos found that in these plays. Of the four important Chekhov plays, *The Three Sisters* is probably the most pure expression of it. But no one I know of ever saw that before Nikos. Everybody always thought of it as this autumnal play. It's about as autumnal as the Fourth of July!

I remember every moment of that rehearsal process. I don't know that I ever had a better one. Some things I've done in the past few years, I feel as good about the result, but the rehearsal process wasn't like that. Everyone was so energized from everyone else. You felt it was like, in the early days, when people talk about Jose Quintero directing O'Neill. You got the feeling from them – and what I think that we all had in *Three Sisters* – that you were working with *the* director anywhere. It was like a master conductor, whose specialty was Mozart, conducting a symphony by Mozart. I mean, he knew what everything was there for. And those kind of people are so assured that they don't need to be autocratic about it, they just had to tell you, that's all. There was no anxiety about it.

JEAN On one of the tapes, Nikos talks about having directed Chekhov so often that he no longer knew *why* he wanted certain things or why he did certain things. He said that if he was pinned down he could come up with an answer but by that point, it had all become rather unconscious for him. And that same thing happens when an actor gives a great performance. The actor no longer remembers if a moment was something the director put in or something he or she put in –

AUSTIN Right, right.

JEAN – That you know you've done a really great performance when you come off-stage and don't remember what you did.

AUSTIN I always felt that in rehearsal with Nikos. It was extraordinary. I even felt it in the rehearsal of *The Cherry Orchard* with Colleen, as turbulent as that was. Still I felt those energies. It was thrilling. I would not rather have been anywhere else. And that was remarkable, because from my point of view, first of all there was a leading actress there who was – radiantly – unhappy! In a way that kind of cast a glow around the whole room! And having just directed the play, I had a very fresh set of images. Even with all of that going on, the joy of Nikos interacting with that material was thrilling.

JEAN What was special at Williamstown in the Chekhovs, from what I saw, was the abundance of very alive, very unusual physical behavior. For example, when you played Vanya you were on the floor a lot of the time.

AUSTIN [With a laugh.] Yeah, that was Vanya.

JEAN How did you come about finding that particular physical behavior for the character?

AUSTIN Well, this time Nikos was not directing, but I think there was just something about working on the play up there. I've played

11

it once before and I've played it since, but at Williamstown it was different, you felt that there was a way one worked on Chekhov at Williamstown, you know? It was terribly physical. I lay on the floor during Vanya's monologue since essentially everything Vanya says in that monologue comes out of the feeling he has that he's hit bottom. So what is there to do, but hit bottom? Again, this didn't go through my head as an intellectual process, you were just sort of drawn to the absolute, urgent physical reality of everything you were saying and feeling, the implicit physical reality of it, which Nikos always encouraged. Otherwise, the characters are just *talking* about their feelings. But no, he's not *talking* about his feelings. He's *living* them. I guess the implication of what Nikos would get at is that the characters are almost seeking out the physical reality of what they're feeling in order to fully confront it. It's not just *thoughts* about feeling. It's: "Here's what I feel, I'm going to go for it!" And the only way to truly go for anything involves some kind of physicalization, in life or in acting. Yeah, everything was physicalized, but not in an arbitrary way. They were the *found* physical things. What would you physically do if you were driven by those particular needs at that moment? That was what Nikos was always seeking out, or encouraging you to seek out.

JEAN Did you ever have any conflicts or confusion about what Nikos wanted?

AUSTIN [He laughs.] You only got confused by Nikos if you tried to absorb what he said intellectually. His directions were not meant to be absorbed in that way, they were meant to be absorbed into the viscera. Also there was no point resisting Nikos interpretively. Nikos, like a lot of master directors or conductors, wasn't into intellectual debate about the play. Nikos knew what he felt the play was about and he encouraged you to live in his feeling about the play. And his feelings about the play were always thought through, and felt through, and they always came from an authentic place in him. So they had an organic logic to them, even when they were a little eccentric, they had an organic logic to them, and in Chekhov I never thought they were even remotely eccentric.

JEAN They weren't constructs…

AUSTIN Yeah, they weren't just playing around. He had really arrived at whatever it was, through his own feelings, and his own life. And in Chekhov they were really on the money. They were that wonderful combination of being on the money and utterly fresh at the same time. And every time he would redirect those plays, he totally rethought them. There was never a sense of: "Oh, it worked wonderfully in 1971 when Joycie crossed over here." It was never like that. He had this tremendous appetite for looking at these plays again and again, to sort of see where he was in his own life, what was different now. Just throw everything out and see where you are now.

JEAN You always seemed especially adept at uncovering the humor in Chekhov.

AUSTIN Well, I think that's the thing that Nikos got onto with me: I am – to my regret a lot of the time – I am a naturally funny person. I have a persona that people are amused by, before I do anything. So Nikos – and this is the oldest rule of comedy but everybody forgets it, I forget it – Nikos always encouraged me to play Chekhov utterly seriously and the comedic aspects would take care of themselves. I have never once in a Chekhov play attempted to be funny, as I have, sometimes, in other material. So that's more just something that comes with what God has given you, the particular set of strengths and the particular set of limitations. I mean, if I go on and play a Chekhov role completely seriously and committedly and passionately and all out, there's something funny about it. It's not even the choices I make. It's just I don't even have to think about being funny.

JEAN So you never have a line you work to get a laugh on. You never have to be concentrating on timing.

AUSTIN That's right. And then what that reveals about certainly the men in Chekhov – I don't know if it's as true about the women – but certainly those men in Chekhov are walking foibles. They are God's fools, almost all of them. They are lost. They are deeply lost guys but they don't know it. And that's – I don't know whether that is me or not, but it's certainly what people read in me when I act. Of

13

course, on other occasions, it has very much gotten in my way, that thing, but Nikos always knew how to turn it to an advantage. And he was, I think, maybe the first director I ever worked with who figured that out. I remember something he would say to Blythe and me all the time, to each of us, individually, separately, he would say: "Don't be vulnerable. When either one of you walk on the stage you look like you're going to be hit by a truck any minute, so don't ever play that, play something else, it will just be vulnerable. Because you don't, either one of you, look like you're going to make it across the room. So don't ever play that."

With me, then he would take it further – see, Nikos understood me so well. The one thing he really understood about me was that I saw myself as a very dramatic actor, and I saw myself even as a romantic actor, in the broad sense of that word. And he always encouraged it and he always allowed it, and he always knew that if he allowed me to do those things and really do them, really fully, that they would automatically have an ironic edge to them just because of the persona that I am. And he was the first director who ever really understood that about me and encouraged it, and so, I think, profoundly shaped all the choices I've made about my career in the areas where I have choices, since. I mean, film and TV I sort of have to accept what I'm given, but in the theater I've followed my own path, and I think it was because Nikos somehow gave me permission to. In the theater I've tried very hard to stay away from what would be called, and what are called "Austin Pendleton" roles. But it was Nikos who encouraged me to do that. "Just play something else and then it will work in some kind of tension with the persona that you have." And probably the most extreme example of that was in the Chekhovs. He never encouraged me to play Tusenbach as a fool. He encouraged me to play Tusenbach as a man in love with his woman. Whereas another director would have tried to use those so-called "Austin" qualities.

JEAN Well, in essence, that was the problem when I saw a recent production of *Three Sisters* on the west coast. The actors were directed more as caricatures than people. There were judgements passed on them.

AUSTIN Yes, Nikos never made judgements. In Nikos' productions

14

everyone was the leading actor. Everyone was the romantic lead, you could almost say. Everyone's passion was utterly acknowledged.

JEAN One strength I've always seen in your work – something I try to emulate – is your ability to be in the moment. Is that how you approach Chekhov, going for a moment-to-moment reality? Or do you develop an idea about an arc for the character –

AUSTIN Never, never. I stopped thinking about arcs in general in the late sixties sometime! Because my worst enemy as an actor is my head, so once I dropped my head, I was able to act.

JEAN How does it get in your way?

AUSTIN Your behavior gets produced by an idea of where you're going with the part and not by what the other person has just said to you. You can't do what you do on stage, anymore than you can in life, except in response to what somebody else has just said or done to you. You can't. And it's that simple. The kind of choices I remember that Nikos would encourage were the ones that could only be done that way, they made no sense any other way. But they made total sense that way.

If the play is any good at all – and it doesn't have to be Chekhov, it can be by an accomplished hack – the line of the character is going to take care of itself. And that was also the way that Nikos approached everything. He had very strong ideas, but they could only be realized in the moment to moment terms of acting. Whenever you tried to match his ideas with an idea of your own, it just was chaos and terrible fights would happen. But if you just abandoned that and abandoned yourself to taking in what somebody else was saying to you and then acting on it at that moment the way Nikos wanted you to, it just would make sense. It was something you could do. And then you find when you started to run through it and perform it that, yes, it did have a line to it but you weren't playing that line, and you hadn't even thought of that line.

JEAN Here's Nikos on the subject, from one of the tapes from his classes: "Thinking has nothing to do with acting. If acting were thinking, we'd all be great actors, and yet I think about it, but I can't act. So don't assume that everytime somebody thinks, it's acting. What you have to do is translate honestly the whole thought pattern into the activities that you're going to do."

AUSTIN Yes, I think Nikos thought that every actor had an extraordinary intelligence to bring to a role, but that that intelligence was in areas of themselves that they didn't know anything about. It was an intelligence in their nerve endings that was uniquely theirs. And that was what needed to be released, not their head intelligence. There are some actors who cling to their head intelligence and those actors always had trouble with Nikos and Nikos with them. Because he thought the genuine intelligence of an actor, – I mean, in life you use your head intelligence all the time, but as an actor intelligence is throughout you. You know what I mean? And it just has to be *engaged* in trying to cope with something else that another character is doing and it will just express itself. He was always implicitly saying, "Don't try to manipulate it, don't try to manipulate the intelligence that you have, don't try to be cleverer than you deeply are." And that's probably a frightening thing to do until you do it and then it's not frightening at all. Then it's like jumping off a high board, once you do it you can't stop.

All the characters in Chekhov want things and they want them very badly. And in pursuing their want for these things they interact with other people and are provoked into an even greater want. And you're okay as long as you stay on that and abandon yourself to it, which again is what Nikos was always encouraging. That Tennessee Williams line, "Make voyages! Attempt them! There's nothing else!" – in a way that became his idea of what the Chekhov characters are about. I mean, in *The Three Sisters*, it is that in a literal sense, "Make voyages! Attempt them! There's nothing else!"

Blythe Danner (Masha) in "The Three Sisters," 1976

"When doing a monologue, you should know what happened immediately before. This is going to be the springboard of the speech, but it is not the full context. I call this 'time-given circumstances,' which has its own depth before the speech. There is a tricky way of doing it for interpretation or for doing it through your soul. Good actors don't use time-given circumstances for the interpretation, they always use them to really get going. That's why it is so very wonderful to work with a very good actor.

"Blythe Danner, no matter what the situation, turns time-given circumstances into an advantage for her acting. Everything is a springboard for her to be fuller as an actress. You could say, 'Oh, let's not see the scene this way, let's see it that way,' but she would still use either direction as a springboard, though a different kind of springboard each time. If you can use the circumstances as a springboard rather than as a corset, you're okay. They will not limit you, they will give you freedom, the freedom to work."

Nikos Psacharopoulos

THE PLACE OF INSPIRATION
Interview with Blythe Danner

Ms. Danner's first role at Williamstown was Nina in *The Sea Gull* in 1974. Since then she's returned to WTF almost every summer, appearing in 12 plays directed by Nikos as well as 9 others. Her other Chekhov roles were Masha in *The Three Sisters* in 1976, Dunyasha in *The Cherry Orchard* in 1980 and Yelena in *Uncle Vanya* in 1984. Blythe and I talked at her home in Santa Monica, occasionally interrupted by her son Jake and the family's two golden retrievers.

JEAN I think the problem a lot of young people have with Chekhov is that the plays are confusing on the first read. Until I saw a really good production – actually, your *Sea Gull* – I wasn't able to connect to what they were all about.

BLYTHE Well, Nikos, for me, was the only director I've worked with who got it – really understood how these brilliant plays should be done. The problem with so many productions is either the comic is overstressed or the tragic, and very rarely do you have the melding of the two. And that's when it works, I think. Really, there are very few writers who create that dichotomy that we see in life - the surprise of the comedy coming simultaneously with the tragedy, or one directly on the heels of the other; the absurdity of those opposite emotions happening at once. I think, this paradox Chekhov draws so beautifully comes from a very accurate observation of life.

JEAN *The Sea Gull* was your first Chekhov at Williamstown.

BLYTHE Yes, and then *Three Sisters*. The one I felt the least good about was the *Uncle Vanya*. Jeff Bleckner was a wonderful director, but I just couldn't get my footing with Yelena. I have no idea why except that I didn't have the familiar ground that I had with Nikos, who knew my own particular neuroses and insecurities and how to deal with me, and who also gave me the freedom that no other

20

director has given me.

JEAN You mean freedom to explore –

BLYTHE Yeah, Nikos was the one who not only allowed me but pushed me. When he first offered me Masha, I said, "No." I said, "No, I can't possibly do that. I can't plumb those depths, I don't think I have them!" I knew I'd have to tap into an even deeper emotional place with Masha than with Nina. The prospect terrified me.

JEAN And when he offered you Nina?

BLYTHE The fact is that he didn't really want me for Nina. He didn't know me and I'm sure he had other people that he'd worked with that he wanted. Why not? He wanted Lee Grant for Arkadina and we had the same agent. I think my agent said if you want Lee Grant you have to take Blythe Danner. And he said, "Who's Blythe Danner?" He was indignant that somebody would dictate to him. It was his theater, I can understand how he felt.

JEAN What I heard is that Nikos went to see a movie that you were in, stayed for three minutes and said, "Okay, she's Nina."

BLYTHE I heard he said, (affectionately, with Nikos' accent:) "So, I saw her; so, she can cry; so, okay." So that's how I got there.

JEAN Did you feel that your training had prepared you for approaching Chekhov?

BLYTHE I was fortunate to have two great teachers at Bard - Charlie Kakatsakis - another Greek! - who concentrated on method work, and Bill Driver, an Englishman who breathed life into Shakespeare and the classics. So I had a strong bridge between those two disciplines that helped me eventually with playing Chekhov. But when I played Irina in the *Three Sisters* right out of college, I felt I didn't have a clue. It wasn't an inspired production, no passion. My Chekhov revelation came when I saw Rosemary Harris play Nina in *The Sea Gull* in Ellis Raab's production at the

Bucks County Playhouse in Pennsylvania. I was a teenager. I came out of the theater reeling. I couldn't get over the power of the play and Rosie's performance - that's when I knew I wanted to act!

I was very scared, though, when I came to WTF to play Nina - I had my doubts as to whether I could cut it. I'd been a rotten Irina a few years before, Nikos was a formidable person and it all felt like unknown territory. I was very grateful that Olympia and Frank were there, they had great humor and spirit. The whole company was splendid, I remember everyone was very loose. And watching Lee in rehearsal - I was so impressed with her freedom to explore. At first I cowered in a corner, terrified. Then, the first time that I let loose with the emotion, I was very proud of myself. But Nikos lit into me, and yelled, "Crying is not the key to Chekhov!" I thought, what is he talking about? I finally cried, I touched my emotions. But he really wanted something deeper than that - a pain that went beneath tears and he wouldn't settle for less than that.

I think with Chekhov there was a great pairing of Nikos' passionate, Greek temperament and his sense of the theatrical. So that he never got too "Method" with it. When the work was in danger of getting too self-indulgent or too small, he would try to goose us, get us to play on a larger scale. We had many battles about this, because I felt at times he wanted *opera* and I'd yell, "I don't feel *real*, Nikos!" But he didn't want to waste rehearsal time finding reality - that was to be done on our own, with each other outside of rehearsal. He only had a few weeks to get these productions up and he trusted us to find all that by the opening. Of course he led us there by his own circuitous route.

JEAN Nikos often said in classes that he rarely rehearsed the last scene of the *Sea Gull*. He felt that if the whole play was on the right track, the last scene would sort of take care of itself.

BLYTHE I never felt ready to do that scene. Every day I'd say "Could we not do that scene today?" It was cowardice, I think. I was afraid to jump into that scene. But that's true, you really have to have the first three acts in order to play it.

I think the reason the role is so incredibly appealing to actresses is the great contrast of Nina's enormous innocence and purity in the first three acts and her darkness in that last scene, being catapulted into that darkness. There are very few roles that have that much of a range. Which is why, I mean, she's supposed to be seventeen, but very few seventeen-year-olds can play her because it demands so much depth and life experience.

JEAN Why do you think it's not Nina but Trepleff who kills himself? I mean, at first glance, she's the one who's more undone.

BLYTHE Well, first, it's a brilliant dramatic devise - the surprise of it. Trepleff sees his pure angel girl, the love of his youth, trampled by Trigorin. On the other hand, he sees she has strength and courage, a resolve to carry on. Nina says, "We must endure", the line I think of as Chekhov's signature. In his cowardice, he's hidden away from life. He realizes he can't save her or himself, and in that scene he sees that all the dreams of his youth are destroyed. I don't think anyone in the audience knows that Trepleff is going to kill himself, though. If that's really played properly it's a tremendous surprise, don't you think? That's the wonderful, elusive thing about Chekhov – it is so unpredictable, like life. Certainly with Nina – she comes into that last scene so undone and she might very well put a gun in her mouth, and the opposite happens.

JEAN I've seen this scene done in class many times and usually Nikos' critique always had something to do with playing against the emotion, and making it a fight for sanity …

BLYTHE Yes, it has to be that. For Nina, Trepleff's the person she shared her youth with, the time that was innocent. The sea gull, I think, represents that for her, that freedom and complete purity and innocence. It's being with Trepleff that evokes the memories of her youth, all that wonderful lightness that she had then in contrast to the darkness of the past few years. She's been dragged through the mud, really. If she's a sea gull she can transcend all that, she can fly away and return to her youth. That's why she goes back to the speech from the play within the play at the end of this scene. And that's a theme throughout the plays – the flying, the freedom of flight, of escape.

I'll never forget something Nikos did during *Three Sisters*. In Act IV, Masha looks at the birds flying overhead and says, "The birds are already flying south. Those are swans, or wild geese. Fly away, my dear ones, so free, so free from care." In other words, "I'm here under this yoke, and I'm imprisoned in my own agony, but you birds are free and you can fly, fly away!" Well, that moment could be done, you know, very poetically. And I remember so well having trouble with that moment and Nikos jumping up on stage, and yelling, "Birds, birds, birds – you want them to escape – fly, fly, get away while you can!" And it wasn't poetic at all, it was – active, impatient! As if he were just – shooing them away. So I tried to do that, I think it might have been the first preview, and he came back with tears in his eyes and said, "Where did you get that moment, the desperation in that moment?" and I said, "From you, from you!" He seemed so surprised!

Whenever I have to play a scene that requires that kind of emotion, I always use my memory of Masha. Something dropped in me with her, I remember feeling emotionally fuller in that role than I've ever been before. It was wonderfully refreshing to feel so rooted with Masha.   Now, when I'm on a film set and given a very short time to get to an emotional result – and you just feel so at sea with all these people around – I go back to Masha and Nina, and I go back to Nikos. He helped me find those moments in a way that no other director before had ever been able to.

JEAN Can you be more specific? Was it just in the kind of direction he gave you?

BLYTHE Well, it was somehow more elusive. He gave me permission...to be bad. I had always been a very "good" girl with most directors, I would never be impolite, I always blamed myself if something didn't work. He encouraged the opposite in me. Actually I *wasn't* completely grateful to him for this, because he let loose a sort of – monster – in me at times. And I realized that happened because he gave me permission to use all of myself, not just the "good" girl. Which was the only way I could get to those raw, raw moments.Until then I'd never trusted anybody else enough to let all of that out, to release all of that.

JEAN The plays also require that kind of release, don't they? The circumstances generate that, too – I mean, in the last scene of *The*

24

Sea Gull, Nina hasn't slept, hasn't eaten, she's been walking around the lake, in the cold –

BLYTHE The lack of sleep was very helpful. When you haven't had any sleep a lot of times things will be unleashed, maybe because your guard is down, you're too tired to censor yourself. When we were putting *The Sea Gull* on tape for PBS, I think we had to stop shooting the last scene at midnight for a crew break or something and we came back at about four in the morning, and I thought, "I can't do this, this is just absurd!" And, of course, that's what the scene needs.

JEAN Did you feel that the TV version caught your best performance of that scene?

BLYTHE No, it felt better on stage because then it wasn't so disjointed. It came out of what preceded it. It's that same old problem when it comes to film vs. theater. I thought I did it much better on stage – but everyone else was just as true. But, when I saw it the last time, I thought, "This is pretty good!", you know?

JEAN What about Masha in *Three Sisters*?

BLYTHE Masha was the one that I resisted the most and the one that Nikos practically had to boot me in the behind to do. I kept saying, "I'm not going to do this, I'll play Irina," and he said, "No, no, no." He had faith that I could do it. Like a child, the actor wants to please the parent, the director. And if the director gives unequivocal love and trust, then the actor gives completely, too. Masha was really a turning point in my life. I always thought of her, in this orchestra of characters, that we all played, as the cello, the contralto. I think of her as having a very deep resonance or passion, which is why I call on her when I have to find a difficult moment in a film.

I tried to stay in a very low, deep place for this part. A place that connected me to her sensuality. Working on Masha I found a very visceral sense of her center. It's interesting. I've talked about this with a variety of creative artists, not just actors. About this place in

25

the body where inspiration comes from. I think that the creative urge, the purest and most creative urge, comes from the place in the body where we all begin, where we create life, our center. I found Masha's center came from – emanated from – that place where I gave birth. My brother, who's a glorious tenor, says that when he hits a high C, he sings his best, it comes from that place, from the groin. When I said Masha's line: "My man, where's my man?" – it used to give me goosebumps! Not that I thought I was being so wonderful, I just felt – here was someone who could just grab Vershinin, take him behind the hedges and make passionate love, whose heart was – whose soul was just – dripping with passion and with need. [She pauses.] Somehow though, talking about it, the words suggest only one aspect, and it's not just that. It's not just the sexual need. It is more than that, it transcends that. It is really – the hunger to fill one's soul.

JEAN Yes. That drives so many of Chekhov's characters.

BLYTHE It's the essence. Chekhov's genius is that he can articulate these universal longings so precisely, so simply. He leads you where you need to go. And then when you find the moment for the first time, the moment when you really connect to that place deep within yourself that mirrors the character's longing - it's incredibly exciting. My frustration is my inconsistency in reproducing the first time. I know we're not supposed to think about repeating a moment the same way every night, but when he gives you those tremendous cathartic moments, you want to always be full. The thing is, though, it stays in your muscle memory. Once you've found it, it's there. You begin to have faith in it, you begin to know that even if it isn't there every time you call upon it, it will come again, because you have found it. At some point you learn to trust it.

JEAN What was the point of contact? What did you use to get yourself there?

BLYTHE It was that moment of putting myself in the place of – of being trapped on earth and wishing I were that bird that could fly away. I tried to put myself into those images that Chekhov gives in the text. It's funny, in my own life at that time, I, Blythe, couldn't have felt happier. I'd just given birth to Jake. I was nursing. And I remember feeling so complete, so full. But something about this was also very essential for me in working on Masha. Maybe because I had just given birth a short time before, I was very much in touch with that earth-mother, primal place within.

JEAN It sounds like both things were operating for you with Masha – the image of her being very earthy, and, at the same time, the need to fly, to not be earthbound.

BLYTHE Well, yes, it really is both. Which shows, I guess, that a truly great role gives you all the colors of the spectrum. When I conjure up "Masha," I don't feel like a five-foot-seven, basically skinny person. I feel like I'm somebody who's five-two and weighs a hundred and thirty-five pounds. I had a great – settled – feeling with Masha, which went right through my being. But, on the other hand, there's that sense of being entrapped, there's the longing and the desire to be the bird, to be flying, to escape, to go heavenward. Yes, the role that fulfilled me most in my life was this character who touched on all of it.

JEAN Yelena in *Uncle Vanya* also has the same image – "If I could just be a bird and fly away from all of you, from your voices, from your talk..." It's really a recurring theme with these women.

BLYTHE Absolutely. I just didn't feel anything as kindred to Yelena as to Masha, just because that experience was so different. I felt like a stick figure. I felt like I was six-two and all elbows! Like everybody was looking at me and I didn't know where to put my arms, you know, like Nina's line, "When I stood on stage I didn't know what to do with my hands." When I played Yelena, I didn't know what to do with my hands.

JEAN Let's follow that through to Masha. How did you use your hands with her? I remember Nikos saying that he didn't want you, as Masha, to touch any of the other actors in *Three Sisters*.

BLYTHE Yes, as Nina in *The Sea Gull*, I kept touching everyone, making contact, and it made me feel very secure. But Nikos wouldn't let me do that in *Three Sisters*. I hated it at first, I felt so alienated. He wouldn't let me interact as I had before, and that was very disturbing to me. But it really helped Masha. She is a character who's very lonely and feels separate from the rest. That's always been one of my covers, when I'm insecure and don't know what do, I'm always trying to touch everybody, trying to make contact. And Nikos knew this and didn't allow me to do it. What that did was force me to go deep within, take a dive down inside myself, because I wasn't allowed to syphon off – Blythe's – nervous energy through touching. The nervous energy was no longer being wasted, let out in an exterior manner, but forced to go back onto itself, inside myself. Almost like imploding, building tension. So that helped a lot. Nikos was so intuitive to know how that would work. "Don't touch, don't touch," – until, of course, that moment at the end when he had me throw myself at Vershinin.

JEAN Steve Lawson told me that was one of the most athletic moments he's ever seen on any stage, that you just were like a projectile, hurling yourself across –

BLYTHE And with a big start, from very downstage, all the way to him, and Ken Howard was way, way, back against the wall –

JEAN How did that moment come about?

BLYTHE Nikos wanted me to do it! The first time he told me, I said, "What?!" I think I said, "No I could never do that, I won't be able to make that believable." You know, I used to always throw things in his path all the time, I don't know how he put up with me. "No, I can't possibly do that!"

But then, of course, the freedom of it! Oh, he was so smart with those things. I mean, it was so raw. The audience – there was always a gasp! It was a beautifully orchestrated moment; he knew really what he was doing there.

The other time I felt that was seeing Roberta Maxwell as Electra in Nikos's production of *The Greeks*. She had a glorious lashing out – I remember thinking he tried to get that same kind of thing behind it – a sense of losing, of losing this forever, and fighting – fighting loss with one's last breath. And – just go with that! Flail the

28

floor, whatever!

That's what I always found so incredible with Nikos and what I feel I'll never, ever have again with anyone, was this thing of being able to take a risk, of making a complete fool of yourself. The thing that I as a person and as an actress am loathe to do. Which is to just have it all be there in all its ugliness and all its freedom, in whichever way it would come out, and to know that it would not be judged. Nikos had faith in us. He gave us faith in ourselves.This was a great experience for me, not only as an actress but as a person. For myself, in my life, it was a great experience.

Tom Brennan, Nikos and 1962 company of "The Sea Gull"

"Chekhov defies interpretation. It's so brilliantly written. Only the most arrogant people believe they can go to a rehearsal ready to do Chekhov, they fall flat. I always find new things in Chekhov. I learn more than I teach. If you come to rehearsals with your five set ideas, you're sunk. We all should go to our junkyards and come back with three thousand things, try them out, to find out what works. You can't recreate the world of the play according to what you already know, only according to what you're discovering. I used to separate things. I would take my 38 books on 'Othello' and work up a preparation. I don't do that anymore. Rather than sharing information, I'm trying to open up the world of the play. By now my whole life is preparation for the text."

Nikos Psacharopoulos

MULTIPLICITY AND CONTRADICTION
Interview with Tom Brennan

Mr. Brennan, a longtime WTF company member and past Associate Director of the theater, went to school with Nikos at Oberlin University. In 1962, he played Medvedenko in WTF's first *Sea Gull*; in 1963, he played Trofimov in *The Cherry Orchard*; in 1964, he directed a production of *Uncle Vanya* as well as playing the Professor; in 1965, he played Andrei in *The Three Sisters*; in 1983, he played Lebedev in *Ivanov*, and, in 1984, he again played the Professor in *Uncle Vanya*. Tom and I talked at his home in Montclair, New Jersey, a few weeks after the birth of his third son, Nick.

JEAN How did you come to Chekhov? Had you seen any Chekhov before acting in that first one at Williamstown?

TOM Yes, seeing Chekhov, that's what influenced me as a young actor. Just before we did our first *Sea Gull* at WTF, the old Phoenix Theater did it with Montgomery Clift and Maureen Stapleton, George Voskovec and people of that ilk. I'd only seen it before in college, a production that was akin to moving in slow motion. It was so lugubrious and heavy that I had no reaction except a negative one. But when I saw the Phoenix production, as stylistically varied as it was, I was floored. By turns, depending on who was acting, you had all these different styles: you had Voskovec, from the continent; you had Judith Evelyn, who was an English actress; you had Maureen Stapleton and Montgomery Clift, both very American. I'll never forget, somewhere near the end of the first act, Maureen Stapleton as Masha went over to Voskovec, playing the doctor, and she laid her head on his chest, and she said, [He speaks in a low whisper.] "I don't know why I'm living." The tears started running down my face. And I was standing at the back of this theater, I'd come down from my seat in the balcony so I could see it better, and tears were running down my face. And I was saying, "This guy's great! This guy's great!" Meaning, of course, Chekhov.

And then, the following summer, Joyce Ebert suggested *The Sea Gull*. Nikos was very wary of it, mainly as a producer. "It's going to be a dead seagull at the box office!" That sort of thing. Well, we talked about it and I recounted my experience seeing it, and Joyce had done it very successfully at Carnegie Tech as an undergraduate. Ultimately we said, let's go ahead. The production was very successful, and Nikos was very moved by it. And that, I think,was the real starter for him. I think initially he was going along with Joyce and my strong feelings about Chekhov, but in doing that play he ran into something that he never expected. When he first started directing he always was involved with "style" plays. Anouilh, Giradoux, that kind of thing. This was the first time he moved to a more emotional realm. And from then on he became a champion of Chekhov and Tennessee Williams, and another whole side of himself emerged.

Then, the next season, we did *The Cherry Orchard*. Louis Zorich played Lopahkin. And Louis did something brilliant with it. He had that speech in Act III about buying the cherry orchard, about being a peasant becoming an entrepreneur, about having grown up in this household and being treated like a serf, second class – which was the way they were treated. And now, buying it, and buying it from a woman he loved! Well, all these contradictory things were happening in the acting of that speech. Louis was angry, he felt guilty, he was proud of himself for getting it. He was like an angry peasant about how long it took him to come into his own. He was laughing about his delight in it. He was crying for her. Ten, twenty different things happened in the course of that speech. Many years later I saw it at Lincoln Center – Andrei Serban's production with Raul Julia playing Lopahkin. I've seen them both do some wonderful work, but in this it seemed to me that all he was directed to do in the speech was smash furniture. He played only one thing, the anger. And that, to me, was an interesting lesson about playing Chekhov and also about what was going on with Chekhov at Williamstown.

JEAN You've directed Chekhov as well as acted. What's central for you about these plays when you're directing? What do you go for?

TOM The basic action, or the basic impulse in the plays is the longing for a better life. Nemirovich-Danchenko, who co-ran the Moscow Art Theater with Stanislavski, states that impulse was the core of what they found. And that longing is expressed in all different ways. For Lopahkin, it's buying the cherry orchard. In *The Sea Gull*, the longing for a better life is expressed through the artist. Everybody in that has some relation to an artist. The actress, the writer, the would-be actress and the would-be writer. Even the foreman of the place talks about opera! He was an opera lover. Everyone has some relation to the arts. In the last scene Nina says, "It's not the fame, not the glory, but ability to endure." Now that is a very harsh statement of what life is all about if that's the bottom line. But I think once you accept that, or once you know that, or once you experience that, then suddenly life does become happier. Once you realize that that *is* life, that the struggle *is* life. And Chekhov had the daring to more or less say that. It's the same thing in *Three Sisters*; what does he do? He takes these people, their longing for a better life, gives a possibility of it for each of them – but then those things that spell happiness for each one of them disappear. And they're left very simply to endure. Same thing in *Vanya*. "We shall rest, we shall rest." That beautiful last speech in Vanya.

JEAN Blythe used that word "longing," too. That sense of longing you described in the plays seems to require the actor to really hook into his or her own deepest longings. And the combination of the two often creates an unexpectedly powerful response.

TOM That happened for me on stage in *Three Sisters*, when I played Andrey. Bill Hansen was playing the doctor. And we had a scene together toward the end of the play and he says something about, "Come on, come away with me. Run away with me and don't look back!" And I'm wheeling the baby carriage, and my wife, that peasant Natasha, is taking over the place. And when he said that, something just welled up in me! Because I couldn't go with him. I couldn't go with him! And I felt like I was choking – I couldn't go with him! It was one of the best feelings I've ever had on a stage in my life. One of the best things I've ever had in my life because I tapped something that way, something so significant. I was stuck in this place and [He whispers harshly.] I couldn't get out! I was devastated.

That emotional response wasn't something I figured out the character should have at that moment. It was just something that hit me from being in the world of the play. It wasn't rationalized. Chekhov says that in an excerpt in *Playwrights on Playwriting*. He says, "Rework. Make a mosaic out of it. Don't polish. Don't finish it off, don't make it slick. Leave rough edges." Chekhov wants that stuff of life that you can't rationalize, that you can't pin down and say, "I'm going to play this here and that there." You just kind of instinctively get a sense of it at a certain point. Of the potential in the material. Lopahkin comes back, he's bought this estate and when he was a kid, he was only allowed to come into the kitchen! For an actor to be given those circumstances! For an actor, for anyone interested in life, it's dynamite.

Also, in *Playwrights on Playwriting,* he says that the Russian temperament, if you could graph it, would be a high peak of excitability and then a sharp drop to exhaustion and boredom. And then up again. That's how you graph the Russian temperament. And that's why I think so many mistakes have been made in playing Chekhov.

JEAN How so?

TOM Well, the bland leading the bland. Just doing it naturally. Actors being so intimidated by the whole Actor's Studio thing that all they ever did was just say the words simply and naturally, but without that excitability. Without that Russian temperament.

Another thing is that actors tend to put Chekhov on too much of a pedestal, as I myself have done – making too much of the subtext. Here's a wonderful quote Chekhov says, "I write an act as if it were a story. The action goes on quietly and peacefully but at the end I give them a heavy jolt. All my energy was spent on a few brisk forceful climaxes, but the bridges joining them are insignificant, loose and not startling." Well, in this vein, Nikos was quick to tell a Vershinin, "Look, when you ask for tea, it doesn't mean you want to sleep with Masha, you're just thirsty!"

The best Vershinin I've ever seen was Sandor Szabo.

JEAN Who's that?

TOM He's a Hungarian. He was in one of those old productions that David Ross down on the East Side used to do with people like Franchot Tone. And when he came in, in that first scene in *Three Sisters*, when he gave those women that speech about what life will be like in the future, three hundred years from now – I mean, those women were fascinated, every one of them! He was so – ebullient and full of life that you knew that in three hundred years it was going to be just as he said! And he finishes. And there was a silence – like a sigh! And then Masha says, "I think I'll stay to lunch after all." And I've seen actors play that speech like [With a yawn.], "Oh, here we are in another provincial town, and my wife doesn't love me and this and that." All very bland or psychological, concerned with Chekhov's "message." No, Vershinin's just delighted to be there! But that's too simple, I guess.

JEAN I thought Chris Walken had a lot of that same thing in his first act of *Three Sisters* at WTF.

TOM Yes, Nikos' last production of *Three Sisters* had a lot of good stuff in it. Here's an interesting thing. He had Blythe in the one before it, playing Masha. And she was just sublime. And I thought, well, you know, he has Amy Irving this time, ho hum. But she was terrific! He got something from her that I never suspected and had never seen before or since in her work. Not that she couldn't do it, I just hadn't seen her be tested like that, I hadn't seen her talent challenged like that before.

JEAN And how was Nikos, do you think, getting this kind of work out of actors in these plays?

TOM Well, I think it was a revelation for him as to where his feelings lay in the work. So there was something very personal for him, and that transmitted itself to the cast. But there was also something about the way he went at it. A lot of times Nikos is kidded about his kind of double talk – you're left with your mouth hanging open, and it's like, "What exactly did he say?" Because of the way he would weave around, in and out of something. But I think that's what Chekhov means when he says a mosaic. Because you get the richness of life, you get contradiction, you get it from different points of view. Unless you see an event with the multiplicity that Louis did in that speech – as opposed to Raul Julia who played one thing – "I am smashing this household for treating me like that," – you're in trouble. If you let the life of it simply happen it's amazing the life it takes on. But the minute you pin it down and say it's just one thing – and Nikos was really good at not doing that. He was a master at not doing that! He would just take off on something. He would start at this point. The next day he'd give you a direction for the scene that seemed to contradict the day before. And again the next day. But by the time he got through, you had a whole picture, you had all the contradictory elements.

JEAN Isn't that really what the comedy comes out of? That juxtaposition?

TOM Yes. At one point Chekhov says, "I've been able to resist making anyone a villain but I'm not sure I've been able to resist the clown." When Chekhov says, "Don't be afraid of being foolish," he means being foolish like we are in life. This was something that Nikos permitted and encouraged. Trofimov, which I played, in *Cherry Orchard* gets so upset with Ranveskaya that he runs out of the room after a conversation with her and in front of everyone promptly falls down the stairs. This is all funny! He's a young, idealistic person who's very naive about life. And in that fall down the stairs, Chekhov is saying something about how silly he is. And, again, then I saw it at Lincoln Center and he was played as a hard-nosed revolutionary who gets no pleasure out of life, who's not foolish at all, a man who has got a back-bone of steel! And it's just so un-Chekhov!

JEAN Someone who would never fall down a flight of stairs.

TOM Yes! And Chekhov does that moment so beautifully. Trofimov makes a dignified entrance to the other room and falls down the steps! And Nikos understood these things. Nikos could be very disciplined, but he also appreciated the opposite. You told me something he once said about wanting one undisciplined actor in every cast. Well, that to me is the essence of somebody who sees reality very deeply with all of its paradox. Paradox. That's the core of it. When Chekhov looks at life, he can't tell you it's a happy ending. But he can't tell you it's a lousy ending, either. People manage to care for each other, have a compassion for each other. And there's a beauty about life, too, in these plays.

That's another thing Nikos understood, the beauty. The beauty wasn't just in the sets and costumes, although he always had marvelous sets and costumes. But more than that he was in touch with the beauty of the expression of the soul in Chekhov. I mean, that last speech of Sonya's! Do you have it here?

JEAN Yes.

TOM I mean, listen to this. Well, actually it's a woman's speech, why don't you read it?

JEAN (as Sonya)

"Life must go on. And our life will go on, Uncle Vanya. We shall live through a long succession of days and endless evenings. We shall bear patiently the trials fate has in store for us. We shall work for others – now and in our old age – never knowing any peace. And when our time comes we shall die without complaining. In the world beyond the grave we shall say that we wept and suffered, that our lot was harsh and bitter, and God will have pity on us. And you and I, Uncle dear, shall behold a life which is bright and beautiful and splendid. We shall rejoice and look back on our present misfortunes with feelings of tenderness, with a smile. And we shall find peace. We shall, Uncle, I believe it with all my heart and soul. We shall find peace. We shall find peace. We shall find peace.

"We shall hear the angels, we shall see the sky sparkling with diamonds. We shall see all the evils of this life, all our own sufferings, vanish in the flood of mercy which will fill the whole world. And then our life will be calm and gentle, sweet as a caress. I believe that, I do believe it. Poor, poor Uncle Vanya, you're crying. There's been no happiness in your life, but wait, Uncle Vanya, wait. We shall find peace. We shall find peace. We shall find peace." *

* Translated by Ronald Hingley. Reprinted by permission of Oxford University Press, Oxford England

TOM Yes. My God. There's a beauty of expression in it. And a lot of that is out of fashion in today's theater. That is so much less expressed, now. Characters express themselves now, more often than not, in monosyllables and, for God's sake, as an actor, don't dwell on the word because that's too phony! It's not that you play Chekhov sentimentally or poetically. You've got to somehow make the thing real and at the same time get the beauty of expression that he's written in it. That's what I love about Williams, too. That's where they are so similar for me. The beauty of expression, the soul comes out in the speeches the characters have. As an actor, if you have any soul at all, you want to do Chekhov.

And for Nikos, doing Chekhov brought out his soul. Before that, he had expressed beauty by using the outer form, in the so-called "style" plays. From that first Chekhov he realized the beauty in the substance as well. And it became a preference for him to do Williams and Chekhov as opposed to the other.

I remember when we did *Three Sisters* the first time. During a dress rehearsal I went out and sat out in the house after I was through. So I saw the end of the play, with the three girls grouped there. They finished the last scene, and I went up on stage and I congratulated Joyce Ebert and Carolyn Coates and Laurie Kennedy, and I was just crying. I was saying, "Oh God, it's awful, it's just awful!" And they said, "What do you mean, the play?" I said, "No, I'm just so moved by the damn thing, it's awful!." I meant, "It's so awful to take!" Pure and simple, he's the most moving of playwrights and I think that's what got Nikos. I really think he discovered something in himself, because he was the driving force from then on for doing it all the time.

It's funny, I think right after we did the first *Sea Gull*, it was either that year or the next, that Jimmy Noble and Carolyn Coates and Joyce and Mike Ebert and myself and all the actors came to Nikos and said, "Somehow, this Chekhov work has to go someplace. We have to take it out into the world." Well, Nikos did that, by doing these plays again and again over the years. He took them out into the world. Because nobody else in this country has done that much Chekhov, nobody. Before or since.

*Olympia Dukakis (Ravenskaya), Charles Siebert (Gayev), Joyce Ebert
(Varya) in "The Cherry Orchard," 1969*

"Chekhov monologues are spectacular. What really makes a good monologue, such as one by Shakespeare or Chekhov, is that there is a moment of a certain intensity which becomes personal and transcends the public event. So, if Hamlet is going to say, 'To be or not to be,' if he is going to ask, 'Do I kill myself or don't I kill myself,' he has to do it alone, right? There's no way around it. If the doctor in 'Three Sisters' has to say, 'I killed somebody on the operating table,' he has to do that alone. If people are around, they might not even understand. That's true in all the great Chekhov monologues; Ranevskaya talks to Trofimov; Andrey talks to the old deaf man that comes from the town council, who might as well not be there, because he doesn't hear.

"In Gorky's 'Enemies,' there is a great speech that the actress has, one of the greatest monologues in the history of the theater, which is delivered to a drunk husband who is more or less out of it. So the greatest monologues are moments when the sense of privacy becomes public. Those are the moments in theater when a playwright allows himself to go overboard. All the great actors have made their private worlds public, and that's the difference between a good actor and a bad actor. That's all it is – giving themselves permission to appear to be silly and ridiculous and emotional and human and glorious."

Nikos Psacharopoulos

CLAIMING THE SPACE
Interview with Olympia Dukakis

Ms. Dukakis did six Chekhov plays at WTF: Olga in *The Three Sisters* in 1970 and 1976; Paulina in *The Sea Gull* in 1968 and 1974; Charlotta in *The Cherry Orchard* in 1963, and Ravneskaya in the same play in 1969. She also played several of these roles at The Whole Theater in New Jersey as well as Yelena in *Uncle Vanya*. Another notable WTF and Russian role was that of The Actress in Gorky's *Enemies*, also directed by Nikos. I interviewed Olympia over lunch at a restaurant in Manhattan's theater district.

OLYMPIA My first contact with Chekhov was at school, with a wonderful teacher who made it very revelatory to me. His name was Peter Cash, and we did a production of *The Sea Gull* in which I played Arkadina, and that's when I fell in love with Chekhov. Later, working with Nikos, I began to trust myself more and more in Chekhov. It was a combination of two things: one was Nikos, seeing him come from such very personal, unreasonable places when he worked, so that I "got it" more often by example rather than by specific things that he said. Although there were specific things he said that were very important. The other was watching Louis [Zorich]. For Louis, Chekhov was like a second skin, he knew how to go from lightness to darkness, from seriousness to humor, from being withdrawn to being convivial. He always brought in all these changes which was really what Nikos was always after, because he wanted it to be Greek! So, it was this aspect, encouraged and supported by Nikos and demonstrated by Louis, that I eventually looked into as we worked.

It was Nikos' support of that in Louis. And Louis claiming it, totally. I think there have been two actors that I stood on stage with and stopped acting – and you know me well enough to know that that is something I don't give up, ever! But to Louis and Bill Hansen, I did. In the third act, of *Cherry Orchard* – Louis came in, as Lopakhin, and with Nikos' total support, he didn't play it as a catastrophe. He was laughing! He was falling all over the furniture!

He was going the whole emotional distance with it. For me, those two – Nikos and Louis – were inextricably joined in my perception, in my sense of what was possible, of where you go and what you could do in Chekhov.

JEAN I think you've just defined why Chekhov is so satisfying to play: there's so much range in every role.

OLYMPIA It's incredible to be in the world of those plays, to get to the point where you stop trying to impose interpretations and let the play take you. Which was the thing that Nikos was always wanting. When he would say, "Don't be intellectual," he meant, "permit the play – the structure of the scenes, the way they move and the sequence of the scenes – permit that to take you; go into that world and let it control you." Of course that's good acting, period. But somehow in Chekhov that's especially true. You can't get any pleasure out of playing Chekhov unless you do that. Because that is so important to the fabric of it. And Nikos knew that. I don't know that he knew it right away. I think he got it gradually. I think he got it because he thought about it and related it to himself and his life. I think he got it because he watched actors and saw when it was working and when it wasn't working. He got it. And I go around saying, well, who's going to do Chekhov now?

JEAN Yes. We seem to have cultivated an approach for doing Shakespeare in this country, but with Chekhov it's pretty hit or miss.

OLYMPIA It's like we're imitating the Brits. That's what Chekhov in this country is like. It's Chekhov that is "in-the-tradition-of." And somebody's decided the way the Brits do it is the way you do it. Very clean, you know. There are moments of emotional whatever, there's a kind of lightness, but it's not the way Nikos did it. You don't get the feeling that you did in Nikos' productions that these people are really on the edge. They're on the edge! Things are scary for some of these people, if not all of them. That's an important element, that their lives are not in balance. But it's not there when you see other productions. Stephen Collins said something and I think it's so true – it's "adjusted." As opposed to being mal-adjusted.

I remember my brother and I came to New York when I was in

college and saw *The Sea Gull* with Maureen Stapleton as Masha. That was the one with Mira Rostova as Nina. And in this production, when Nina said to Trigorin, "Do you think I ought be an actress," people in the audience, more than one, yelled "No!" Unbelievable!

But in that production, Stapleton was, like, *on* it, on the edge. I still remember the very first cross she made across the proscenium, trailed by Medvedenko, just barely enduring him, and finally he says the line, "Why do you always wear black?" And she says, "I'm in mourning for my life." She said this like: "Oh my God, I've got this creep following me, asking me questions!" You could see that it was funny, but underneath there was a motor running, the clock was running here. And I think there is that sense of the clock running on these characters – time is running out on these people.

JEAN   Yes, the element of time is a constant in both the fourth act of *The Cherry Orchard* and *The Three Sisters* –

OLYMPIA   The clock is running on these people, and when that element is there, people behave unreasonably, and things happen to them. Like Epihodov in *Cherry Orchard*. He drinks the water wrong and it goes down wrong, and he comes out in the end of the third act rasping, and Lopakhin says, "What's the matter with you?" and he says, [breathlessly:] "I swallowed water!" I mean, the guy is anxious! Everybody's leaving, there are all these departures and arrivals and lines like, "When are they coming from the station, when are they due?" This enormous thing about time which must have been so a part of Chekhov's life.

JEAN   I've read that. At many points in his adult life he was told he had only a year or two to live. No wonder the sense of time running out is so pervasive.

OLYMPIA   It's so brave. I mean, here we are knowing that we're going to die and we get up – it's like Beckett's *Happy Days*, the woman says, "Another happy day, so far!" and she's buried up to her neck! That play is to me Chekhovian. I know that sounds crazy. But when I say "Chekhovian" I mean what we're talking about here. Because often when people talk about "Chekhovian" they mean a kind of sentimentalized mood, they don't mean *character* which was something else that Nikos got. The sense of character was important to him.

JEAN How so?

OLYMPIA In *The Three Sisters*, he was interested in what made them different, he didn't worry about what made them sisters. He dealt with their characters, in the way in which people deal with life reveals character, the actions they choose to take at any given moment. Not only what they do but the way they do it. For example, death happens and we mourn, but people mourn differently and how they do it determines their character. He was on to that. He wanted actors whose sensibilities moved toward character. Not a concept about something "Chekhovian." That's the killer. You've really got to let the play take you. If you're into proving your craft and playing actions and objectives and stuff, all that has to live in you, but you cannot do that. It's about not having a plan – you have to know what's going on, but it has to be so much a part of your body that you can't work at it, or make it the reason you're on stage. The reason you're on stage is to seek your happiness, in some way. All those characters want somehow to fulfill their lives. That's all they want.

You know what happens? Actors read Chekhov as an audience member, as opposed to reading him as an actor. You take in the fabric, you take in the whole and you feel all these things, but you're being an audience. Then what you need to do is go into that one character and permit yourself to be a part of that fabric which the audience will then take in. You have to just do your part, you don't play your sensation of the whole play. You can't bring into it the burden of all that you perceive as an audience member.

JEAN You mean all you feel you know intellectually about the play?

OLYMPIA Oh, even all that you feel that you know about life, it's not going to be useful to you, you only need what that character has, that's all you need. Chekhov, of course, gives you such a big plate, so you want to fill it up, but that isn't what you need to do, you only need to put your part of the meal down there and let the audience sit down to everything.

JEAN Sort of what Nikos said about not trying to score points with this material as an actor, that Chekhov scores the points.

OLYMPIA That's right, that's exactly what I'm saying.

JEAN So you don't know so much what the whole is all about –

OLYMPIA No, anymore than we know in life. That's what so great about it. You're just living. What's that line? "Life is something that happens to you while you're making your plans."

JEAN Would you talk a little bit more about Olga in *The Three Sisters*? You once said something about her I found fascinating – that she feels like she's the younger sister, the one least capable of taking care of herself.

OLYMPIA I found that through the crying. The first time I did it, I started to cry in the first act and Nikos wouldn't let me. The first time Nikos wasn't trusting and stopped the process for me. But Nikos learned and grew as we all did through doing it. So the next time we did it I said to him, "I have to cry." He was afraid the crying would dominate the scene or whatever, and he had an idea of what it should be. When he spoke so eloquently about the importance of not having ideas, intellectual ideas about the material, it's because he once had a lot of ideas and he knew what went wrong. It wasn't only that he observed it with actors, he observed it in himself. He permitted himself to be a student as well.

JEAN So it was through the crying that you realized –

OLYMPIA It was the crying, but it was also Nikos telling me to keep talking, so I was crying and talking at the same time. So Olga became this funny little creature, this little girl, whose feelings were just bubbling up! Her younger sisters weren't crying and carrying on; one was involved in a marriage to an unbearable man, and the other one was trying to figure out what her work and her life is about. And there's Olga, trapped in her head about her father. She didn't get past that moment, that time in her life. That was the thing that liberated Nikos and me from the idea that I was the older, responsible one. That doesn't mean that I didn't *try* to be the older, responsible one, I did. But that other creature was always there underneath. That's why during the fire she gets so upset, so sick to her stomach. She's upset about Masha's affair with Vershinin because she can't handle it! She can't handle these so-to-speak adult things, and.they know this about her, both her sisters know this about her and they watch out for her.

In the first act, when Vershinin comes in, it's Olga who's the most gaga and flirtatious. She's doing this whole number, she's like a teenager. She's shy about it, and wanting, wanting him to notice her. I think she has to start from there so that you understand that she also, by the end of the play, has resigned herself to the fact that there are certain things that will never be available.

JEAN I think a lot of times directors who don't trust the play accentuate the obvious, they put those things in from the beginning. But if Olga is the spinster from the beginning, then there's no place to go.

OLYMPIA That's the way we did it the first time! You see the advantage, the great gift that Nikos gave us all was that he kept working on them. He did them again and again and again, and he kept learning by doing them, and we kept learning. Who's now going to do *The Cherry Orchard* every three or four years?

JEAN It's the continuity, I think, that's so valuable. Most of the time actors and directors don't work with each other enough to –

OLYMPIA – Create relationships.

JEAN And build trust. So that one can really work.

OLYMPIA The best, of course, are regional theaters where people keep going back. We had that at the Whole Theater, where people would come back over and over again, and the Arena stage has it. It does exist. For me it was there in Williamstown long before the others were there. I felt the same thing with the Public. You know what it was? The continuity of your work for the most part is in your own hands and also in the perceptions of your closest friends, but at Williamstown it was associated with a theater and an on-going process of doing plays and doing parts.

For example, I thought the work we did in *Enemies* was very important. Nikos said to me, "I want you to be beautiful, I want you to look beautiful, play a part in which you're physically beautiful." He would get a feeling about what would be exciting or challenging for me to move to next. And it wasn't just me, I saw that with a lot of people. He wanted to be present and part of that step or that growth. I felt that with Joe Papp, too, because he'd seen my work so often. He saw me in *Electra*, he saw me in *Peer Gynt*, he saw me in *Titus*, in *The Memorandum* and in *Curse of the Starving Class*. And then we got to *The Marriage of Bette and Booh*, and he said to me something like, "It's an extraordinary thing – all that passion and power is there, but it's like everything else, the character work, the technique, is riding on top of it." I mean, for somebody to know your work as intimately as that!

Nikos would also say things to me like that. He would have a perception about me and it was like a mirror, it helped me *claim* it. When I did the actress in *Enemies* and he talked about wanting simplicity in my work, he kept track of certain moments and said, "Your work is so simple there." And in his saying it, I claimed it. So it became part of my work, it became part of my machinery, because he named it. He put it in focus. He told me to stand still, just stand there in the dress and just turn my head slightly. He said, "Do three things only." And I said, "That's it? You think I should just do only three things?" And he said, "Yeah, just fool around with those three things." I got this kind of stillness and simplicity, and then, of course, the character I was playing – the Actress – got stature. The part I was playing got stature. Because anybody who can stand dead center on the stage and take a great deal of time, and say a word and then turn slightly and say four more words – you think – well, this has to be a great actress – which is the character. Then I could have that in other parts, that simplicity to just stand there and act – not do things, not run around – just stand there and just let it come pouring out of me. It had become part of my essence.

JEAN That reminds me of something Nikos once said to me in

class, "Could you please have the courage to be boring on stage?" Which meant, of course, feeling the freedom of not having to do something in every moment.

OLYMPIA   Finding that courage came from trust – from being a part of his process and seeing him change. And also, I knew he would *never, ever* let me make an asshole of myself. I knew that. He would never, ever permit that! He would be there to stop it. He would not let it happen. He would fight me, he would wrestle me to the ground before he would let me do that. And sometimes I had to be wrestled to the ground.

Basically, what he couldn't stand was someone trying to be right, someone trying to control the stage. That was wonderful, because I knew he could be totally trusted to stop that. He did not permit that! He was onto it like a hawk! And that was good. You know that great expression from the sixties or the seventies: he made a safe space for these kinds of things to happen. And if anybody tried to fuck around with that, he was on them.

For example, something very interesting happened the first time I did Paulina, in *The Sea Gull*. She comes to them in the third act, and says, "here are the plums for the journey." And when I was researching it I thought, why is she giving him plums for the journey? It always seemed like she was a batty person! And then I began reading what it was like to go on a journey then. There was a long time on the train, it was very difficult, the food was very bad, people would get diarrhea, constipation. And when I read that I knew what it was! Bowel movements! So, I mean, I could play that! That's something that's a private thing, you don't announce it to everyone. I mean, if I came up to you and you were going on a trip and I said, "Here's some Ex-Lax," I wouldn't make a big announcement! I would try to be confidential about it. So that helped me with how the moment should be acted. But even then, I thought the audience doesn't know this, they don't know that that's what plums are about. The line should be prunes! An audience will know prunes.

Now the word in the text is plums, there's no getting around it, the specific literal translation was "plums." At least that's what I was told again and again by Kevin McCarthy. Because Kevin had been in that production with Mira Rostova, he considered himself the big

Chekhov expert among us. He didn't think it should be changed. As usual I didn't go up to Nikos and say, "Listen, I think we should change this, blah, blah, blah." I just did it one day in rehearsal. Nikos fell over with laughter! He said, "That's great, that's wonderful." Well, Kevin was apoplectic. But I felt – it's not the specific word, that's true, but this is the spirit of it, this is what's intended, this is what Chekhov wants the audience to know the woman is doing. Well, Kevin made such a fuss that Nikos backed down. He said, "Well, maybe you better not do it." This is what I mean by we all moved and evolved together. I thought, okay, I won't say it. So, then we had the compulsory run through in front of everybody, you know, in that little room, what was it...?

JEAN The "Ex."

OLYMPIA The Ex! You know what it was like when everybody came for that run-through in the Ex! Everybody'd be packed in, lined up against the walls, sitting on the floor, people in the show performing that week, people working in the next show, or in the one at the other theater, maybe people who were visiting. Directors. Your peers. Just everyone, you know? And you really felt like everything's on the line. Nikos loved it because he created all this excitement. This heightened thing of something *really important going on*! So, I came out to do the scene and at the last minute I didn't say "plums," I said "prunes"! Well, the place fell apart. Nikos fell apart. I remember Peter Hunt almost fell out of his chair laughing. Nikos waited till Kevin had given me my scolding and left the room and then he came over and said, "Keep it in."

JEAN That story reminds me that on the tapes Nikos says that every Chekhov production should have one completely undisciplined actor, and then he talks about you. That the rest of the company never knew what you were going to do, where you'd be on stage. He said that in a great way, it threw everyone off.

OLYMPIA I think they wanted to be as free as they thought I was feeling. That's interesting he thinks that of me. I thought I learned about that kind of thing with Louis.

JEAN Do you mean that from watching Louis you learned to give yourself permission to be that free?

OLYMPIA Yeah. I was too reverential with Chekhov at the beginning. Also I had no idea that there was this range in Chekhov, that there was this kind of palette that he painted with, to use Nikos' metaphor. He said the palette was so varied, so rich, in any given character. And Louis let me see that. Whereas before I thought, well this character only has this little area that she gets to work with. I realized that that was an "idea." But the freedom Nikos talks about – I've always felt that. A lot of actors – it's interesting – they feel careful and worried about what a director will think and what other actors will think of them, and if they're going to change something they have to get permission for it, or approval for it or clearance for it. And it's true, I didn't feel that with Nikos. Why didn't I feel that? Why did I feel that I could go any place and do anything in his rehearsal room? Because, at some place I knew he *valued* it. He valued that spirit. He valued it. He valued that independence. He valued that kind of individual – taking – claiming the space, he *valued* it. And that's why he'll call me undisciplined, but there's love in it when he says it, because he valued it.

JEAN I know for myself, and I think this is probably true for a lot of actors, that one of the reasons we act is to reclaim that – freedom of expression we once had. And which in many cases was *not* valued in our early lives.

OLYMPIA Yes, or we had it but then we were civilized. But we remembered it and loved it so much that we never let go. So we found a way in which we could live and work so that we could have it again.

JEAN And it is moving to find someone who values that and encourages it. Blythe talked about feeling like she no longer had to be the "good girl" in rehearsal –

OLYMPIA He wanted her to be the undisciplined actress!

JEAN That's right. And she talked about, for the first time in *Three*

Sisters, finding this physical place within her where all that raw stuff came from, hunger and –

OLYMPIA   Aggressiveness?

JEAN   Yes, aggressiveness – and, for the first time, with Nikos, that she felt permission to let that out. And encouraged to let that out.

OLYMPIA   Browbeaten to let that out! Ridiculed!

JEAN   Not suppressing it or pushing it aside.

OLYMPIA   Yeah. It makes you not somebody who's there to serve the director's concept, but someone who is there to participate in the life of this play.

Nikos was so happy in the rehearsal room when we did *Three Sisters*. That's what I remember, the happiness that he felt, being in the room. And that's when he told me he only cared about being in rooms with people that he loves and wants to work with. He was so happy to be in that room with those people, doing that play, finding out more things, it gave him such happiness. That's what I remember, his face. And then at the end – and you know what was great? By that time it was great because we trusted him. He was, like, totally trustworthy. Maybe because he trusted us, I don't know. But by the last ten years or so of working together, I didn't step back and think, "So. What is he saying?" Or, "What does that mean?" I didn't care if it was reasonable or unreasonable, I would do anything he told me to do by that time. But that was *earned*. We all earned it.

And he earned it. He did. And he earned it by making mistakes. He earned it by doing things that fucked things up. And we earned it by making mistakes and fucking things up. But that was the gift, that you would do it again and again, and the fact that you fucked up something and it didn't work quite right once, didn't mean that we couldn't all try it again. Whereas that is not the case in ninety-nine percent of the rest of theater. I mean, he worked like a dog to keep that theater going, I know the sacrifices he made, but he took the pleasure he wanted from it, he *took* it. He really took it.

And I think it's a mistake and it does Nikos a disservice not to recognize how he grew and learned, because he was the student recognize how he grew and learned, because he was the student always – in that sense he looked to see what he could learn about Chekhov and about the process. And he permitted that of you.

People talk about him like he was this great expert on Chekhov, they talk about him like it's a *fait accompli*, but it was that process of *his* learning and discovering and doing things that were not accurate and sometimes really fucking things up, that mirrored my own experience. Because I did all those things, I made mistakes, etcetera, etcetera. But that was permitted, that process was permitted, and we all grew out of that. And of course Nikos became so absorbed, he was so full with it all – he was there for all the performances, learning, teaching.

I always got him. Even though, I mean, the literal things he'd say were often deceiving! The last time I worked with Nikos, people would say to me, "Can you understand that man?" And I would say, "Yeah." And they would say "What do you mean?" And I'd just say, "Well, I just do everything he tells me to do." Because by that time, you see, there was that kind of trust.

Louis Zorich (Dorn) and Olympia Dukakis (Paulina) in "The Seagull,"
1974

"I think somebody must have told actors that being efficient is great. When they come into an audition they change shirts and open bags and move chairs and readjust - all these things that are totally unnecessary. Also, they like telling you things. For example, someone comes to an audition and says, 'This is a speech from Hot L Baltimore, and as you know, Hot L Baltimore was written by ...' or 'this is Saint Joan, and Saint Joan was a soldier ...' and so on. This information doesn't really matter, because most of the time a work of art is or should be self-explanatory. I love somebody to come in and do it with a sense of ...not a sense of efficiency, but a sense of proportion, to just stand up there and use themselves in the best possible way."

"When I see that actors are in the process of discovery, that's 'working.' Peter Brook has an example of somebody going into a cave, an archaeologist, and first they find the legs of a horse. Then they might find the neck and so on. They don't go into the cave saying, 'First I find this, then I find that, then I put it all together and have a horse.' You find things, and then eventually you put them together."

Nikos Psacharopoulos

GOING UP TO HIT
Interview with Louis Zorich

Mr. Zorich, who spent many seasons with the Festival, played
Lopakhin in *The Cherry Orchard* in 1963; Vanya in *Uncle Vanya*
in 1964; Dorn in *The Sea Gull* in 1968 and 1974; Chebutykin in
The Three Sisters in 1970 and 1987. He has also played all of
these roles at other theaters around the country, including The
Whole Theater in Montclair, New Jersey, which he founded and
ran with his wife, Olympia Dukakis. Louis and I talked on a
Saturday morning over cappucino at a restaurant in Los Angeles,
where he was working on the television series, *Brooklyn Bridge.*

JEAN In the years that you were at Williamstown, do you feel that
some kind of collective vision for doing Chekhov evolved between
Nikos and the actors?

LOUIS Yeah, I mean, as I was coming here to meet with you today
I realized that one of the things that stuck with me was that there
were few people who were doing these plays more than once.
Except Nikos. He just kept doing it. This is what I find fascinating. I
used to be a little stupid. Years ago Olympia and I would be picking
shows to do at our theater, and she'd say, "Well, let's do such and
such." And I'd say, "Well, I did that already." "Oh! you did that
already! Oh! So you mean you've really done it?" And I realized
what she was doing. "Okay," I said, "But I don't like to do plays
over and over, there's so many plays out there." But now I know
what she meant. You can't really do a play only doing it once. It's
impossible.

I often wondered why Nikos did the plays two, three, four times
– I can only guess that he did them, number one, because he loved
them, and he felt that he never really realized fully on stage what
was in his head. So, as a result, people like myself, Olympia, Blythe,
Austin, had the great opportunity to do these parts again and again.
It has its drawbacks! One time I was playing Chebutykin [in *Three
Sisters*] and Nikos wanted me to do something and I didn't quite get

it, so we did it again, and I couldn't do it. He wanted me, when the doctor talks about killing that person in Act III, he wanted me to actually simulate a doctor before surgery, there was a bowl in front of him and he's washing the way a doctor would before he goes into surgery. Later on I discovered that this was something Bill Hansen did when he played the part. Something incredible happened with Hansen and he remembered it and wanted me to do it. It was a little unfair!

But the virtue in doing these plays three or four times, wasn't just for the actors but for him. Each time Nikos did one again, I think, he also did it better, more colorfully. In crowd scenes or family scenes, you got a sense that Nikos wasn't so much interested in each line being clearly heard, but in a swirl of movement, of life. Like in that game we were playing, that game in the fourth act of *The Sea Gull*. I remember very clearly being worried about getting my line in, and he said, "Oh, no, no, everybody kind of overlaps." So what you got was the tremendous sense of life, of vitality of these people. I think a lot of directors don't do that because they're too careful. Nikos discovered the overall life of the thing, that's what I carried away from it. You weren't aware of what each actor was doing. You were aware of a group of people in a certain situation. As an actor, you got a real feeling of being part of an ensemble. I think this is exactly what Chekhov is all about.

I've often said, "I'll do any part in Chekhov." Because each part is so wonderful. The smallest part. Even that pilgrim, that pilgrim that crosses in *Cherry Orchard* – he's just there for a moment. But he's striking! There's something striking about him.

JEAN Olympia said that she learned how to do Chekhov from watching you. From your ability to turn on a dime from emotion to emotion. How did you know to do that? When you picked up the play for the first time, did you just know that that was what was required?

LOUIS Well, even though I'm not Russian, I'm Slavic and that's part of their character. That's why there are other plays I can't do. I really feel uncomfortable doing certain plays that Olympia does very well. I think, of the two of us, and I'm not putting myself down, but she's the brainier person. I've seen Olympia in plays, even in rehearsals – that mind of hers! I see the wheels going around. We did a production of *Godot* with women instead of men. And even when we were previewing I watched her on stage, and as she was going through the motions of the character, her mind was working all the time. I can't do that, I don't have that faculty. I just sort of throw myself in.

JEAN   What makes a bad production of Chekhov?

LOUIS   I hope I don't sound like I'm speaking out of both sides of my mouth, when I talk about this, but a few years ago I saw Peter Brook's *Midsummer Night's Dream*, which was brilliant. And it wasn't done in period, it was done in kind of a white box on stage with step ladders, swings, like a big sandbox. I don't know if that was his metaphor but I remember thinking that. But his production of *The Cherry Orchard* – if you've ever been to that theater, BAM, you sort of think it's a perfect setting for *Cherry Orchard*. Because they've left that theater deliberately unfinished, so immediately you get the sense of decay or transition between one class of people and another, which I loved. But I don't think Peter Brook trusted the play. He didn't trust it. I may be prejudiced since I'd done Lopahkin a couple of times, but Brian Dennehy just seemed to me like a football coach up there. At one point Olympia counted how many times he did this – he'd walk into a room and [He gets up to illustrate: throwing his arms out in front of him and then clapping.] She counted how many times he did that and he must have done it fifty or sixty times. And then, of course, in the last act Trofimov says to Lopakhin, "You're a wonderful guy but you wave your hands too much." Well, he took that too literally!

In his first speech Lopakhin says, "I'm a peasant, I'll always be a peasant, look at these yellow shoes." He says in his opening monologue that he reveres this woman, he's in awe of her, she's like aristocracy. Well – and this I believe is the director – this Lopahkin walked around like he owned the place. If I'm talking to you and you're Jackie Onassis, I'd behave differently. I wouldn't be as familiar as I am right now. There was no sense of character, I didn't think, in this production. And then what stunned me, what stunned me, was that Frank Rich in his review said that this was the definitive Chekhov! I couldn't believe it.

JEAN That sort of brings us to the British vs. the American approach to Chekhov...

LOUIS For my money, the British have no conception of how to do Chekhov. The reason I'm saying this is because I have a fetish about *Cherry Orchard* and Lopahkin. I've seen it in Canada. I've seen it in London. I went to London some years ago to do a movie of the week and naturally I went crazy going to the theater. I think I saw twelve, fourteen productions in two weeks. And one of the first shows I saw was – guess what? – *Cherry Orchard* at the Haymarket. I think it was Joan Plowright doing Ravenskaya and Frank Finnley doing Lopahkin and I forget who else. And believe it or not, the guy who stole the show, according to the critics, was Pishchik! Pishchik? "And center on the stage, outstanding, was our old friend" – this character actor who was a former vaudevillian, in real life. Let me tell you what this Pishchik did. It's the scene where Charlotta enters with the dog. They're all crossing the stage to go to the next room. And when she comes with the dog he sort of looked at the audience and winked – he was commenting to the audience about the play! This is the guy who walked away with all the reviews for the show! I said to myself, "What is wrong with these people, they don't have a clue!"

Many years ago I saw a production of *Uncle Vanya* with Olivier doing Astrov and Michael Redgrave doing Vanya, and I think Plowright was in it, playing Sonya, and there was so much expectation about this one, but to my mind it really missed the mark.

JEAN Why?

LOUIS Well, this has to do with my interpretation of Vanya, it may not be *the* interpretation of Vanya, and I know this is presumptuous, but when I watch a production of *Vanya*, I can tell by the first two or three words what kind of production it's going to be. Sounds presumptuous but here goes. In the first act, Vanya comes out, he was taking a nap and his first words are "Yes, yes, yes." Find me one actor in the world who makes that moment work. What is it about? Chekhov doesn't tell you what it's about. But I found something. Throughout that first scene, he's acting very strangely – his mother even says, "Vanya, what's wrong with you, what's wrong with you,

59

Vanya!" And Serebryakov, the learned brother, is coming, and the mother talks about how wonderful he is, and Vanya could just kill him! Vanya could go for his throat the minute he walks in! Well, this has to be going on underneath. It's not, [Yawning and stretching, casually.] "Yes, yes, yes." As if the only thing is those words!

A lot of times the Brits play Chekhov theatrically, or they only play the boredom. They think the characters are bored, so they are boring. No, all these characters want something! How can anybody like people who are bored! I think the mistake is they don't understand the temperament, they don't understand Russians. The feelings are here! [Rubs his hands over his arms and chest.] They're here! They don't hide them. They don't fucking hide them. I mean, when I think of Vanya – I can even do it right now! I'm not doing an actor's trick but, when I just remember what Vanya went through! [He begins to get visibly upset.] He worked for this bastard twenty years! Twenty years! All of a sudden it's like [Serebryakov] says, "Fuck you Vanya," And for Vanya, it's like, "I'll kill him, I'll kill him!" When Vanya comes out on that stage at the opening of the play he wants to kill that guy! He's sitting on something, there's something underneath that propels him through that whole scene! Through the whole scene! It's not this [Casually.] "Yes, yes, yes, I've just had a nice nap!" And if those first three words aren't there, nothing's ever going to happen.

JEAN So, from just three words you can sense –

LOUIS Yes! In fact something happened in that production of *Vanya* at WTF that has never happened to me since. And I don't know how it happened, I don't know why it happened, I mean I didn't prepare, I didn't do a damn thing, but I remember, from the beginning of that play right through to the end, everything happened the way it should have happened. It was seamless. You couldn't say, well, here I did this or here I did that. The minute the play ended – I don't know how to say it, it wasn't perfect or idealized – but every moment was there. It just happened. It happened for the first time in my life and after it was all over, I'd think, "What did I do?" I had no idea. It was one of those magical moments when – Well, it loses in explaining it.

The thing I find, over the years, is that you can't *think* on stage.

Acting isn't thinking. I hate to say it. They used to make a joke about Yogi Bera. Have you ever seen the baseball bat? There's a label on the bat that says where it was made, and they used to say, when I was a kid, when you're batting you can't have the label face the ball because if the ball hits the part of the bat where the label is, the bat will crack. So you got to know where the damn thing is. So, somebody asked Yogi Berra, "When you go up to bat, do you think where the label is?" And Yogi Berra says, "I don't go up to bat to think, I go up to hit." And that summarizes it. It's instinctive! Well, you're an actress. How many times has this happened to you on stage, when you start really thinking about the words on stage, and then you fuck up the speech. Did you ever do that? All of a sudden you're thrown. That's not a perfect example of what I mean, but really, you can't think on stage.

JEAN Yes, I know what you mean. Nikos often said in class the best actors never remember what they did when they come off stage.

LOUIS That's what happens if you let yourself get up to your neck in the passion, the real passion of these people. Somehow with a lot of the Chekhovs I've seen, especially the English ones, it's all about language, and it's all pictorial, it's all about stage pictures, rather than – passion. Not everyone, I think Anthony Hopkins – and Finney's a very passionate actor. It's somewhere codified that acting stands for a certain layer of English society – but it's not all of English society. Sometimes the most exciting work comes out of the slums of England, look what's happening in some of those movies, in some of those stage plays, it's very visceral. Those kids are screaming for their lives.

In 1976, I was in Canada, doing a play called *Eve* with Jessica Tandy. And, since I was part of the company, I was able to see all these plays. So there I was, in the first or second row, seeing a number of things, a Restoration play that Jessica was doing at the same time, and a few others, and then they did *Measure for Measure*. I happened to be living next door to one of the trustees on the Board of the Stratford Festival. He and his wife owned the big furniture store in town, so they were sort of the money people of Stratford. One day he invited me over for dinner, with some friends of his who were also members of the Board. *Measure for Measure* had opened a few nights before and I had seen it, and the reviews mentioned something about the passion, the passion of this play. And they were all talking about how wonderful it was and then this man turned to me and said, "Don't you agree, Louis?" And I was like, [Under his breath.] "Yeah, yeah, yeah." Finally he realized I wasn't overenthusiastic. "Louis, what is it, what are you really thinking?" I said, "No, no." "No, come on, what are you really thinking?" I said, "Frankly, shit." "What?" "What!" they all said. "I'll tell you why, damn it." They talk about the passion these people have. At one point Isabella's talking about Angelo and the reviewer made a point of one moment where she walks upstage and takes some water out of the pitcher and she did this: [He pours a little water on his fingertips from his glass and gingerly touches his forehead.] And the critic talked about how at this moment she was inflamed with passion. [His voice rises.] THAT'S PASSION?? At another moment, she's standing downstage and Angelo embraces her from behind and touches her vagina. Which is fine. Now I'm sitting in the second row. Watch my face, I'm Isabella. [He sits motionless for some seconds, until I get it. Then, in a low whisper:] Nothing! Nothing! Nothing! Not a thing! I swear to God. Where's the passion? Where's the passion? What passion? Show me the passion and then cover it, and then catch yourself, do something, but let me see it! They read into it! The critics read into it. It wasn't there!

The thing that I felt, going back to Nikos, I really feel – this passion was part of his personality. He wanted that. He wanted it, this was what he valued in actors, this was what he valued seeing onstage, because I saw it in Williams, I saw it in other plays he did. That *Crucible* that he did. That *Crucible* was like one straight line, there was so much tension in it. When I watched his production – from the very beginning – I sat like this – I was hanging on to my seat! It was like somebody just pulled a string tighter and tighter. You wanted to say, "Release me!" But it never stopped, it was one straight line. I don't know where he got the idea, but again it was there, the passion underneath it, and I don't think that ordinarily directors see that or do that.

JEAN That's sort of a recurring theme so far. That Nikos had an instinct for the life underneath the words, especially in Chekhov. It wasn't about a "subtext" underneath, but about an abundance of life underneath. And this translated into some very exciting behavior on stage.

LOUIS Well, it's like in *The Sea Gull*, Olympia did something and when she first did it I was shocked! I think I had a bunch of flowers in my hand or she had a bunch of flowers, and she took them and – [He mimes tearing them to pieces, stamping on them.] I died! I died! It wasn't – it was messy! It was ferocious! And no one expected it! She sat on the fucking jealousy for so long – I guess Dorn and Paulina had this affair, it's evident in the script and she thought that I was trying to make it with Arkadina. It wasn't even that she took the flowers and threw them, she had to tear – them – apart! Like she wanted to tear me apart! All the great things in the theatre I'll never, ever forget – had nothing to do with language, nothing at all to do with language.

JEAN I remember seeing you play Chebutykin in *Three Sisters*, and even in the fourth act when he's moved into this completely existential realm, lost all sense of hope or meaning – even then, what I got from your performance was a great deal of – inner activity. Like there was a volcano underneath your words. How did you get there? What's going on with that character in the fourth act?

LOUIS It's like the way I feel about the New York theater scene! When I was a beginning actor, when I first came to New York, if a theater closed, it pained me. Pained me! My daughter's doing an off-off Broadway play in New York. Sometimes I can barely communicate with her because I see how hard it's going to be for her. Because – it's not there anymore. At least when I got to New York, all those theaters, doing all those plays – what a great thing it was to do a play off-Broadway. But today – everyone's out here [in Los Angeles]. I mean, it's not entirely gone, but most of it. And there's such a sense of loss, when you've poured so much optimism into it, so much hope and all of your own ambitions that you've poured in it – and that's the thing about Chebutykin. This family is everything to him. And by the fourth act, it's gone. That's one of the things I also wanted to say about Nikos, that's how he connected to Chekhov, as family.

I grew up in Chicago. My mother and father came from

Yugoslavia. And when I was very young I'd come out on the back porch and all of a sudden this guy's there. Maybe I was eight years old. I'd walk in the kitchen and say to my mom, "Who is that man?" "Oh. That's Kimme." "Who is he?" "Oh, he's a distant cousin, he's going to stay with us for a while." And he'd stay a couple of months and then he'd leave. Then a month or two later, another guy. Chime! Or Misha. That's the way I feel about Chekhov: it's like an extended family. And Chebutykin was one of those. He's in on the family history, the family is his whole world. I never thought I made that scene work, that moment when he brings out his gift for Irina, that samovar. I once saw – believe it or not, every time anyone does Chekhov, I go see it – I saw *Three Sisters* once at the Arena Stage, and there was a wonderful actor doing Chebutykin, and he had the same problem with that damn samovar as I did.

JEAN The scene between Lopakhin and Varya in the fourth act of *Cherry Orchard* is another example of a scene that has very little going on on the verbal level but so much life underneath. What happens in that scene? All through the play everyone's been talking about Varya and Lopakhin's marriage. It seems almost a given that this will happen. And yet when the moment comes, the last moment when they're all leaving forever and it's Lopakhin's last chance to propose, he doesn't do it. Why do you think? Is he just too afraid?

LOUIS Yeah, absolutely.

JEAN And he really loves her.

LOUIS Yeah. It's that simple. He doesn't know what to do with a woman. This is also probably why he idolizes Ranevskaya. In his first speech he says something that she did for his father – that she wiped the blood off his face. Things like that you don't ever forget. She's on a pedestal. This is what enables him to shut his mouth. This guy's driven, this peasant is driven, but he doesn't override everyone else's feelings, he pulls back. I think with Varya – he's afraid to commit himself. I hate to sound like *Cosmopolitan*, but he's like that.

JEAN It's such a moving scene. And it's so short – but it's like a lifetime of loss is contained in just those few moments. How do you feel when you walk off stage after playing this role every night? Is Lopahkin a satisfying part to play?

LOUIS [After a pause, his eyes fill up with tears.] You see what happens? It's incredible. If you can play a part like that – any great part like that – [And then, after another moment, he laughs.] I cried for him. I cried for Sonya, all these fucking people. I mean, we see it in our parents, we see it in our children, things that – it's the essence of Chekhov, the longing, the longing, such longing. Even this gesture now – when I was in therapy, I never forgot this – it was called Bioenergetics therapy. I was talking about my mother, my family and the guy says, "Come on, reach. Reach. Reach." And as I reached – [He stretches out his arms, reaching out and upwards, and releases a long "AHHHHHH."]

Incredible! What is it? It's a gesture, it's a gesture of longing. I was devastated. When you tap into that, that's what it's all about. Not in everybody, but there is – even this laughable son-of-a-bitch, the guy with the horses in *Sea Gull*, Shamrayev. Incredible character! People ask me, what do you want to do? I never say it, but it's a secret desire of mine, and again, it's presumptuous, it's arrogant, but I've never seen a Pishchik the way I envision a Pishchik. I want to play the Pishchik that's in my head. I may never be able to do it. And Shamrayev. These incredible characters. Years ago, Olympia saw the Moscow Art Theater do *The Cherry Orchard*, and she said Pishchik did something she'll never forget. He comes in with the rug and all that and finally he says, "Give me water, water, water!" And Pishchik goes – [He drinks a glass of water with both hands, gulping it, spilling it all over his face.] He played the longing, he WANTED water. How badly did he want water? It was like life and death! He wasn't just – [*sipping.*] But he, he – WANTED water, he wanted fucking water! And some of these things, when you see actors really connected, you never, ever forget. A glass of water? A glass of water? His whole life was in that glass of water! It's incredible.

And there was a similar moment with Bill Hansen, in the last scene of *The Cherry Orchard*, it's hard to describe, but the way he pulled up that deformed foot at the very end, when he was left in isolation on stage, when they'd all forgotten him. God, it was just so moving.

Bill Hansen played Nonno in *Night of the Iguana*. I remember we were working in that little room downstairs, the Ex. I think some of the greatest work I've ever seen was in the Ex. Anyway, I was playing one of the Germans, and I watched the rehearsals, and when Bill Hansen began to recite Nonno's poem – I had to leave the room. It was so naked – the guy knew he was dying and the words came out – like he was just forming them! It was the same thing with that gesture when I went to that shrink. It was like – he was out there going – [Pause. Shakes his head.] What is the word?

Well, maybe there isn't a word for it. Maybe it's in the body, the gesture. The reaching. But Nikos allowed those things, those things you don't have words for, he allowed them to happen.

Lee Grant (Arkadina),William Swetland (Sorin)
in "The Sea Gull"

"I think you should give yourself the chance to be boring up there. If you only keep hitting the big moments in a scene, you lose the trip, you lose the process. Don't make it easy to watch. Unfortunately people in the theater have made things so easy to watch. But, you know, make it difficult for people. Why don't you make them bend forward to see you and listen to you rather than relax back in the seat saying, 'that's fine'? You don't have to move from important moment to important moment. Great painters do little things here and there in the painting that they enjoy and nobody else knows what the hell they're doing, only the art scholars look at the little corners and say – 'look at these little leaves or look at somebody's name or sombody's moustache.' Take the time to say, 'I'll just stand here and I don't have to do anything, I'll bore them, but I'll just stand there.'"

Nikos Psacharopoulos

THE LIFE IN BETWEEN
Interview with Lee Grant

Ms. Grant, known for her work as actress and director in television and film, worked only once at Williamstown, playing Arkadina in 1974 in *The Sea Gull*, both on stage and for PBS' "Great Performances" Series. We talked on a winter afternoon in the kitchen of her West Side apartment in New York City.

LEE My first experience with Chekhov, ever, was at Williamstown. That's why I came, because it was an opportunity to take a chance in that kind of setting, away from the so-called pressures. Although Nikos betrayed me – he had the *New York Times* there for opening night! I could've killed him for it. But to have an opportunity to do it in a far away place, with great people – Frank Langella and Blythe Danner and Olympia Dukakis and Louis Zorich – just a remarkable group of people – with a director that came out of a Chekhovian way of life, was incredibly appealing. Nikos knew about a style of life, a texture – it was his own style of life in Greece. He told me how when he was young he would get off the boat and servants would come and meet him and take him to the house. He lived in Greece in a feudal way, from the way he described it. So he understood the canvas, the tapestry that we had to fit into and was able to give me a sense of it in a way that I couldn't possibly know on my own. I understood the character of this woman and what her conflicts were and what she wanted very, very well. Nobody needed to tell me anything about that, I was very strong-headed. Nikos had certain ideas – for example, at a certain point he wanted a Madonna and child thing, me sitting there with Frank Langella on my lap, he had a vision and it wasn't something that I could do. I knew the pain, I knew the selfishness, I knew the being in love, I knew the elements that made up this woman so well, but I had to be given my head and allowed to explore. I think he was very pleased with what came out.

JEAN I'm surprised to hear this was your first Chekhov, because I've watched the tape of this play many times and you seem so

70

completely at home in that world.

LEE I am. I am. I'm very comfortable in it. I would happily do nothing but Chekhov the rest of my life.

JEAN Had you any trepidations that first time?

LEE No. Not for a minute. I knew it was my home. I'd read it so much – my mother was Russian, she came from Odessa. The levels of how contemporary Chekhov is to life today, the humor – these things were so close to me that I couldn't wait to get into that water and swim in it. It was like a pool I'd been waiting to jump into all of my life. Each year Nikos and I would talk, he'd say, come back and do *Three Sisters*, come back and do this, come back and do that, so Williamstown became my Moscow in a certain sense. "To Moscow, to Moscow!" Each year I hoped I would make it back because it was really what I was thirsty for and needed very much as an actress and Nikos knew it was something I needed. "To Williamstown, to Williamstown!" And to Nikos, really. And it really is one of my deepest regrets that I never did make it back, because I needed it.

I've never seen a production of *The Sea Gull* that's as good as the one we have on tape. And I'm usually very self denigrating, and I'm not talking about me; I just felt that everything about that production came together in a very remarkable and a very fresh way but also in a very traditional way. Nikos understood the life, it was not the typical American production of Chekhov. It was a well integrated production with a great look and a great point of view. The relationships were so "found" in it.

JEAN Was that something to do with the combination of actors?

LEE Yes, I think so. When you look at Blythe and Frank and myself and Louis – we are actors who are as comfortable in comedy as in tragedy and who cross those lines easily. I mean, there's a sense of the absurd that we all have. That split second kind of transition that Chekhov always has is something that's very available to all of us. Moving in a split-second from feeling that the world is coming to an end to connecting with something that fascinates you or interests you or to just being silly.

JEAN What made it so satisfying for you personally in playing Arkadina? Did it have something to do with the agility you just described?

LEE Well, first of all, Chekhov is a great playwright. To be allowed to enter into that world and explore people like that is something that you don't often get a chance to do. As an American actress who made a choice to go from theater to film, I've found that opportunities to play in things that are that rich and have that kind of depth – are limited. Not that I haven't been very grateful for the film roles I've had, but this pushes you that extra yard that you always want to be pushed as an actress. You're forced into a much more challenging area. This woman, Arkadina, this actress comes to relax at this dacha in the country and finds that she's in danger of losing a great deal, especially the man she's in love with. That whole sense of being in love with a man, taking him to the country, manipulating, using everything feminine in yourself to entrap him and then finding that he's attracted to a young girl, is something just marvelous to explore! All the ways of holding onto him, of being charmed by the young girl yet knowing she's a danger.

Chekhov chooses never to have Arkadina confront Nina, to confront the situation, or to confront the man. She always manipulates, manipulates, and at the same time she has to deal with a grown son who's getting in the way of this love affair. She loves her son but he's getting in the way of it! She has to deal with taking care of a brother who's sick and out of money, yet she knows that she's getting older, she has to watch out for herself. She's selfish: even though it would take so little to give something to her son, to give something to her brother, she doesn't. She says, "I can't do it, I have to watch out for myself!" It's the joy of all of these elements that are so contradictory and yet make up such an extraordinary reality.

JEAN That's what I saw that I thought was extraordinary about your performance. You were so full of contradictory impulses. At the end of the first act and the beginning of the second, I could see your impulse to be generous with Nina, but in the same moment, the opposite impulse came through. And in the scene with your brother, I could see you both wanting and not wanting to help him.

72

LEE Yes, you have to be very hooked into all possibilities in the same moment.

JEAN You turned what's sometimes played as just a selfish woman into someone much richer – someone who goes with the selfish choice, but is tortured by it.

LEE Tortured by it, yes, tortured! And Chekhov always makes his women – put it aside, it's like, put it out of your mind, like Scarlett O'Hara, we'll see what happens tomorrow. In *The Cherry Orchard*, too, Ranevskaya comes to a certain point and then says, "I can't, it's too painful, I'll deal with it some other time." When we were filming, I was very dissatisfied with my scene with Kevin McCarthy, who was playing Trigorin, and I begged to do it again. I think I had the flu or something the day that we were doing that scene and I was out of it, I wasn't in it. And it's so important, that scene, in which she goes down on her knees to him, she kisses his feet, she resorts to anything in order to keep this man. It was so important for me to go as far as I could – to get to that place of being tortured by it! And I couldn't get in it.

JEAN What happens in that scene with Trigorin? How does she turn him around? Immediately before she has the argument with her son, she's completely thrown off and then Trigorin comes in and says he wants to leave her. Yet in the end she somehow wins Trigorin over, doesn't she?

LEE She wins. She wins in a way that I never could, never, never, never! She is so good at covering, at dissimulating, at knowing the spots, the buttons to touch that will reach this man or any man. And it's such an interesting difference between a woman of today and a woman of that day. You did not confront, you did not say, "I know you are in love with a young girl and either it's her or me!" Never, never, never! There's never that kind of confrontation. It's always a suggesting rather than a confronting. She talks about his talent, she talks about how wonderful he is, she talks about what she wants to do for him, so that what she does is soften him and he eventually says, "I'm so weak, I have no will of my own." Because she disarms. She melts down for him, she gives him a total melting

73

down of love, so that he's got nothing to fight against. She disarms him, she takes away his weapons. Fantastical! It's nothing I've ever known how to do. But she knows.

JEAN These two very heightened scenes come right on top of each other in the third act: she has an almost violent argument with her son and then moves into the scene with Trigorin where she has to shift gears completely in order to keep him.

LEE Yes, she's powerful. It's interesting because it wasn't long after that that I did Regina in *The Little Foxes* and playing Arkadina threw me off entirely in playing Regina.

JEAN Why?

LEE I see Regina, who was never touched by anybody, as totally manipulative, totally doing things for money. Arkadina, on the other hand, is a *fool*, she does everything for love. And she knows what a soft touch she is. She hangs onto her money because she's such a soft touch. Whereas Regina has no heart at all. And what a contrast after playing Arkadina, who is a working woman, she's supporting her whole family as an actress, she's supporting everybody on the estate, everyone's looking to her for everything. I thought to myself, why did Regina sit on her ass? This southern lady was manipulating men for their money in order to get her freedom, whereas Arkadina was going out there and making it for herself. And who is stronger, Regina who did the manipulation, or Arkadina who did the work? I never was able to enter into Regina or to give the Regina what most people wanted to see because I saw her as being smaller than life instead of bigger than life.

JEAN Yes. Chekhov also suggests that Arkadina is a woman capable of great acts of generosity and selflessness. It sounds like that's the difference between the two women – with Arkadina, it's being able to use the whole range, the whole spectrum.

LEE Yes. And to have those real conflicts. To have a real conflict. Not to act in one particular way throughout, or act in another particular way throughout, but in one minute act one way and in another minute take it back. Chekhov is such a master of inconsistency in a character. Not consistency. *Inconsistency*, which is so delicious to play. All his characters, especially his woman, have short attention spans.

JEAN Nikos once said in class that the success of the scene between Arkadina and her son in Act III depends on the length of the bandage. How did that moment inform your relationship withTreplev? How did you find the behavior in this scene?

LEE I think these things came out of the tremendous conflict about my son. I felt that he was a grown child, that he had not found himself yet, that he was competing and comparing himself to my lover and endangering that relationship for me. The work that he did I thought was ridiculous and as a professional I had an obligation to express myself to him. This, of course, would destroy him and then he'd act like an adolescent. I knew that he had a terrible need for me, but he wasn't a baby anymore and it was draining for me, and he was always draining me, he was always attacking me, he was always trying to get between me and the pleasure that I was having. So it was a very troubled relationship. On the other hand, there was that bond that I had with him, he's my only child. Yet I was so wary of him. And Frank Langella and I got into fights within character in rehearsal that were – very violent, you know? I remember when he was telling me how selfish I was, and I was telling him that he had no talent – he threw a book at me, and it hit me in the chest, and I kept that sense about him, that he was irresponsible in terms of what he could do to me. When we did the scene on stage I was wary of him. So when he asked me to do his bandage, we were for a little while again in a safe place where he could go back to being the child and I could go back to nursing him, it was a safe place for both of us, where we needed to rest, we needed to make some contact with each other that was nurturing and wasn't always tearing each other down.

JEAN That's what Nikos meant about the length of the bandage, that while the bandage was being done they could have that closeness. The end of the scene then gets very reckless, doesn't it?

These two people say things that go beyond what they intend to say and become cruel.

LEE Yes, the things that happen within every family! It's definitely a dangerous scene, you feel the danger when you're playing it.

JEAN How did your working relationship with Nikos unfold?

LEE I think we were feeling each other out, because it was the first time in a long time that I'd done theater and also I came very full, very close to this, and I wanted to run. I was really like a wild horse, I needed not for any hand to be on me, or anyone to be riding me. I really needed to run with it as far as it could go. Nikos had put so much thought in it and so much work in it and had done so many *Sea Gulls* and already knew more than I knew. But I needed to find out for myself, not from the master but from the running with it. And maybe bumping and falling down and having to get up and go back to places again. So for a little while there was, I felt, a need for him to put his vision against my need not to have any vision, and to just see where I go and to surprise myself and to surprise him. And at a certain point he said, "Okay, you go with what you want." And then we formed a very, very close bond. It began with the usual testing each other out – but then loving each other.

After that, the direction that he would give me, the guidance that he would give me, made me understand the kind of relaxation this woman has. This ability she has to pass the time of day, to make small talk, which is not an easy thing for me personally. All these people, and this woman particularly, have the ability to just pass the time of day in the woods with somebody and have a conversation and explore the moment to moment reality without knowing where it's going. Unhooking myself from the love story, unhooking myself from the son. And just allowing that kind of Chekhov thing of being in the moment and being in the woods. Which is hard for me but was a very, very important gift that he gave me. It was part of Nikos' understanding from his background, of being in a situation where people just sit and make an art of conversing. An art of pleasing each other with the sounds of words and the closeness which you take the time to find. Because in all the high, emotional moments, there was nothing that I needed except to be told if it was too much.

But it was in the least needy moments, when I had to relax in the hammock and talk about the dresses, and the little things, and just *be* in that place, that's where he gave me the most.

And in relationship with the servants. Olympia had a terrible time being a servant, it drove her crazy, she just could not understand inequality and she couldn't understand accepting it, and reveling in it, and being joyful in serving someone. It just went against every bit of her nature. And I could feel these things coming from Olympia so that when she smiled her resentment was like fire. You know, it was where the Revolution came from. But Nikos understood that those relationships not only existed then, but for him existed in his home, where he comes from. Where there is a place that people have a servant class and they love serving. That's very difficult for us to conceive of. But that is what he created, he created that world in which people had a structure, they had a feudal structure that they occupied and when their masters or mistresses took care of them and looked after them, they were happy. And that's a slave situation almost, but he understood that. And without that structure created, there's no way of doing Chekhov, because that's what people accepted and lived by.

JEAN So Nikos helped you find a way of exploring the life that goes on in between the big moments.

LEE I think Nikos' way of rehearsing – small chunks, deliberately out of order – was his director's way of tricking us into getting away from the "arc" of the character. For me, I need that arc, I need objectives and actions and I need to wonder what's coming next within the character. Those are my little life preservers, the line of where I'm going. But he was so helpful to me in releasing me from always feeling I had to do something to somebody or something to myself, releasing me from acting objectives. In this particular period, in this particular time, people floated.

Yes, the life in between. That was his great gift. I remember in the party scene in the end, when he had the gambling and he had that wonderful little caged piece that had the dice in it that went around. There were always games, and it was something that both Chekhov had and that Nikos pursued further and further. People were always involved in some kind of game, some kind of playing with others, which made you fill each moment up. In small behaviors, in small choices. I mean, during so-called important speeches, we were slapping flies away, I was playing with my umbrella, I was whispering to the doctor about something else, and there was always so much life going on. I remember Frank Langella, as Treplev, had to fight our inattention, our boredom, all the time. That's what the whole thing is about, especially in the first act, and that's what was so insulting to Treplev.

Always, with Chekhov, and I think Nikos understood it very well, there is a flight from boredom. I think boredom is always there, but I think what you're always trying to do is fly from it, to defeat boredom, by being in love, by fighting, by looking at dresses, by moving on, by leaving, by talking about leaving. Because boredom is the enemy, the adversary that you're always running from. I think it's very much a part of the fabric.

JEAN Unlike most work in theater, this one's on record. When you look at the tape of *Sea Gull*, how do you feel? Is there something you'd do differently if you had to do it again?

LEE I wish I could do the part again and be a little bit more absurd, and a little bit sillier. I know that Nikos had seen me in the film *The Landlord* when he wanted me to do this, and the woman in *The Landlord* was a very silly woman. And I think he wanted more aspects of my being ridiculous, more silly. Whereas I wasn't able to give up certain places that I wanted to go to. But I would have the next time I played it.

JEAN How so? Is there some specific scene you think of, are there specific moments?

LEE I think even with the character, starting with the character being more of a foolish woman to begin with, just to see where it would go. Because a lot of times you look at your own mother, or at someone you know who you might call eccentric, and they're even more absurd, even more eccentric than you'd dare play them on stage! It would be a fun place to go with it. And I think that elements of the character from *The Landlord* could be transported in Arkadina.

JEAN What's the difference, for you, between the English sensibility about Chekhov and the American sensibility?

LEE I think it's the director. I think it was Nikos' sensibility in knowing the work so intimately and in making great choices in casting American actors who had all the elements. And in allowing, not the showiness and not the staging, necessarily – although I thought his staging was remarkable – but the heart, the humanness to come through. I always felt the British productions I've seen were empty and rattling around in comparison to what Nikos was doing. Now, I think that if Nikos had gone over and worked with British actors, and there are so many of them that are remarkable, so brilliant – he could've made it happen. I think it's the director.

JEAN Yes. Blythe told me initially she wasn't so comfortable diving into those very emotional, very raw feelings Nikos wanted. And that he gave her permission to touch that place in herself for the first time. But it sounds like you didn't need that permission, it seems like you came to your role –

LEE Wanting to devour. Yes. But he didn't just permit it, he encouraged it. And that's where your director either says fly, you know, without a net, or come down and don't make a fool of yourself. And he encouraged us to fly.
  For me, working on *The Sea Gull* with Nikos was one of the most enchanting times of my life. And I was very glad that we taped this. I mean, when you're in it, you have no sense of what you're doing. So I'm very glad it's on record. Of course, I was overwhelmed by Blythe's performance and by Frank's and by that entire production. I thought I was okay. But to see it all together, was very – comforting. You know – the word inspiring really has to be connected to Nikos because he was an inspirer.

JEAN In the sense of being a teacher, or ...

LEE Well, I don't know about him being a teacher, but he had such theatrical energy himself. He was such an eccentric himself, such a darer, a doer, a naughty – provocateur! So the mirror he held up to you was one that was exciting and shaking and not down or dour. It was always – up, you can rise to it! And there are few people that have that kind of – I think that was his attraction, you wanted that mirror to say, "That's good!" "Exciting!" "Wonderful!" "Fabulous!"

George Morfogen (Gayev), Maria Tucci (Varya), Jerome Collamore (Firs)
Colleen Dewhurst (Ravenskaya), Kate Burton (Anya), Tom Atkins
(Lopakhin), and in "The Cherry Orchard," 1980

"When we are doing any kind of a play – even if there's a contrast of the characters, there cannot be too much of a contrast of understanding. A lot of times when plays are done in this country directors cast individual actors independently of how they mesh as a group. Always, as a director, I find that very wrong. I never say that. I say – if I can get those ten people together I'm fine, but if I can't get those four, I'm going to change the other six. It isn't that there is anything wrong with the other six, it's that the sensibilities of certain actors, the scale of certain actors match up and don't match up to others. You say, this actor goes with this actor, but this actor doesn't go with them. And I think that's the trick of it, somehow. I know that sometimes when a production that I've done has worked better than I thought it would work, or worse than I thought, it was to a great extent because the two people have not played well together. Or because the two people have played so well together.

"But it's more, really, than choosing actors. It's the way people respond to people, the way some actors respond to certain other actors. You can be on the same wavelength as characters but not on the same wavelength as actors. I try to chose people to work with who are – in process, or in sensibility or in temperament – part of the same family."

Nikos Psacharopoulos

BEING UNSOLVED
Interview With Kate Burton

In 1980, while non-Equity at Williamstown, Ms. Burton played Anya in *The Cherry Orchard*. She returned to WTF as an Equity actress in 1987, to play Irina in *The Three Sisters*, a role she'd done previously at the Hartman Theater. While an undergraduate at Brown , Kate played Nina in *The Sea Gull*; at Yale Drama School she played Masha in *The Three Sisters*, and she took the role of Sasha in the Broadway production of *Wild Honey* (Michael Frayn's adaptation of *Platonov*). Kate and I talked over lunch at my home in Los Angeles.

KATE I was always, always fascinated with Russian literature, Russian people. I started studying the Russian language when was I thirteen at the United Nations school in New York. I'd started reading Gorky in my childhood, I remember reading *Father and Sons,* by Turgenev, at UNIS – United Nations International School -- when I was thirteen. And I started to read historical things like *Nicholas and Alexandra*. I wrote papers about the Russian revolution – I was definitely obsessed with all things Russian.

The first Chekhov I saw was the film of *The Sea Gull* with Vanessa Redgrave. I saw a production of *Uncle Vanya* at Circle in the Square with George C. Scott as Astrov and Nicol Williamson as Vanya when I was a teenager. I remember seeing Alan Bates play Trigorin in London. Of course, since I grew up in a theatrical household, there was a lot of exposure to this. My father, I believe, played Treplev once, but I never saw that, it's on one of those kinoscopes. It was live television with June Havoc. I remember there was one moment with the Circle in the Square *Vanya* where there were a lot of problems and there was a possibility that my father was going to play Astrov – a role, of course, that he was put on the planet to play. But he never did do much Russian theater, except for that one thing.

By the time I got to my first year at Yale Drama School I realized how much Chekhov was in my bones. For me, reading Chekhov was like lying in a hot bath. It felt that familiar. One of the things that's been wonderful for me is that I can hang in there with Russian, I can read it in the original. And that was always helpful because it's actually very simple writing, it's not very colloquial. The first time I did *The Cherry Orchard* with Nikos we used a translation which I think was his with a lot of amalgamation, but I always came to rehearsal with my Russian version. John Glover, who played Epihodov, was reminded me recently that I spent as much time in rehearsal with the dictionary as I did doing scenes!

I didn't quite realize until we started talking just how much Chekhov I've done. It's such a part of my life, these Russian plays, and Irish plays, too – they seem to be the plays that come the most naturally to me. It's interesting because they're very different. In Irish theater people always think that everybody's very touchy-feely with each other, and very warm – but that's untrue. It's very much the opposite, they're very hard people, trying to come to terms with their lives. Whereas Russian theater, and I've also done one Gorky play, is much richer emotionally. These people really want to affect each other.

JEAN That summer we were in the non-Eq company together, when you did your first Chekhov at Williamstown – what was that like for you?

KATE Well, I was twenty-two and it was perfect that I was playing Anya in *The Cherry Orchard* because, at that time, I was very much where she is in the play – it was like I'd died and gone to heaven. To have gotten that part, to work with such a wonderful company – I felt that way when I played Irina, too. I really have no sense of whether the actual production worked or not. I'm not really sure if either of those shows were the best productions of Chekhov at Williamstown. All I know is that I felt so incredibly lucky to work as a young actress on this *Cherry Orchard*.

Nikos worked on it the way he did most plays – he would work on little chunks, out of order. Little pieces of puzzles, that's what it felt like to me. It's funny, I don't feel he treated me any differently in 1980 than in 1987, which was quite wonderful, because then I was a student, I'd only done one year of drama school. I remember it was a little bit hard to understand what he wanted exactly, but one was willing to jump off the cliff for him. It was all very active and very unintellectualized. He would literally walk through the scene and do it for me and I would watch him and then I would copy him. Of course, it was hilarious to have this Greek man with espadrilles playing Anya! John Glover actually said to me one day, "I think Nikos really wants to play Anya, maybe we should let him go on for a performance!" There was a trunk onstage in the first act. And I remember Nikos said, "Hon, you come in, you see the house, you have missed the house, and you throw yourself over this trunk." And he was, like, draped over this trunk. And here I was in my little shorts and my round face, looking at him and thinking, "What exactly is this man doing?!" And just sort of knowing that whatever it was, I was going to do it.

When I first auditioned for Nikos, I had just played Masha in *Three Sisters*, and I did one of her monologues. The monologue from the third act, of course. And he sort of worked me through it, and then he said, "Hon, you have one problem." And I said, "What is the problem?" And he said, "There's no Vershinin." And I said, "What do you mean, there's no Vershinin?" And he said "You have no Vershinin in your head." And I went, "You're right." I had done the worst production in the history of Chekhov, with the worst director, my first-year acting teacher at Yale, and I don't care who knows it! He had no sense of fun, no sense of the humor of the play. I played the whole thing in posing. I probably didn't have an honest moment in the show. And in that moment, Nikos knew all of that.

I might be wrong about this, but I got the sense that Nikos chose you because he cared about the way you rehearsed almost more than he cared about the way you performed. When he chose me for Irina, he had just seen me in rehearsal for *The Rover*, a Restoration comedy. We'd been rehearsing for exactly one week and Nikos came to a run-through for which we were completely unprepared, we were a wreck. And for the first time in my life, I just thought, who cares! It's a run-through! And because I just let go of having to do well, I was funny! Everything went wrong and I just didn't care! I think that's when it clicked for Nikos, watching me do that, and he asked me very soon after to do *Three Sisters*. He just wasn't that interested in people who came up to snuff in performance but who, in the rehearsal room, were a total nightmare. This suddenly came to me. I noticed that. To a point of ludicrousness, where it's like, "Nikos, get over it, they're money players, they come up with the goods!" Because rehearsal for him was the milieu. Especially with Chekhov.

Doing *The Three Sisters* at Williamstown in 1987 – I had some interesting experiences doing that play, one of which was I got pregnant before the first preview! But that, and doing the Brian Friel play, *Winners* at the Roundabout – were probably the two most fulfilling acting experiences I've ever had. I was so happy because I'd already played Irina once. And I know sometimes that Nikos liked to cast people who played the part before, and that was a very wise thing, especially with a part as huge as Irina is, it's an enormous role. After I played Irina for the first time, I worked with Laurie Kennedy in *On the Verge* at Hartford. And Laurie had already played Irina three times at Williamstown. And I'd just done it for that first time, feeling like I had just put my toe in the water. Laurie talked about her process of "solving" each one of the acts for Irina the three times she played it, which was both fascinating and frightening to me because I guess I didn't feel like I'd solved much of it at all! As I get older I realize the less embellishment the better, but actually, now that I think about it, I often feel that the better I am, the more unsolved I am.

That's the biggest thing that I've discovered for myself as an actress and I think that actually that seed was put in me by Nikos. The times where I've been in plays where I truly have no idea what I'm doing are probably my best work. I still don't know that intellectually. I'm the classic Virgo, I still want to have it all in little compartments. For example, before I did *Three Sisters* at Williamstown, I did *Wild Honey,* and – you were there, remember – we all went to the opening party afterwards, at that place with the thousands of oysters! Nikos came up to me and said, "The scene that you had with Misha was gorgeous, absolutely gorgeous, emotional, all of it." And I had no idea what I was doing in that scene! In that whole play, according to the reviews and to people I respect, I did very well, but that was truly a time where I had not a clue about what I was doing. That, and *Some Americans Abroad*, were the two plays I had the most critical success with and I was very unsolved about both of them.

JEAN How was that seed planted, that not knowing what you were doing?

KATE Well, I think it started that first time that I saw Ni over that trunk! When I knew I would go for that even though I didn't quite get it. And my coach at the time, Harold Guskin, helped me. Harold's biggest thing as an acting coach is to allow you the freedom to not make the obvious choice. To really explore what each thing can be about. The humor, always finding the humor, in any situation, even the most tragic. It's like in *The Three Sisters*, at the end, I mean, these three girls have really had a bad day! And Natasha finds the fork on the table and starts screaming and yelling and they all start laughing, or when Kulygin puts on the beard, and in the midst of all the loss, it's *really* funny and Masha *really* laughs.

There were so many wonderful aspects to playing Irina, not the least of which being the company of actors I got to work with. The moment when Christopher Walken came on in that first act was heaven on earth, to be on that stage, as Irina, with Chris Walken. Just listening to his Vershinin make that speech about what will happen in a hundred years – I mean, I'd already heard this speech a lot, I'd been in two productions of this play before. But Chris – he's such an incredible presence – and I remember when he started to talk about our house – "look at this house, it's so full of flowers," – he took our breath away. So when Masha says, "I'm staying for lunch after all," the laugh in the audience was just so wonderful because the audience was spellbound too. The whole audience fell in love with him.

And then, of course, the famous third act scene – this scene we always worked in longer rather than shorter chunks, and it always felt endless, because we were all onstage for such a long time. One day in rehearsal, Chris did the big speech, and as usual, it was just brilliant. This is the fire scene, and there's a lot people on stage and we're all sort of half asleep, and Chris went through this long, long speech and finally at the end he said, "Oh my God, Nikos, I'm standing here, I don't know what I'm doing. I feel like Ed Sullivan!" And of course we couldn't do that scene again for three days, because every time we got to that point all of us who were supposed to be asleep would just crack up.

JEAN What else about Act III? It's a huge turning point for Irina, isn't it?

KATE Yes. That third act scene, to work on, is living hell. It's a scene of complete unleashing, of the agony of getting it out, it's total despair for Irina. And funnily enough, I always found it very easy to do in rehearsal, but then we always did it about three times in a row. So when I got to the third time, it really worked. But in performance it didn't always work and then I just stopped being so hard on myself about the actual H_2O coming out of the eyes. It's so much pressure to put on yourself to have to hit that in every performance.

What I loved about Roberta Maxwell's Olga was that she was rough with me in this scene, she was fierce. It's amazing to me, some plays I've been in since this I can hardly remember but I remember all of this quite clearly. I remember doing these scenes like it was yesterday. I remember Nikos giving Amy Irving [Masha] a direction about her speech in that scene, and he said, "You know, it's not such agony for you to tell them that you love Vershinin." He said, "It's not agony, you're releasing it, it's coming out, you're telling your sisters all your truest feelings. You're making it into, 'I can't tell you.' It's not, 'I *can't* tell you.' It's 'I *want* to tell you, I *want* you all to understand, you won't understand, but I have to tell you.' "

JEAN Something as simple as not playing the negative. Playing the positive, making it more active.

KATE In the first act, in my moments with Masha, he always wanted me to make it more active. Irina wants to make Masha feel better, I want her to be happy, I don't want Masha to be depressed all the time. And Nikos would do it, of course, he would act it out for me! And he would act it out for me with just those words, "I want you to feel better, I don't want you to be unhappy." And I would say, Nikos, I understand what you're saying, but those aren't the words that Chekhov wrote here. But he wanted that underneath and so the speeches became more active.

The second act ends with Irina saying, "To Moscow, to Moscow," and there Nikos really didn't want me to do anything. He wanted me to sit there as if I had no energy in my body, to not even attempt to communicate with people. Fascinating. Because it was almost like – he directed in such an instinctive way, and I think unconsciously he wanted me to be – *not* active there – because we already are seeing what's happening to her, her enthusiasm for life –

disappearing. John Heard, who was playing Kulygin, said he had trouble with that, with what I was doing, because he said, "It's like you're a zombie." He said that quietly, just to me, and I started doing something a little differently, but Nikos spotted it right away, he knew very specifically what he wanted.

My favorite act in the *Three Sisters* is the fourth act, always. Even when I played Masha. It's something about giving up, we've all given up. So everything is so easy. John Guare said what happened to me in the fourth act, from what he saw, was that all that my youthfulness just disappeared. My favorite moments are not even when I'm talking, it's when I'm walking in the back in the birches, listening, hearing Andrei talking with the baby. And then of course, the scene with Tusenbach. The simpler, the less weight you put on it, the lighter it's kept, the better, which Nikos always emphasized. He never wanted me to get too dark in that act.

I remember always being very affected by the moment when Masha falls apart. I went to see *The Three Sisters* at the Moscow Art Theater, which was a fairly meat-and-potatoes production. The Irina was a bit ditsy. I always think it's more interesting to have an Irina who's not the quintessential ingenue; it's better having someone who has a little bit more weight. Irina is a more pure version of Masha, perhaps a little less intellectually acute. But aside from that, I remember the actress was quite wonderful who played Masha, I'll never forget one moment in the fourth act. In Russian, there was something more powerful about Masha's line, "When my man comes, tell me," [Kate says the line in Russian and it becomes very staccato, like she's spitting out each word.] – I remember just being knocked out by it. Every single person in the audience responds to the despair Masha feels in the fourth act. That's what it is about, the fourth act. The emotional fulcrum of the play is the third act, and then the fourth act is just the acceptance. What was exceptional about Nikos' productions is that the emotional work wasn't self-indulgent in any way. Certainly Masha was allowed to scream and yell and cry and do her thing. But they didn't get sloppy.

Since I didn't see our *Three Sisters,* I can't judge it really, but the best production I've seen of *Three Sisters* was the Irish production with the Cusack sisters. Sinead Cusack did not miss a trick as Masha. She's Irish, so there was no sentimentality at all. It was a wonderful production, full of humor, and I'm looking forward to seeing Adrian Noble direct more Chekhov, it's the first time I felt: finally, another director who really understands what this was all about.

JEAN How does a good director help you, personally, as an actress to results? To giving the kind of performance you want to give?

KATE My two directorial mentors were Nikos and Mark Lamos. Nikos was a great deal about giving up control and Mark Lamos is more like, control is everything. He said to me once that as a director he tends to turn the screws too tight, and he knows that's one of his problems as a director. And I said, I have the same problem as an actress. I still think it's all very ephemeral. I think that's what makes it exciting and frustrating. You don't ever know. I don't ever know when I walk on a stage if it's going to be a great performance, or if I'm going to be great in a show, forget it! I never know. I always think, "Dear God, get me through this because it is so scary."

It's interesting because I'm feeling some ambivalence now about acting in theater, which makes me nervous because I think, "Oh, no, maybe that means I'm not meant to be an actor." But when you have an experience of working on Chekhov with a truly gifted director, which Nikos was, and with such a company, an experience that so enriched and informed who I am as an actress, it's the ultimate. Maybe my ambivalence is that there's not enough of the ultimate experience.

In Williamstown there was also something about the bucolic atmosphere – I mean, it's not like Nikos planted all the trees outside the theater, but there's something about that atmosphere that was Nikos and that was Chekhov. It's the feeling of the outdoors, it's lush; you can imagine Nina running out and through the field behind the theater and starting that speech about how wonderful life is. It's conducive, it's a very conducive environment.

Amy Irving (Masha), Kate Burton (Irina), Roberta Maxwell (Olga) in
"The Three Sisters," 1987

*"I learned how to be very courageous from – Mr.
Psacharopoulos. On the opening night – after the first preview of
'The Greeks,' he said to me, 'You didn't let that speech go.' Big
speech! 'Let it go. Let it go.' I said, 'I can't. I'm afraid.' He said,
'Let it go tomorrow night.' I said, 'I can't. There are going to be
critics out front tomorrow night. I can't.' He said, 'If you're going to
fail, fail trying to be successful. Don't fail because you're too scared
to be successful.' "*

Roberta Maxwell
from a CBS Cable documentary on WTF

APPROVAL
Interview with Roberta Maxwell

Roberta Maxwell first came to Williamstown in 1981, to play Electra in *The Greeks*, directed by Nikos. The following year she played Maggie the Cat in *Tennessee Williams, A Celebration*, and in 1987, she played Olga in Nikos' last production of *The Three Sisters*. When I reached Roberta, she was in Toronto preparing for the national tour of *Lettice and Lovage*; we talked over the phone.

JEAN Can you remember your first reaction to Chekhov?

ROBERTA I think because the first production I ever did was a Chekhov – I played a maid in *The Three Sisters* at age fourteen – I was taken into it on a very personal and visceral level, it came very naturally to me to become part of that family. I'm Irish and there's great similarities in the Irish emotional makeup to the Russian, I think. But, it's very different doing Chekhov with an English group of actors as compared with an American group of actors.

JEAN What are the differences?

ROBERTA The English, of course, are very much involved with form. I think the English enjoy doing it because they can let down on the technique, but still that's always very high on their list of priorities. Just in how they approach their work. It's much more formal in process and finally in production. I remember seeing Peter Brook's production of *The Cherry Orchard*. It was his celebrated production. And I remember feeling very dissatisfied with it. I think because of the formality of the translation, although they emotionalized the life, it somehow was superseded by the sound that was created, the tone of the English, the vowels would take over. Whereas I've felt, from my own professional involvement with Nikos, he was never interested in the technique, it never satisfied him either in rehearsal or in performance that one was able to do just "so." You always had to go much farther than that. Even if you failed, he always expected you to be reaching for the impossible. At least I felt those were his expectations for me. Perhaps coming from my background, he felt that he could trust me to do certain things and he wanted me to abandon those things.

JEAN But obviously you'd done a lot of that emotional work in your career before that. What was so different with Nikos?

ROBERTA Well, no, my forte has always been understatement and restraint and repression.

JEAN That's funny, I think of you as just the opposite. I think of you as being the kind of actress who can really let loose.

ROBERTA He brought that out in me. My great success was in the play *Ashes* and this character just ground glass from the beginning of the play to the end; it was all grinding around inside her and she was swallowing so much. Whereas he just uncapped it, he wouldn't have any part of that. It started in *The Greeks*. I could not go far enough for Nikos. It was just a challenge every day to go into that rehearsal room. You know, I never had a problem with my voice in *The Greeks*. And you would've thought with that much going on vocally that I would've been wrapped in cotton and gargling with honey and water. Never. Because it was truly connected to – he always guided you to that primitive place and it came out – effortlessly. And I felt so safe because – one was never embarrassed by excess. It's not that he encouraged indulgence, because I felt that he was very, very stringent when he ran a rehearsal. He didn't really put up with too much personal indulgence. He wanted you to get it out and make use of it for the play, it was always for the play, it was never like having a therapy session. Absolutely not! He was not the therapist director, no.

JEAN How was is that you felt so safe, how did he create that?

ROBERTA Approval. [Pause.] Yes. And never feeling that anything I was showing was going to be rejected, that it all had a place and a time when it would come together, because he trusted that each rehearsal one was finding a kind of truth that wouldn't eventually be discarded. He had no time to waste, you see. Every rehearsal had to pay. So I always went for broke in those rehearsals.

JEAN What exactly does that mean for you, going for broke?

ROBERTA Really giving him everything that he wanted and felt that I could bring to it at that particular time and place. Never holding back. He would not ever put up with me saving it for the next rehearsal. Give it to me now.

JEAN Was Olga, in the Three Sisters, a part that came easily to you, that you connected to right away?

ROBERTA No, I don't think so. I think that it was a much harder thing for me to come to. I'd played Natasha so I understood the family from outside, from the point of view of somebody wanting to get in, so I came with a kind of lack of familiarity...and I think I resisted being inside the family because, you know, you had to work very personally, and Nikos demanded that you tell the truth, and so for me it wasn't a comfortable place, it was never a comfortable place to be with Olga. It may have worked, if it did work, because that place is not a comfortable place to be.

JEAN You mean in terms of the character?

ROBERTA I never worked as if it was the character and then me, I always had to find those places in me where the two life energies found the same force, myself and the character. I don't know if that's instinctively why Nikos cast me in the role, but my own sort of family situation was not dissimilar to that of the sisters and so consequently not a place that I always wanted to be! I personally always wanted to get out. I think perhaps, if it did work, that must have come through, "Let's get out, let's get away from here, it isn't working." I never longed for the past as Olga, and perhaps if Nikos approved of what I did and the way I worked, it's because Nikos always wanted you to go forward. He wasn't interested in the mood, the sentimentality of the past. If a mood came, it was a mood of wanting things, very, very much. He wanted his actors – at least to me – he always emphasized the action, the verb, the desire to live, the hunger to get through it and go on. That's the difference in some of the English productions. They emphasize much more the relationship to the past, which manifests in a focus on the tone of the piece, the holding onto the past rather than abandoning yourself, as one had to in Nikos' productions, to the mission of the characters. The English productions long to recreate the past – perhaps it's like England! Recreating that picture from the past, the time when life was. And it's done through sound and text, the way it's spoken, the word, rather than through a more Russian sensibility, the emotionality, that passion in the living sense of the moment. Nikos was all about survival, he cast people from very, very different backgrounds, very high profile people. You couldn't rely on everyone speaking in the same beautiful way. The unifying force of these productions was the sense of mission, the life going forward, in their energy for the future. When you think of Rob Lowe – that was probably the finest moment in his life, to play Tusenbach. He really probably did the best work of his life so far, and Nikos gave him a future, something to aspire to.

JEAN In the fire scene in Act III, Irina has an outburst, she's in despair about her life and about her brother, Andrei. And then Olga tells Irina to – give up, almost, doesn't she?

ROBERTA Do you remember how it was blocked? I took her down and I sat on the trunk with my back to the audience. Actually I sat on the trunk and she kind of moved around it. First of all, although I was the oldest of the three, I felt that there was an equality, that we were equal in many ways in our stations within the family. That I was not the head of the family. I didn't take that position at the beginning of the play. By the time I get to that scene, I do what I'm forced to do, what I've never wanted to do, which is, I have to take control. Whatever else has happened in our lives, we are, within our own experience, the three sisters. When I created the myth of what our childhood had been like, we were always the three sisters, "Oh, there go the three sisters." And then when it becomes so painfully obvious that Andrei is not the head of the house and that everything is lost, I felt I was forced into this position of totally giving myself over to her and being completely honest about the loss of the dream, facing the illusion.

JEAN It's a real act of courage then for Olga, isn't it?

ROBERTA Yes. For that moment. But then at the very end of it, the end of the third act Irina does say, "Let's go, oh, let's go to Moscow." So she's able to still hold onto it, to see hope. But for Olga, when she observes both of her sisters in this scene really lose everything; for me, with my back to the audience, it was a process of just letting go of everything, giving myself over to them, and finally, the horror of hearing Masha say that she loves this man –

JEAN And that horror for you was because –

ROBERTA I knew that he was a bum! I hated him. I was, in fact, in love with him when he first comes through the door!

JEAN Yes, Olympia said Olga is almost more giddy than the others are when he first comes in.

ROBERTA Yes. Yes. She had such hope because of her father. And here is someone, Vershinen who knew her father, who she must have loved very, very deeply. And it was the end of girlhood, it was the end of my girlhood in that scene. I had to pass over my womanhood, I had to go from girlhood and, well, become a woman, but become a spinsterish woman. I felt such anger at him for taking advantage of my sister. And watching it – I had no control, you see, I gave up all control at that point. It was a kind of death for me, that scene. You know, I say I'm 28 when the play starts, and then four years have gone by, and I look in the mirror and I look old and tired and – everything is finished at the end of that scene for her. I give everything over, all expectations, everything.

JEAN So if her rebirth is at the end of Act IV, you're saying this is the death scene.

ROBERTA Yes, it was a very interesting experience for me, and as I say, it was a private thing that was going on with me at that time, but I think – I know that Nikos was very aware of my feeling for Vershinin. And by the end of that scene, I was so angry, after having loved him so much at the beginning and seeing what he had done and what he represented. The failure that he represented for me. So when I came to the last act, I just wanted it over so that we could begin our life again.

JEAN Several actors I've spoken to have said they had a sense of Nikos sort of intuiting what was going on in their personal lives and wanting all of the fall-out from that in the rehearsal room. But that this was never explicitly stated, it was never intruded on, as you said.

ROBERTA He never would talk about it, he didn't have to talk about it and you didn't have to talk about it. That's why you felt so safe, really, in using it. He knew that I would survive. He knew I would survive and he knew Olga would survive. And he knew that I was very, very concerned as to whether or not Masha would survive under those circumstances.

JEAN Were you and Nikos ever at odds in the process?

ROBERTA I felt that I never got the speech in the first act. The opening speech. I don't know why, I just never got it. Perhaps because I resisted the father dying in some way and I would attempt to escape that, because of my own situation with my own father! I just couldn't commit myself to not having my father alive. Somehow I could never bring myself to experience fully, to talk about what it would be like not having him there. I could work through it in the other scene because I had an action to do, but to actually talk about it – I never got it. Oh, and we worked on that! We worked and we worked and we worked.

JEAN What was he working towards?

ROBERTA He thought I was relying too much on the structure of the speech to carry me through the emotional line. I would go from sentence to sentence, the verb in each sentence, how I felt through each sentence, but I never stopped really reading it off the back of my eye. So it had this quality of control. Not that he wanted me to be out of control, but there was never any question that I'd actually gone through that, because I couldn't bring myself to go through that. We worked and we worked and I never felt I got it, but he never forced me to a result that he wanted. However, we both knew that there was much more there to get. But if he had forced me, of course, you see I wouldn't have been able to go on with the rest of the play.

JEAN It sounds like it was allowed to just keep growing and be what it was, it didn't have to reach some kind of image that he had in his mind.

ROBERTA That's what I mean about the technique that's expected in English productions that I've seen. I was very privileged to be part of the Robin Phillips/Maggie Smith production and that group of actors because Phillips too always went under the text. But most directors, especially the English – I mean, the critics raved about Peter Brook's production.

JEAN Several people have talked about that. What was the big mistake?

ROBERTA I think because there was great, with quotes, acting going on. I mean it was a "great" director. With the expectations of a "great" production. And "great" acting. It wasn't about the little things that go on in life, the moments. I think the English have this enormous burden where they have to be as great as the old group were or greater because they're trying to create something new. It can be very hard to have a famous father because you have to live up to him. And that's what I feel about so much of their work. Perhaps not so much now as ten years ago.
 There's a sense of going for anything that doesn't involve the real emotional core of their being, whether that means focusing on the beauty of the text, or the vocal tone, or some kind of intellectual response. One day in rehearsal, very early on, Chris [Walken] came on and he was doing something extraordinary and it was my turn, or I was supposed to do something and I was just caught in the moment of watching him. And Nikos said to me, "What?" And I looked at him and I said, "He is so wonderful! Isn't he beautiful!" And Nikos just – "Yes, yes!" he said, like he knew where I had to go. That was

the hundred and ten volt charge, put my finger in that plug and it would carry me along. I could make a life with that for Olga. It wasn't about the words that Vershinin was saying, it was about who he was, what he brought into the room, the electricity. It was, to a great extent, about the core of his being connecting with the core of mine.

JEAN Nikos often deliberately rehearsed all the scenes out of sequence. Did you have any problems with that?

ROBERTA No, I loved that, it never, ever bothered me. It meant that you had to know your character upside down, inside out, in your dreams. That one scene did not depend on something having happened before, that you could be dropped into the middle of the character's life. They were there because they were there. No subtext. Life is to be lived in the present tense. Even if you're thinking about the past, you're experiencing it in the present. That, in fact, you may not be remembering anything except a memory.

JEAN When I saw your performance of Olga, it was as if you were doing all the "Olga" things, being the headmistress, trying to be the more stable one, but there was an inner life that very much went against all these things.

ROBERTA Well, I think Nikos really knew something about that secret life of hers. And he never intruded on it, but he indicated that he understood what was going on so it was even more important at the end that she say, in the face of loss – Masha says we must live and Irina says we must work and Olga says one wants to live and our life isn't over yet and we shall live. Vershinin, when he comes and kind of blows my sister's life apart, says something like, "I wish I could prove to you, tell you how unhappy life is, that there isn't any happiness..." but at the end there is that rebirth, which is what I think Nikos understood and admired so much about human beings and characters in plays. Olga doesn't say, "we're unhappy," she says, "Listen, the music is so gay and so full of joy." She hears it, she has the ability to rebirth herself, which I think must have been Nikos' great love for them and his great admiration for Chekhov. Everytime I finished the play it was great for me because I survived! I got through. And I reaffirmed each time that I came off stage, that it was possible to have that moment and have it be truthful.

It was never like Nikos was working for himself, for his own little production. It was a big thing, it was a life experience being part of those plays. It changes you. Changes you, those kinds of experiences. They were very life-affirming and lifeforming times which you draw on when, you know, you have to go in front of a camera at ten o'clock in the morning with your hair all poufed up to do a commercial audition. What is it that Olga says – that those that come after us will benefit from what we're going through now. And of course it's true, that's exactly what's happened for us as actors, too, having those experiences.

Diane Wiest (Sarah), Christopher Walken (Ivanov) in "Ivanov," 1983

"*...Try to find what eventually become 'mannerisms' of people. In a good sense. The sort of idiosyncratic things that some actors do when they respond to something happening. I think the more you look at good actors the more you find out that they come with a bunch of physical and vocal characteristics that someone like a reviewer might call 'mannerisms.' And they become mannerisms when they have no meaning. But if these things are done with a purpose then, as an audience, then you identify. And as you keep watching, you find out that the actors who are functional up there are just not as interesting. They are just not as interesting on stage as people who cultivate these things.*

"Chris Walken does something with his shoulders that somebody might say is a 'mannerism.' But it's not, because it's so much a part of him. He doesn't just do it on stage, he does it all the time. It's organic to him. But if anybody else tries to do it, it's just funny, it becomes the musical comedy version of Chris Walken. With the really good actors you work with, after a while you find out there are things they do, things that people can do take-offs on at parties! But these things are theirs, rather than borrowed from somebody else.

"Now, if you don't find these things inherently in yourself, if it doesn't come naturally, sometimes we have to help it. The greatest way of helping yourself develop your own idiosyncratic mannerisms, for want of a better word, is by sending your imagination to a junkyard and collecting the most pathetic, sick details you can ever imagine! You know what I mean? Just bring all of that in and let it play on you so that your task somehow becomes to reach for this. Allow these things in your imagination to conspire to help stimulate the words. You see, nothing is really interesting about a mannerism that is borrowed from someone else or from your image about someone else. So don't go for mannerisms; try to find your own manner of doing it."

Nikos Psacharopoulos

TRUSTING IN CHAOS
Interview with Christopher Walken

Mr. Walken first came to Williamstown in 1975, to play one of the leads in Tennessee Williams' *Summer and Smoke*. In the Chekhovs, he played the title role in *Ivanov* in 1983, and Vershinin in the 1987 production of *Three Sisters*. Other Chekhov roles include Trigorin in *The Seagull* for the New York Shakespeare Festival and Astrov in *Uncle Vanya* at A.R.T. for director Robert Brustein. At the time of our interview, Chris was on location with a film; we talked over the phone.

JEAN Tell me about working on Chekhov with Nikos.

CHRIS Nikos and I worked very well together. How you define that and name why, I'm not sure. I was always very comfortable with him. We didn't really discuss the work too much – in rehearsals he would say something brief and I understood him, it was nice and simple. One of the things about working at Williamstown on any play was, of course, how quickly it had to be done. And Nikos, in the way he ran the place, was exciting. In that he would decide things quickly and just put them together quickly. I worked there a couple of times when only about a week before beginning rehearsals I'd get the call to come on up. I always got a kick out of that. It was very intense.

JEAN Yeah, I always thought the whole Festival was a very good reflection of Nikos' unrelenting energy.

CHRIS You said, "Yes, I'll come do it," then immediately you were up there, learning your lines, rehearsing long hours, and of course it was such a beautiful place to be. And then you were on. And just as quickly it was over. The audiences were very loyal audiences, I think. People who came back year after year. And a very giving audience, I always felt. Well, they knew they were going to get a good show. Every time I worked there the place was packed. I don't remember ever being there when there were empty seats. I think that he had that audience knowing that every ticket would be a tough ticket to get.

JEAN Nikos talked about how he thinks it's always great to have, in a Chekhov play, one "undisciplined" actor. And he mentioned you as an example. That, in a good sense, no one else in the cast ever knew what you were going to do next.

CHRIS He actually said that to me once, words to that effect.

Yes, I know he liked that. There was always a great deal of spontaneity in our rehearsals. He used to always say to me, "I see you watching." I would sit and watch the other actors, and I'm a very good audience, I would laugh and really appreciate them while they were doing it, and Nikos was that way too. And I think that that contributed to the energy of the shows, that the rehearsals were fun. Everybody got the impression from Nikos that they were doing a good job. There's nothing worse than getting the impression that the director thinks you or someone else could be doing it better! And Nikos was always very encouraging.

JEAN So what about doing Chekhov? How do you, Chris, go about it?

CHRIS I approach doing all plays pretty much the same, Shakespeare, Chekhov or a contemporary play. As far as I'm concerned, and it's been said before, but they really are new plays. I try not to think of them as anything I've ever seen or read, just as if a new writer had just handed it to me, whether it's *Coriolanus* or *Ivanov* or *Hurly Burly*. That it really is a matter of opening it up and looking at it new. My process usually involves just reading it over and over and over, and to some extent out loud, until I notice something. I always think of it sort of like getting my foot in the door, or like a little crack appears, where you see, suddenly, something that you can really get in touch with, something that's – similar. I play a lot of villains in the movies and obviously what I have to do in order to do that is look at the guy and try to find someplace where we touch. To personalize it. I don't know what other actors do but that's pretty much what I do.

And certainly that's true with a writer like Chekhov, who, to my mind, is right up there with Shakespeare. Even though he wrote so few plays, those plays are just – perfect. If you're a good actor, you can hardly help but be entertaining. That's another thing that Nikos was aware of: those Chekhov plays are funny. Whatever else they may be, they've got tons of jokes in them. They all do. And they're good jokes. I read somewhere that Chekhov once reprimanded Stanislavsky for taking all the jokes out of *The Sea Gull*, he said something like, "you've spoiled my play, you've made it all heavy and morbid."

Every one of the four that I've done is like that. In *Uncle Vanya* – I mean, some of those lines of Vanya's torture, his jealousy are really hilariously funny. Somebody once said that jealousy is the seasickness of the soul, that you think you're going to die and everyone else thinks it's funny. And I think that Chekhov often contains just that. And Nikos got actors who could do that, balance those two things. Blythe Danner is perfectly aware of how to do that, as is Austin Pendleton. It's the comedy of human dealings.

JEAN   How do you start character work? Take Vershinin in *Three Sisters*.

CHRIS   In a way, I was well suited for that part. I think of his easiness with the women; that Vershinin is comfortable with the women, that he likes them and they like him. I always felt that that was an important part of Vershinin, that he was easy in the company of those women. And he's funny, too. I'd only seen it once before, and the Vershinin was very good, but different. I have, you know, a natural, undisguisable, New Yorkness; a kind of from-the-streetness, and sometimes that's hard to overcome in a famous play such as by Shakespeare or Chekhov. I think very often my own from-the-streets-of-New York quality comes through no matter what I do about it. And I suppose that could be a drawback for somebody watching me, but it doesn't really bother me at all.

JEAN   When I saw your Vershinin, you seemed to have found Vershinin's vulnerability, rather than having the character exist just as sort of a mouthpiece for Chekhov's philosophical view of life. And I don't think it's usually done that way. I just saw a production of *Three Sisters* at an important regional theater here in the West, and every time Vershinin made one of his long speeches, the director pulled down the lights, put a spot on Vershinin and played some very eerie music underneath. As if to say, this is Chekhov's message.

CHRIS [Laughs.] That doesn't sound like a good idea.

JEAN When you did it, all of his philosophical speeches seemed so personal – not at all axiomatic. For me, that made the character much more – vulnerable, more human, than I've seen before.

CHRIS Well, Nikos encouraged people to behave and to speak like life, and to avoid heavy-handedness, absolutely.

JEAN What were you working on, for example, in Vershinin's big speech in the third act?

CHRIS Well, it's a very long speech and a very active one, and it's sort of crazed at that point in the show, with the fire and everything else going on. And I was just sometimes trying to remember my lines! If there was a certain panicked quality about it, which I think was correct, the panic was partly character and partly the actor trying to get through it.

But with any role, any speech, one of the hardest things an actor ever learns – if he's lucky enough in his life to learn how to do it consistently – is to tell the truth, to simply tell the truth. And, of course, truth is relatable only to one's own experience. But if you can take what's happening in the play and equate that with your own life, to speak it in the way that you understand it in your soul, and not try to figure out what anybody else thinks about it, that's it. Because one's own vision of something is different from anyone else's in the world and the trick is to find that in yourself. Somebody has said that what an actor has to do is be clear, and in order to be clear as an actor, you have to be clear to yourself.

I don't think it's possible to be a good actor without some very distinct center. I think a good actor has got to be, in a way, almost like a priest. That there is a purity of spirit involved which makes it possible for ideas to be conveyed through that person to the audience, that the actor becomes a kind of conductor or a medium, or a way of transferring something abstract and indefinable to an audience. And that's why the great writers make the most interesting evenings. If you sit and watch a production of *Coriolanus* or *Three Sisters*, what you're really doing is spending an evening with Shakespeare or Chekhov. Because every time somebody opens their mouth in one of those plays, whether they're a man or a woman, what you're really listening to is the mind of the person who wrote it. And I think important actors connect with important writers.

JEAN Do you think it's necessary for a director, or even for an actor, to come to a play like *Three Sisters* with ideas about ways to do it differently than it's been done before?

CHRIS No. I always think that the role and the production will reveal itself to me, will show me what it is. I never go into a play with a – I always go in knowing what I mean when I speak, but I never have any idea about the total. I think that's the way to do it. Nikos was a director who sat down on the first day and heard the cast read, and then slowly realized what the strong things were without having decided in advance what he wanted it to be. There are things you can see that are strong and you go after them, and there are things that probably won't work and you just let them be.

JEAN What were Nikos' strengths as a director? How did he help you?

CHRIS Well, I always got a lot of encouragement from him. I mean, Nikos could be tough. But he was never that way with me, even sometimes when I obviously wasn't doing something right, he let me be. I always found him very articulate and even eloquent. Once he started talking he could become quite poetic. He actually sometimes reminded me of Tennessee Williams when he spoke. He was very inventive with speech.

JEAN What was the process with *Ivanov*?

CHRIS I loved doing that. I'd like to do that again, actually. It's a much better evening than it's given credit for.

JEAN What happens with that man? It seems like he starts from a place of complete despair and then just goes lower and lower.

CHRIS Yeah, but, I mean, he's so funny. There's a scene in it where I think he stands on stage and doesn't speak for about fifteen minutes. The party scene in the second act. He says nothing, he just stands there and watches everybody. And I used to get a lot of laughs in that scene! He's so ridiculous. I saw it once, and I won't say with who, he was a very famous actor. Well, it was a very long evening. And I don't think it should feel that way. There's all these crazy people, like that guy with the firecrackers, and, of course, Ivanov himself, his depression. I always felt that suicide – unless you're really sick, unless physically you're incapable of sustaining life – that a suicide for a young, healthy, strapping man with everything to live for, is really an example of narcissism taken to its absolute limits. The selfishness of an act like that, the self-centeredness of such misery – when the guy should really be thanking his lucky stars! I always thought that was kind of Chekhov's joke, that the play itself is a rebuke of Ivanov, and that Ivanov is a ridiculous character. And I felt that, too, I thought he was ridiculous. And I think that's why he's so funny.

JEAN He seems to have a great deal of sanity, too, that the other people around him don't have.

CHRIS Yeah, he's a very smart guy. He's just miserable. [Laughs.] He's a very intelligent man, and everybody likes him, and he has no reason to feel that way, he just does.

JEAN There's no real hope in this play, is there, the way there is in the others.

CHRIS No, *Ivanov* is really just the study of a suicide.

JEAN When a Chekhov production goes wrong, what do you think is the mistake?

CHRIS One of the best productions I ever saw of a Chekhov was *Uncle Vanya* in Hebrew at the Habebin in Tel Aviv. I knew the play so well that it didn't matter that it was in Hebrew, I knew every scene, and the actors were really superb. And, being mostly Eastern Europeans and Israelis, they had a real sense of that part of the world. They were very robust and spirited, passionate people. They were big actors, the men were big, heavy guys and the women were big, heavy women! And they all had huge voices and they were really – out there! I think those characters in Chekhov really are right, as they say, in your face. They are big people, they are the kind of people that you notice when they walk into a restaurant. They are life loving and fun loving and they love to eat and drink and fight and cry. As Americans, it's a little bit difficult for us to do that, even though, in many ways, we're closer to the Russians certainly than the English. I think American people are a working kind of people, and I think Chekhov's Russians are like that, too. And passionate, capable of big mood swings, and a little bit larger than life. Any kind of reticence, I think, doesn't serve Chekhov well.

JEAN Nikos often talked about the best acting being sort of "messy" or "unfinished." "Unfinished" meaning never fully accomplishing the task, that once you accomplish the task you give yourself as an actor, something gets "set" in the performance and then the spontaneity is lost. Can you speak to this?

CHRIS Absolutely. I mean, I'm a big fan of chaos. I operate off it in my life and in my acting. One has to have a kind of trust in chaos. I believe, you know, that chaos is a real fact at the center of many things that we think we control and that we think we have the strings on. One of my favorite feelings, before walking on stage, it's something that happens to me only in the theater: I'll be in the wings waiting to go on, and there's a sense of – "I have no idea what's going to happen now as I step into the light." I don't know what's going to happen, and I don't care! If I forget my lines, I don't care. If the whole thing gets screwed up, it doesn't matter! All that matters is what's happening, and is it interesting. And if the audience senses that, they're going to be looking at you, they're going to be paying attention, they're not going to be thinking how maybe that they should be someplace else.

In other words, I guess we're talking about something dangerous. Which I think is a very important aspect of watching acting, especially on the stage. And that, for me anyway, comes out of a surrender to the notion of chaos. And I rehearse that way, too. I trust that I've done my work and when I go out there, it's there. Once I walk on I don't think about anything. And it's a dangerous thing for me, too, because it doesn't always work. But by taking that chance you can make some sparks. And audiences appreciate it, too. An audience doesn't want to watch an actor being careful. One can make mistakes in that respect and be criticized for it but I've always thought that the other side of it, the part that balances it out, is much more valuable. For me, connecting to something deep inside is really allowing that – what I think of as sort of a higher intelligence in me – to take over. I always reach a point where I'm just not smart enough to think about it anymore, so let something else do it for me, I guess that's what they call intuition, or whatever.

I don't believe most people are capable of figuring out, let alone articulating, complex human situations. How can you? You can't even explain your own life! The person you're married to, your mother and father, your brothers and sisters, what do you really know? All you know is that when you see them, something happens. That's why sitting down and saying, in this scene you realize that's what this is, that this is what the playwright's doing, is pretty much useless. I think it is important for an actor to know what he wants – you know, where am I, what am I doing, what do I want in the scene. It's important to think about those things, but only to get your foot in the door. Once that's established, it's useless. It's a hindrance, really. Because if you lock yourself into that, you can't surprise yourself, and if you can't surprise yourself, you're never going to surprise the audience. I believe that. I think that one of my most valuable assets on stage is that I'm never quite sure what I'm going to do next, so how could anybody else be? Because you do telegraph that, if you know exactly what you're doing the audience knows it. You know, some actors are very good at that, but that's not my strong point. You don't know what's going to happen next in the play itself, you know? What's next?

When I played Astrov in *Vanya,* we had that scene between the two of us, Vanya and Astrov, toward the end of the play. And some nights we'd be laughing and rolling on the floor, other times he'd cry in my arms, sometimes a combination of those things, sometimes I'd run off the stage and come back on my hands and knees –

JEAN – The scene where Vanya wants the medicine –

CHRIS – Yeah, he wants the morphine and I'm hiding the bottles, and the whole thing was ridiculous but it was right, too. And it never was the same from night to night, I know that.

JEAN A lot of actors I talked to felt like Nikos allowed them the permission to do that for the first time. But it kind of sounds to me that you've always felt that permission –

CHRIS It's the only way I know. But, you know, I've run into directors who did not encourage that. And that's difficult for me.

JEAN It must be.

CHRIS As a matter of fact, some directors don't like that at all. But usually they don't hire me in the first place.

JEAN Nikos was always so elated after a day of rehearsal with you. I think because he was always happy when he discovered another actor who liked to work the way he did.

CHRIS Yes. And he was fun. He was fun to be with. To me that's important in a director. I think rehearsals should be fun, even if it's the biggest tragedy ever written, if you're rehearsing *Medea*, the rehearsals should be fun. And I think the actor's position too always has to be one of being in a *play*. I think that the illusion that what one's doing is really happening is something you sort of give up once you're ten years old. There's a quality of the experience of a show that's participatory, and everyone knows what's going on: we're all there for a purpose which is to put on a *play*. And let's use this word "entertainment." No matter what it is, it's got to be entertaining. Nikos was aware of this. He was aware of the fact that people were going to be sitting there and, in addition to being moved, enlightened or whatever you want to call it, in addition to seeing a great masterpiece of literature, they also had to be entertained. And that is a mighty responsibility. That's probably why I've never directed anything.

JEAN Because?

CHRIS I can entertain as an actor. I'm not sure I could put the whole machinery together and make it entertaining. Nikos could. Nikos loved it. He liked being a cook, you know? Putting it all together like some fantastic meal.

Laila Robins (Sasha) in "Ivanov," 1983

"When Thorton Wilder was asked, 'Who's your best friend?,' he said, 'the wastepaper basket!' When you look through all the notebooks of Michelangelo, or de Vinci, or Picasso, there's a hell of a lot of pieces of paper, yet in between you still imagine that for each sketch, at least ten sketches were torn out. You're coming to class or rehearsal to do a sketch, just one quick sketch in front of everyone, right? The point is, you have to create for yourself, you have to create the conditions to go up there and do the work like a sketch, with much less reverence and much less expectation. Accept that automatically things happen, and at the end you don't ponder over your sketch, wondering why it's not quite right, instead you just take a quick look and say, 'Oh, yeah, I messed it up.' Or really, you don't even remember it. Because you're on to the next one.

"When the time comes that you go out of a performance and you don't remember if it was good or if it was bad, then you know you're working. If you really worry all the time, saying 'this is good' or 'this is bad,' just forget it, you'll just screw up. I mean, it's just not worth it or even that interesting! There have to be many more interesting things for you to do as a person. You can have a drink, a meal, you can go on a trip, see nature, why should you go through this agony? Unless of course you get your kicks that way!

"Don't worry if something goes wrong or right. If you worry about it, it's going to go wrong. Do it kind of as part of your existence. Next Thursday it doesn't work, the Friday after that it works. Some people need to do twenty a year, some need three. But if you worry about it, there's not going to be that sense of throwing the work away. It's going to matter."

Nikos Psacharopoulos

117

A WINDOW OF OPPORTUNITY
Interview with Laila Robins

Ms. Robins, as a non-Equity actress, played the role of Sasha in the 1983 WTF production of *Ivanov*, directed by John Madden. At graduate school at Yale, she played Natasha in *The Three Sisters*; and she's played Nina in *The Sea Gull* twice – with Olympia Dukakis for The Whole Theater Company, and most recently in a production directed by former WTF associate director, Bonnie Monte, for the New Jersey Shakespeare Festival. Laila and I talked over lunch at my home in Los Angeles.

JEAN What was the process of working on *Ivanov*? What attracted you to Sasha?

LAILA When I got to Williamstown, my first summer, and found out I was playing Sasha – I thought my whole world had changed, my whole life! I felt like I was in a dream, I was just so thrilled. I kept saying to my friends, "Is this my life?!" And of course Sasha is the same, the ingenue full of life and hope. And when I found out I'd be working with Chris Walken, I had this image – I sort of felt about him much like Sasha feels about Ivanov. That there was so much wonderful stuff in him but at the same time, a degree of self-destructiveness. It was very parallel to how Sasha feels about Ivanov and very useful.

JEAN How was working with Chris?

LAILA Three days before we went into tech he turned to me and he said in this really – sort of ominous – way: [In a low whisper.] "This is going to be a catastrophe." And I said, "No, No! This is my first professional play, you can't say that!" And then at that tech rehearsal he, of course changed everything. We came off stage after one scene, and I remember trying to catch up with him and saying, "Don't you remember how we rehearsed it? Remember how we blocked it?" I was filled with terror! I thought he might do *anything* onstage and he

118

did, he did! Chris hated when the air conditioners were on in that theater. And he told the stage manager time and again, "Don't turn on the air conditioners, they make that white noise, I can't act with that." So one night during the Act III scene between the two of us, suddenly he looks at me. And he goes sort of cross-eyed. And then he holds his index finger out to me as if to say, "Wait just one minute." He leaves me on the stage alone! He walks through an imaginary wall, to the stage manager's desk and says, "I told you not to turn on the air conditioning!" And the stage manager says, "No! It's raining!" It was the rain coming down on the tin roof! "Oh," says he. And then he comes back on stage and proceeds to do the scene. And this was my first time on a big stage, I just hung there with my mouth open, waiting for him to come back! It was terrifying! He was very unpredictable.

He did something wonderful in that scene. Sasha has a line: "Exactly, that's just what you need, to break something, smash something." And Chris did this brilliant thing where he then took a pencil and broke it in half. When she says, "break something," I feel that Sasha means for him to throw a vase or a chair or something like that! But Chris just did this little, impotent gesture which was so hilarious. And then his next line is, "You're funny." I felt every night when Chris said, "You're funny," it was really heartfelt. It was like he was looking at my terror as an actress and saying, "You're funny!"

And because I was young, I also had one of the most powerful experiences in a rehearsal period that I've ever had. We were rehearsing the last scene where Ivanov goes off and shoots himself. And I'm saying, "No, somebody stop him, somebody stop him!" And one day in rehearsal I just started weeping uncontrollably. The rehearsal was over and I went over in the corner and just sobbed and sobbed and I remember John Madden, the director, came over, and comforted me. I mean, it's a young actress thing to do and kind of silly, but I'll never forget that. Something had really dropped in for me emotionally.

JEAN Finding that kind of emotional connection is one of the gifts in Chekhov, I think. The material makes it possible.

LAILA Well, the beauty of it is, it's there, and if you just open yourself up to it, it will resonate very deeply. When I look back on this I realize, Sasha and Ivanov *were* Laila and Chris because Chris kept telling me, "This is going to be awful, this is going to be a catastrophe," and I kept going, "No, no! It's going to be a wonderful play, you're wonderful in it!" It's exactly what Sasha does to Ivanov. "No, life is wonderful, don't give up, you're a brilliant man!" It was all so parallel.

JEAN Let's look at the scene you mentioned between the two of them in Act III . The one that's famous for being done so frequently in acting classes.

LAILA I auditioned for Nikos the first time with the monologue at the end of the scene.

JEAN There you are. Let's sort of go moment by moment and explore what's going on for her. The last time we've seen Ivanov and Sasha together was at the end of Act II, discovered, by Ivanov's wife, in an embrace. It's two weeks later and Sasha's coming to see him. Why?

LAILA He hasn't come to visit her, she's worried about him, and she's in love with him. I think she's also come to say, "Look, I can wait, stay with your wife if you need to." She says this at the end of the speech. To sort of tell him that he doesn't have to make a decision right now, to take some of the pressure off of him. And just to simply see him again.
By the end of the play, his negativity really does overpower her positiveness. She loses the illusions of youth. At the end of the second act he embraces her and says, "Oh could this be a new life, could this be it?" And she feels, "Yes, it can, it can, I love you!" I think for her to have that power to be able to change this man, this brilliant man who's lately been very depressed, to feel that she could change his life, is very heady. And even at this point, in Act III, when she comes to see him, she still thinks she can snap him out of it. That's why she says, "Throw something!" Or why she starts talking about the picture of the dog. By the end of the play she's saying things like, "You don't know how you've beat me down, you've sucked the life out of me," and realizes she cannot lift that

120

darkness that's in him. She can't change that, as much as she tries. But at this point she still believes she can.

JEAN I'm glad you mentioned the line about the painting of the dog. It's one of those lines in Chekhov that seems pretty cryptic at first glance, as if it came out of nowhere.

LAILA There's a whole beat at the beginning of Sasha trying to make him come out of it. And then she says, "Oh, it's so exhausting talking to you." And then comes the line about the painting: "This dog is beautifully drawn. Is it from life?" Partly, I remember, I wanted to get a little distance from him so that he could look at me, so that he could look at my young body. Maybe not so consciously, but part of it was, "All right, well, I'm not going to argue with you, I'm not going to waste my time." And then she kind of sways over to the picture and that gives him a chance to look at her youthful body and remember how wonderful she is. And then she talks about the painting. It really is a non sequitur. But it's so wonderful because she says, "This dog is beautifully drawn, is it from life?" I mean, what a wonderful choice of words for Chekhov, "from *life*." It's almost like – we're all play-acting, and he and I are play-acting with each other and there's something almost more real about that dog in the painting than there is about these roles that we're playing with each other! "Is that a picture of a dog? Is that what a real dog looks like or is that just somebody's *idea* of what a real dog looks like? I wonder what the real dog looks like."

JEAN That's fascinating because it's what the scene is about too, Ivanov has all these *ideas* about life that are dragging him down, and she's saying, life is so simple.

LAILA She's saying, "So, you're living this idea, this print of a dog is your idea, but what is it really? What is it right now in this room between you and me. Don't angst over everything, don't – make up your life, just *be* your life." I mean, she wants to get him in the here and now. That's why she says, "break something." An act like that puts you in the moment. If you take something and smash it, that kinetic energy of smashing definitely gets you in the moment. That's what she wants him to do, get out of his head and break something.

To snap him out of his apathy.

JEAN And in the next moment –

LAILA Right after the moment about the painting, he says, "[the dog] is drawn from life, yes. But this affair of ours is secondhand, it's trite: the man is depressed, can no longer feel the ground firm beneath his feet. Along comes the young woman. Strong and high spirited. She extends towards him a helping, loving hand..." When he says this, it's almost like he's outside of life, he's narrating rather than experiencing. He also narrates at the end of Act II, when he says, "Could this be, could this be a new life?" It's almost like he's commenting on his experience. Rather than saying "I love you, Sasha, I've always wanted you, Sasha," it's all about himself. "Do I like myself in this movie? Can I deal with this young girl?" We all do that, but he does it to the nth degree, narrating, watching, judging, assessing – instead of just *being*, actively, with people.

When he says "you're funny," it's really his first reaction that's in the moment, it's the first time I get him to look at me, not look at himself with me in this room, narrating, but the first time he is just being with me. He doesn't give to anybody. I mean from my point of view. Maybe not from Ivanov's point of view.

Then he has this wonderful line, "There's a little dust on your shoulder –" I loved this moment. When Chris did that, it was a very sensual moment, because he touched me. He connects to Sasha in a real way rather than an abstract way. That's the meaning of that moment. It connects to the life underneath.

When I first went to Yale, they gave us a reading list over the summer. I had never read Chekhov, and I read all of them that summer and I felt, "I don't get it." I just thought, what's with these plays, why are we going to study these for a whole year? And I felt really nervous because obviously they thought there was something there! And eventually I was actually the first one to go up with a scene, we did Masha and Vershinin, and I was just lost! I hadn't done any of that kind of work before I went to Yale. And we studied those five plays for a year and realized, what you dig into is the life underneath, which is made up of who they are and what they deeply want. Most of all in Chekhov you have to find that out – but that's the beauty of it. If you have a line coming out of nowhere, like the line, "there's dust on your shoulder," it's the joy of discovering why it's there, and how you make the transition. The challenge of that is what's so great about it. To look at it and get confused and frustrated is a waste of time. And I think for Chris, I can't speak for him, but I felt that when he brushed that dust off, it was a finding of a very intimate moment. He kind of put a pause around it, and then continued.

And this last speech of hers – [She reads from the text:]

"There's a lot you men don't understand. Any girl would sooner take on a successful man, because what she's attracted by is the idea of active love. Do you understand? Active. Men are absorbed in their work and so for them love is lucky to get a place. But for us, love is life itself. I love you. That means that I dream constantly about how I'll draw you up out of your depression, how I'll follow you to the ends of the earth... I remember once, about three years ago, harvest time, you came to our house all covered in dust and sunburnt, exhausted. You asked for a drink of water. When I came back with the glass there you were, stretched out on the sofa, sleeping the sleep of the dead. You slept around the clock on that sofa, and all that time there was I standing outside the door, keeping guard in case anyone should try to go in. And I felt so good, it was wonderful! The greater the effort, the better the love...that is, you know, it's felt more intensely."

It's just wonderful. This is sort of the dialectic of the play. That Sasha *is* active love. Ivanov is inactive, passive, he's unable to come out of himself. This is also, interestingly enough, something Nikos would try to get me away from in my work, that is, imploding with the emotion rather than making it active. He always wanted me to be more active in my acting. And when you're active, you actually offer something to the world, to people around you. Sasha's saying she would rather be with someone she could help and actively try to make feel better and do better. Because that's exciting to her. She's the opposite, psychically, from him. I mean, people can look at this speech and say, "Oh, God, what an anti-feminist speech." She's saying basically she'll do anything for him and follow him around and be his slave and give him a glass of water when he's tired!

JEAN Was that hard for you to justify?

LAILA No, not so much because I think that women are supposed
to do this, but I think that when you love someone you do want to
give everything – but in the same way that a man would also want to
do for a woman. It's just that in this case, a woman is talking about
it. I remember John Madden helping me through this last part of the
speech where I had to really visualize coming in and seeing him on
the sofa. Chris and John and I sat there and did a kind of sense
memory about that moment, about the glass of water, and him
sleeping. And then he has that wonderful line, "Active love, hmmm.
Sounds like one of those dangerous female fantasies!" And he goes
on to make fun of himself. Chris did this so well! This line, "Boo,
hoo, hoo. Boo, hoo, hoo." He did it in a way that was so
contemporary. I, with my fresh-from-drama-school classical
training, thought: "I don't know if that's right." But he really got the
humor of that moment, people really laughed.

And here at the end he says, "You must go, Sasha, we're
forgetting ourselves." That's exactly what he needs to do is forget
himself. He's a little taken out of himself because he does make fun
of himself, but he can't sustain it. He sends her away. And then, I
love this line: "I have that feeling again as if I'd eaten too many
wrinked, old toadstools." He can't sustain it.

One of the things Nikos taught me, and that I used in this scene,
was to hold onto my own personality, to not pick up and play the
other person's energy in the scene. I remember a scene where
someone had to come in and tell me something horrible and I ended
up responding too empathetically and going into *their* horrible place,
instead of being opposite to that. *That* person's having the tragedy,
your task is to do something else. You don't fall into that dramatic
hole where the other person is living. Be something to bounce off of.
I had a tendency to fall into certain kind of empathetic behavior that
was based on the other person's world.

JEAN While you didn't do a Chekhov play with Nikos, you did do
a Russian play – Gorky's *Barbarians* – which is certainly similiar in
style. What else was Nikos dealing with in your work when he
directed you in this?

LAILA Well, mostly, my tendency was to implode, to have the feeling inside, but not to have it come out to another person. He tried to get me to come out of myself a little more. It was easy for me to understand pain and all the emotional moments in a role, but to actually, actively *do* something with the feeling onstage was harder for me. So he would kind of be irreverent with me. He'd say things like, "Why are you staying in the mudhole, Laila? Come out, come out!" That meant, "Don't be so caught up in your own thoughts, your own angst, your own worries, the pain of the part, come out more." I think Carrie Nye was just the opposite, very much that other thing. She was very out there, she was very grand, and everything she did "read" on stage, which was what I think Nikos loved about her.

He'd also say, "Don't complicate things, try to simplify, simplify your work. Don't get so wrapped up in trying to play so many different things, they're all there!" Meaning, have confidence in what you have as an actor, it's already there, don't worry about it. You don't have to "act" the emotion, you've got that. Play one thing and make it simple. And all that other stuff will resonate because of who you are as a person, or because you've done your homework. Don't let all the homework show in your performance. Sort of do the homework, then just let it go, and then just play the one thing that you need from the other person on stage with you.

JEAN It sounds like he was saying,"trust yourself ."

LAILA Yes, right. And that was there from the beginning. I remember auditioning for Nikos when I was a student at Yale, and at first I was very intimidated. But after auditioning for him I felt relieved. I didn't feel like I was being tested in any way. I was just sort of being encouraged to do what I do, and he was just going to happen to be there. He almost made you feel that he already knew you could do it, it was just whether or not you were going to allow yourself to do it *today*. So he instilled a lot of confidence. He talked to you as if all of it was in you already. It wasn't like, "Oh boy, I don't know if she can do this." It was more like, [In a very matter-of-fact, Greek accented voice.] "I think you can do it, you know you can do it, so do it." That's kind of refreshing, because you weren't doing all that angst-ing and worrying. It was really left in your lap, whether or not you were going to get rid of the bullshit and do it. I worked with him on four plays, *A Knife in the Heart, Peer Gynt, Undiscovered Country* and *Barbarians*, and it was always just like that. He had a way of imbuing you with confidence and making you feel capable.

Working with Nikos was also about not having preconceived ideas when you went out on stage, it was more like: "Let's see what happens. We're all here together in this room, let's see what happens." And because of this, he created the atmosphere of – a playground. You felt, "Wow, he's really loose about this, so let's all be loose about this."

JEAN That sense of not worrying about it.

LAILA Yes, this sort of laissez-faire attitude. [Expansively.] You come in, you're glad to be at rehearsal, we'll sit down and see what happens today. And that's a wonderful environment to create in, very safe and very nurturing. Because, you know, if you didn't do it well today, it would work tomorrow. He always had faith that it would work. It was never like, "Oh my God, I'm never going to find this, he miscast me." It was always, "It's in you, and it'll come out when you're ready." A lot of freedom.

During *Summer and Smoke,* which Jim Simpson directed, I remember our first stumble-through and Nikos was there and afterwards I was a basket case, I was just beet red with embarrassment. And I looked at him with sheer panic. But with Nikos, even if on Friday you were completely impossible, he would still believe, he would still be certain that on Monday you would be fine. I don't know, maybe he just knew that miracles happen. He seemed to have faith in miracles!

Another reason I responded so much to Nikos, I think, was his European vision. My parents are European, so I connected to that right away. Because English was his second language, sometimes he would communicate more in gestures and noises than in words; but because of that it was almost as if he was using a universal language. The musicality and the dance and song that he would do let you know what he wanted. It was very instinctual and almost symbolic. He did a movement and a noise, and at first you say – [Somewhat confusedly.] "Okay, uh huh." But then, two days later, you go

126

"Aha!" Your subconscious mind is working on it on a whole other level than your literal mind. So you dream on it a couple of nights, and then in two days you know exactly what he was trying to tell you. But it's been given to you in a code, practically. And many people would get impatient with him because they wanted to know, literally, in so many words, what he wanted. But the process was more suggestive for Nikos. He would, I think, suggest things to your subconscious mind, in such a way that your literal, rational mind would be bypassed.

The other great thing was his sense of glamour. Just the way he'd come backstage right before the curtain on opening nights in the tux and the sandals with the bottle of champagne. And everyone took a sip from his silver cup. And that enormous box of flowers that were passed out opening nights to everyone who worked at the theater, those things. There was a sense of ritual, a sense of occasion, of ceremony. And, for the company of actors, would be the joy of looking forward to that, of knowing that he would always be there with that champagne on opening night. I think he had a gift for creating a ritual, and I don't think a lot of people do. And I feel what we're lacking a lot in life is ritual.

JEAN Rituals are also part of the experience of "family." I never really made that connection before. Everyone's always saying "Williamstown" and "family" in the same breath and one of the things intrinsic to families is ritual. And at Williamstown there were a lot of rituals.

LAILA Yes, and the looking after each other, the nurturing that he did. Thinking ahead about what would be good for people. He had a way of knowing what you might be ready for. Like when he offered me *Summer and Smoke*. He didn't direct it, but he cast me. They were starting rehearsals in three days and somebody fell out, and he came to me and said, "Laila, I think you're ready to do this." And it was almost like, when Nikos said you were ready, you *were* ready. I felt he was very senstive to where actors were in their growth. Or what might be a challenge at this point, or what might be a good idea. And I felt like he knew that about everybody. It was amazing, I felt like he was aware of each individual actor. That he actually took the time to think about every one of them: "What would be good for

127

him or her to play?" And then he'd come up with something that would help them to grow. Usually, you don't have people that – pay attention – to that. I always thought that Nikos really paid attention to people and really watched them and really saw them. He had so many people on his mind, a whole roster of actors. But I always felt I had a special place, and I think a lot of actors felt that way. It wasn't that I was, in particular, special to him, it was that he made everyone feel special.

JEAN Roberta Maxwell used "approval" as the operative word. That Nikos' constant approval made it possible for her work to grow in unexpected ways.

LAILA How rarely we get that. We are just faced with judgment and rejection constantly. That's why I think Williamstown felt like a family, because you don't just get rid of your family! You love them and take them back no matter what. With Nikos you felt that you could go out in the world, the critics could kill you, you could be really very bad – but, no matter what, you could go back to Williamstown. He approved of you no matter how you were received by the world. Wanted you back. And then when you came back, maybe in that moment, you would be able to grow. In that little window of opportunity, in one of those summer months if you were in a show at Williamstown, you could grow. You longed to go back there because you knew it would be a safe enough place for you to grow. All the growing that you knew you had to do all year was too scary! It was too scary, until you got back to Williamstown and then – "Okay, I'm ready to change." And you would be able to change, because he loved you. He approved of you. Roberta's really got it right. Approval.

Louis Zorich (Dorn), William Hansen (Sorin), Joyce Ebert (Nina), Carolyn Coates (Arkadina) in "The Sea Gull," 1969.

"A director can just give you the shape. I don't want to know the limitations before I know the possibilities and the potential. So, I look for potential. I look for possibilities. I look for lack of discipline, frankly. I love actors who go to their emotional junkyard, pick up everything, and bring it on stage. Afterward it is up to me to keep things 'down.' That is my job, to shape rather than to invent. The actor invents. So I'd rather see too many things going on and cut them down, trim them to the needs of the material, size and edit them, than see absolutely nothing and then have to pump energy and life into the actors. I love to see open work, and sometimes I get lucky and see work that is wonderful."

Nikos Psacharopoulos

GETTING RESULTS
Interview with Joyce Ebert

Joyce Ebert, an early WTF company member, played Nina in the first Chekhov done at Williamstown in 1962, *The Sea Gull*, and repeated the role in 1968. She played Varya in *The Cherry Orchard*, in 1963, and again in 1969. And Masha in *The Three Sisters* in both the 1965 and 1970 productions. I reached Joyce at her home in New Haven, and we talked over the phone.

JEAN I've spoken with a lot with actors who were in the WTF Chekhovs during the middle and last part of Nikos' tenure at the Festival – and I was around for a lot of that work myself – but you were there at the start. In fact, you were actually the one who came to Nikos with the suggestion of doing the first WTF Chekhov, *The Sea Gull*. What was it like in the beginning?

JOYCE I think better than towards the end, quite frankly. It was like Nikos had discovered something fresh, you know? He hooked into something that was ingrained in his culture – the temperament, the religion, the emotional range that the Russians and the Greeks have in common. Suddenly, I think Nikos felt at home. I mean, he didn't lose it later on, it was just much more exciting at the beginning because he was constantly discovering things. And besides that, I was really there at the beginning and not in the later ones at all! The later ones, the parts I would've been right for, like Arkadina and Raveneskaya, he used other actresses. He was going on to a different family then. Laurie Kennedy and I were talking about this and essentially Laurie felt that she should have moved on past Irina to some of the other roles, and I felt that I should have moved on, too. But I finally did get to do Arkadina in *The Sea Gull*, I did it at Long Wharf.

To give credit, it was both Mike Ebert, my ex-husband, and I who came to Nikos and said, "This is something you should do." I had done Nina twice before, you see.

JEAN So by the time you did *The Sea Gull* at Williamstown, you already had your feet wet with it.

JOYCE Yes. I really teethed on Chekhov in school – especially Nina. It was a life process doing Nina. The first time I did it I was a freshman. Then, the scene that was most difficult was the last scene. The early scenes were easy. And then when I did it when I was a senior, the last scene was a little easier. But the first time I did it at Williamstown was when it really all pulled together for me. I was still young enough to be able to do the first three acts and experienced enough in life to do the last act. And then when I did it the second time at Williamstown, the last act was extremely easy and the first three acts were a little harder. As I grew older, of course, I had much more life experience, had gone through a lot of what Nina goes through.

JEAN Blythe was saying that it's probably impossible for an 16-year-old to play Nina.

JOYCE That's also true of Juliet. I only did it once, but it requires age. No, you can't pick a 16-year-old to do Nina. They just don't have enough life experience. Or, not enough understanding of the life experience they have.
    Nina is, I think, the best of his ingenues. Irina is also wonderful. Anya, in *Cherry Orchard*, is very difficult, very opaque. But Nina is a very clearly written part. The first time we did it was very exciting. I don't think Nikos had any preconceptions about it, he just sort of plunged in. His discoveries must have challenged him because he did a Chekhov every year after that. The audiences were getting a little sick of it near the end!

JEAN When people go wrong with Chekhov, why do they go wrong?

JOYCE Because they don't balance the humor with the tragedy of it. Usually it's played very darkly and morbidly and people are really bored and the audience is, too! Or they take the exact opposite tact which is to play it all for comedy, play it all almost slapstick. And there's a very delicate balance between the two. One of the only modern playwrights I've worked on that I feel even touches that is Peter Nichols. In plays like *Joe Egg*, and *Passion* and *Forget Me Not Lane*. I've done five Peter Nichols plays, and that's why I love doing them. Because he has you on the floor in one moment laughing and the next moment in tears. And Nikos had a handle on that. The lost lives. The silliness. You couldn't lie around with long pauses in Nikos' Chekhovs unless they were pretty much orchestrated. Which is what you have to do in Chekhov. You can't just: pause, pause, pause, after every line, saying "I'm bored." You have to say "I'm bored." in a way that shows you're looking for something else to do. And Nikos managed that balance very well. Arvin* does too.

It's a tricky thing to go back and forth with that and to have actors that are willing and able to do it. Olympia has that. She's funny when she's crying and her funny moments sometimes make you want to cry. And Carolym Coates had that too when she did Arkadina. Laurie Kennedy was very funny, and a lovely Irina. When she did it the first time she was just an apprentice and she emerged like a little butterfly.

JEAN You've done so many of the plays - is there a role you missed? Something you wished you would've done?

JOYCE I never did Yelena in *Uncle Vanya,* I always wanted to do that. Maria Tucci was the best Yelena I've ever seen. And Laurie was wonderful in that production too, but she was just too pretty for Sonya.

JEAN This was a production where the Yelena, Maria Tucci, felt she wasn't pretty enough, and the Sonya was told she was too pretty.

JOYCE Well, they're both beautiful because both Laurie and Maria have a certain radiance on stage, that's completely aside from the physical characteristics. It's like a halo effect, around certain performers. Some have it and some don't. But when you see someone who has it, and you can see it in both men and women, it's actually very much like the glow of light you see in religious paintings. You can understand where that came from.

* Miss Ebert's husband Arvin Brown (who studied with Nikos at Yale and was his assistant at WTF) is the artistic director of the Long Wharf Theatre in New Haven.

JEAN In the early years Nikos directed all the major Chekhov plays except *Uncle Vanya*. Nor did he direct it later. Do you have any idea why?

JOYCE Well, he always said he couldn't identify with it, but I think Nikos, unconsciously, overidentified with *Uncle Vanya*, and somehow or other didn't want to touch that. I don't think he realized that deep underneath he did.

JEAN Identified in what way?

JOYCE Something about Vanya's dissatisfaction, frustration. Because Nikos could always mask the frustration. I always felt that, because he always shied away from it and I thought there was some deeper reason. Maybe the same reason I gave up singing opera, because it was too important to me, I wanted it too much, I felt if I didn't succeed at it it would make me miserable. I think it's fascinating that *Uncle Vanya* is the only one he didn't touch.

JEAN What do you think about the way Chekhov is done in this country, as opposed to the way the English do it?

JOYCE It's a sore point with me that most critics think that only English actors can do Chekhov. I think American actors are much more true to the Russian spirit of things than English actors are. Because they tend to be not as slick on the surface. Of course there are notable exceptions. But American actors tend not to be as stylistic as English actors are. If there's not a slick surface a lot of critics think it's ineptitude rather than an honest rendering of the character. The character himself or herself not being slick, not being packaged. You get that with a lot of Anglophile critics who just think that the British can do no wrong and Americans can do no right. I think that Americans, for the most part, have a sensibility for Chekhov that is more in keeping with the Russian temperament. The same way that American actors embraced the Stanislavski method moreso than English actors did. And Nikos, being a teacher, of course taught in that way too. Nikos wanted both. He hired actors who were technically proficient but also emotionally honest. And that's, I think, what is required for Chekhov.

JEAN You've put your finger on something I think was characteristic to the Chekhovs at Williamstown – the lack of a finished surface. The value system was about the texture of the work being unfinished, rough.

JOYCE Well, you know Nikos was a very clever at casting, for one thing. Sometimes he didn't have to do that work. He more or less left it up to the actor to fill the emotional moments. Which is really what Arvin, does too, actually. Which makes sense because Nikos was Arvin's teacher at Yale. Although sometimes Nikos could be very Machiavellian in order to get the results he wanted. As he was when we did *St. Joan*. He started yelling at Bill Hansen and me in the trial scene, he would say, "Don't feel sorry for yourself!" And then he would demonstrate how he wanted me to do it, and I thought for all the world it seemed like he was feeling sorry for himself! This happened over and over and eventually made me very mad at him.

He used those same methods that Kazan would use. Which was – he wouldn't exactly bully the actors, but he would sort of very sneakily get the results he wanted by getting the actor upset. And he did that in *St. Joan*. I was mad at him a lot during that whole production.

JEAN Austin talked about Nikos doing the same thing with Blythe, getting her creatively mad. And she said she sort of needed that in order to find those very raw moments.

JOYCE Well, Kazan was Nikos' idol, and it was a technique that Kazan used all the time. But you don't like to always feel you're being manipulated and sometimes Nikos would do that. On the other hand, sometimes it would work very well! I had that same thing when I did *The Trojan Women* with Cacoyannis, who is brilliant, although he was much more of a martinet than Nikos. He would get up there and demonstrate and give you line readings and you knew very well that if you did them exactly the way he did them, it was not what he wanted. He wanted – it was like touching your ear with your elbow. You had to interpret what he wanted, not imitate how he wanted it done. Nikos was much less Machiavellian than Cacoyannis, but it's very Greek, or at least the two Greek directors I've worked with have used it! Sometimes it would get wonderful results. The only problem is that only works when you have a short run of the play and Williamstown was a place of very short runs. It's not a great technique to use over the long runs because that anger wears out.

I remember when we did *Tennessee Williams, A Celebration* – which, by the way, was really a crowning glory for Nikos. The idea of the all the characters from all the Tennessee Williams plays coming together, six hours of them all interacting – what a great thing that was. I was playing Princess in *Sweet Bird of Youth* and, once again, he got me very mad in one scene. I was successful in it but it was hard for me. He was asking something of me that – I really didn't understand what he meant, what he wanted. I got very discouraged during some of the rehearsals. Because I just felt that I wasn't – adequate. I was working off of the frustration of that. But nevertheless, when we got up there, I was good in it. So it paid off.

I worked with Nikos so much that I trusted him, but I also got to know him. So I knew his foibles as well as his strengths. The same as with Arvin. In the early days Arvin didn't have an eye for costumes or technical things. Now he does. He developed that over the years. Whereas Nikos had an impeccable eye for technical things, for costumes and stage picture. He was very, very good at that. Always was. You could always trust Nikos that you wouldn't look bad, and that you wouldn't go out there and make an ass of yourself. He had wonderful taste. Particularly so in casting. He could be maddening and he could infuriate you and all that would come into the work, but he never took it so far that it went beyond the bounds.

The main thing, though, this is something that Arvin said, too – the crowning achievement of Nikos' life was establishing and running that theater. He was a wonderful director of Chekhov but, really, his great achievement was putting that theater on the map as a serious theater where classics could be done and done well. And then getting all these wonderful actors to come and work for him for almost no money. In the later years he moved into more star turns with actors – probably a lot of it was economy and probably a lot of it was ambition, but he did resort to a lot of stars at the end. Which sometimes enhanced the work and sometimes did not. Nonetheless he ran that theater in a way that very few other theaters could touch. Made something really brilliant.

John Glover (Epihodov), Blythe Danner (Dunyasha)
in "The Cherry Orchard", 1980

"As artists, what you have to do is to conjure the promise of what is back there, right? It is like a dollar bill. A dollar bill is absolutely nothing, but the piece of gold that it represents, which used to be in Fort Knox, is much more interesting, that's the thing that has value. The dollar is just paper. In the same way, it is not interesting when your acting is stronger than the life it represents. You must have that kind of promise, that kind of frustration within you of the myriad of things you want to do, out of which you only get to do one. It is that kind of promise which makes for good acting. It is the idea that good actors are unfinished actors in terms of coming backstage and saying, 'Goddamn it, I didn't do it well tonight.' That is absolutely an accurate thing because good actors always have something more to do, and something more to do, than they ever really do on stage. The moment they accomplish what they want to do, they stop being good actors. That is why I am saying that good acting is not about accomplishment, it is about a promise.

"I guess what I'm saying is what I've said many times – the reason things become interesting is that the life represented is always more interesting than the form, or the text you're using. And that the great actors have an ability of communicating that life to you – sometimes they don't even think about it, right? Many, many times we know very good actors who haven't thought what the life is underneath, but they communicate the sense of it."

Nikos Psacharopoulos

THE UNKNOWN
Interview with John Glover

Mr. Glover came to Williamstown in 1973 to play the title role in *The Misanthrope* and stayed on for several other productions that season. In 1976 he played Solyony in *The Three Sisters*, and in 1980, Epihodov in *The Cherry Orchard*. He also played a featured role in another Russian play directed by Nikos, Gorky's *Children of the Sun*. John and I talked on the terrace of his home in Hollywood.

JOHN The thing that first comes to my mind is *Three Sisters*. I came in late for rehearsal, I think I'd missed about a week. I was playing Solyony. And I knew everybody in the show. I knew Nikos and I knew most of the actors. The first scene of this day that I came to rehearsal was the scene at the dinner table, in the first act. We were all around an upstage table. And I knew my lines, I'd learned my lines before I came and the stage manager had given me the blocking the morning I arrived. So I'm doing this scene with the cast for the first time, sort of feeling my way through. All of a sudden Nikos clapped his hands, and screamed – something! – And everybody started running around the table frantically! And I was thinking, what's going on here, what is everybody doing? And this kind of confused, frantic, yet passionate – thing – proceeded to ensue.

JEAN What was it?

JOHN It was action! It was life! He was directing life. And I think this sort of thing is exactly what often frustrated people about Nikos. Part of what life is, *is* confusion and part of what Nikos wanted to create on the stage in those Chekhov plays was the confusion and chaos which gives life passion. There were certain scenes in that production of *The Three Sisters* I used to watch with a kind of awe, scenes which were just astounding, mostly between those three sisters – Blythe, Olympia and Laurie. There was a great deal of passion in this production, starting with this physical love that the three of them had.

Right after I played Solyony in Nikos' *Three Sisters* I went to London to do the film *Julia*. And an incredibly successful production of *The Three Sisters* was running on the West End at the time. It had gotten great reviews, it was doing great business, and I went to see it. And it was the most sterile, uptight, production. That's when I realized how incredible Nikos was with what he did with Chekhov – in bringing out the passion of those characters. I realized that was what we in this country had lost by trying to imitate the English versions. Chekhov had become so cerebral, so heady. People just playing a kind of existential depression. But this thing that Nikos put together at Williamstown was not about that at all, it was about life and confusion and passion.

JEAN How was that passion expressed? In what scene in particular?

JOHN At the very end of Nikos' *Three Sisters*, when the military is leaving and the three sisters are left alone on the stage – well, these three woman did something very extraordinary, very moving. Nobody knew what to do with the ending. There wasn't a moment that ended the play. They practically were in tech rehearsals or the last dress rehearsal before they found it. And the four of them, Blythe, Laurie, Olympia and Nikos, just sort of said, "What are we going to do?" Now, they all knew each other from plays before, so that makes certain kinds of things possible. What they found was – they just kind of started tentatively touching each other and kind of wrapping arms around each other. And this incredible moment grew out of confusion. They didn't know what else to do, as characters and as actresses. Which is what acting is all about.

I have this image of them as – dolphins. They were like these three dolphins swimming together. I remember once seeing two dolphins in the water together that knew each other and they did an almost choreographed ballet. That's what Blythe and Laurie and Olympia seemed to create. None of it was rehearsed, they just sort of improvised it. Because they trusted each other and knew each other and had worked together, an instinctual thing happened among the three of them. This movement blended and went back and forth like those dolphins instinctively communicating without any of our kind of language. There was this – family – meaning to it. It's frustrating to try to put into words a moment like that. It's a mystic thing, the kind of acting that I think is so exciting. There's a mysticism about it, a magic. I get goosebumps just talking about it.

And the other moment that tore me up was the final scene between Olga and Vershinin. Ken Howard played the scene with Olympia and she wants to say "I love you," to him, and she thinks maybe he's going to say that, or at least that's what that scene was about with Olympia and Ken. And then Masha came in and he starts to leave her, and Blythe jumped on him from behind, clutching him. And Olympia, Olga, had to physically pull Masha off Vershinin. It's already been set up for all of us in the audience that Olga's madly in love with him. In reading that off the page, sure, the feelings are there, but the *passion* is not. I used to sneak around to the back of the house and watch that scene from the audience every night. It was spine-chilling to see. But it wasn't until I went to London and saw this highly successful, but incredibly sterile – nothing – that I realized Nikos' genius with it.

JEAN What about the other Chekhovs you've been in outside of Williamstown?

JOHN Well, the others I did didn't seem like I was doing Chekhov. They just seemed like plays about a bunch of depressed people! Years ago, when I was doing summer stock, I met an actress named Mary Finney who had been in a production of *The Sea Gull* at the Alley Theater. And she came to the Barter Theater where I was an apprentice. And I was so excited because I read that she had been in *The Sea Gull* and I'd played Constantine in my freshman year in college. And I came running up to her and I said, "Oh, you were in *The Sea Gull*! I was in *The Sea Gull* in college!" And she said rather dryly, "Oh, yes. I think that's a play the actors like much more than the audiences."

Except when Nikos did those plays. Because he brought life to them. All anyone was used to seeing was a bunch of depressed people, all into themselves. He brought people trying to do things instead of people walking around being upset all the time. I've never seen any other productions of Chekhov approach this. I remember seeing *The Cherry Orchard* with Irene Worth and Mary Beth Hurt and Meryl Streep at Lincoln Center. And again, this was all about production values, concepts. Not about the people.

I did see a *Sea Gull* in London in which Vanessa Redgrave and her daughter were quite brilliant. Vanessa Redgrave was astounding, it was about that passion. I kept thinking that if Nikos and she could get together – I mean, they'd fight like cats and dogs! But I think they'd both know what they were fighting about. I went backstage after the show and saw her, and she was saying that she'd had a big fight with the director because she wanted to be padded as Arkadina. And the director didn't want that. And I asked, "Was it a good fight?" And she said, "Oh, yes, because I won!"

JEAN Solyony in *The Three Sisters* is probably Chekhov's most arbitrary character. He's so important to the play, yet Chekhov gives so little information about him. It's a role that can go in a lot of different directions. What was your process with this? How did you work on this part?

JOHN [He pauses and then sighs.] I don't know! Well, he was an outsider. He's an outsider and someone who doesn't get his love requited, right? I can relate to all that. But really, I don't know. People would tell me that the scenes I had as Solyony with Irina were just riveting and spooky, but I had no idea why! I really didn't know what was happening. I was at sea. The same thing happened in *Children of the Sun. Children of the Sun*, a high point of feeling at sea! I just felt like nobody was getting it, that it wasn't working. One of the actresses in that used to go around to the audience and watch me play a certain scene every night. She kept saying, "That scene was brilliant, John." And I was at a total loss in that scene! It was so painful to go out on stage and play the scene because I had no idea what to do. And that's, I guess, the yin and the yang of Nikos. That's why he upset so many people. He must have had a strong belief in deliberately creating a climate of confusion, so much so that when you went out on stage, you never knew why it worked. When I did *Cherry Orchard* it was the same. Most of my scenes in that were with Chris Reeve and Blythe. And I remember that I'd do one thing one day, and then the next day he'd throw out a whole other thing for me to play, a whole different attack from the day before. By then I would just do anything he said, and do it full out.

In *Cherry Orchard*, I had some sort of understanding of the character so I was able to do what he wanted and not angst too much about it. But *Children of the Sun* was a very painful experience.

There always seemed to be someone in every cast that Nikos was just relentless with and, in *Children of the Sun*, I guess it was me. There was one actor in *Cherry Orchard* who just dreaded coming to rehearsals. I think one of the reasons why Colleen Dewhurst sort of turned against Nikos was because she didn't like the way he was treating this guy, confusing him and being so hard on him. And opening night Nikos sent him a note saying something like: "Sorry I was so rough on you, but you see I was right!"

JEAN Why do you think he became so relentless?

JOHN I think, really, Nikos was trying so hard to get passion and truth out of everybody. But some actors couldn't work as fast as he wanted or maybe weren't as well equipped. Or, like me in *Children of the Sun*, maybe they didn't have a handle on the role. And some people aren't used to working with a mad man! Granted, Nikos was a mad man. Everybody, I think, would've said that. Some of it was genius. But at the same time, it could be infuriating. And confusing. Because it wasn't a heady thing, you couldn't logically figure out what he wanted. It was a passionate thing, it was a gut thing he was asking us all to do, so it required us, I think, to be out there and be naked. Sort of at any time feeling like the rug was going to come out from under us. So when you're out on the stage – I mean, on stage we want to be in control! Actors want to be in control. And I think that Nikos was constantly doing things to sort of get everybody a little out of control. So that it was dangerous on stage. And that's what made it so exciting.

I think that's why Austin is always so exciting to watch as an actor. I mean, he's a brilliant actor, but there's something about the fact that he has a stutter. At Williamstown, Austin was often playing characters who were trying so hard for things they usually couldn't achieve. Usually Laurie Kennedy's love! Or Kate Burton's love. And, on top of that, there is Austin trying just to get through a sentence without stuttering. I mean, working really hard not to. And that became incredibly moving, because of the honesty about that. And Nikos loved this. Because here was somebody not covering anything up.

JEAN Yes, not knowing what will happen next. I always get the feeling with Austin that he truly doesn't know what will happen next on stage in any given moment.

JOHN I remember one night in *Three Sisters*, I did the scene with Irina with this sense of being on top of it. And it didn't work. There was a certain amount of concentration and preparation that playing the scene required. Of trying to make something happen. And of not knowing what was happening. I mean, there was this unknown thing you sort of had to abandon yourself to. And one night, because enough people had said, "that scene is great," I went out and did the scene without the preparation. I just did it feeling like I knew what I was doing, and it didn't work. And then, of course, I became totally confused and didn't know anymore what to do and it worked every other night after that, as it had worked every other night before. The success of the scene involved this kind of fear about being onstage and not exactly knowing. Gave it this spooky, unknown danger.

JEAN Your Epihodov in *Cherry Orchard* was so funny. But not because you made exaggerated character choices.

JOHN No, it was too honest.

JEAN What did the humor come out of?

JOHN The honesty. I think that's why it was so hard for some people to do. Because what Nikos required was for you to just go all out and make a fool of yourself. And not comment on it, not wink at the audience and say, "the character's a fool but I'm not." And some people at some times were not able to do that. So they would get uptight or whatever. It was a strange requirement asked of you. To be honestly foolish and not to comment on it.

For example, when Chris Reeve and Blythe and I were doing *Cherry Orchard*, the scenes were basically the three of us together, and there was a humor that grew out of that love triangle. Epihodov, who I was playing, wanted Dunyasha, and Dunyasha wanted the good looking one, Yasha, and he didn't want anybody, except maybe himself. And we were confused, we didn't know what we were doing and I remember sometimes the three of us would go out and work on our own and we'd all get upset with each other. But when we opened, the scenes were very, very funny. But a lot of times it was Blythe's and my characters who were getting the laughs and not really Chris'. So as the run went on, I think in an effort to feel more in control, Chris would laugh *himself* when Blythe and I would say something, which sort of killed the audience laugh. I don't think it was a malicious thing, or even anything that he knew he was doing. But he was sort of at sea. Which some actors were in Nikos' Chekhov, not knowing what exactly it was that made the performance funny or made the performance moving. Like I felt as Solyony. I'd go out on stage and not know, really, what I was doing. So Chris, in an effort to gain control, would laugh, sort of subconsciously, to let the audience know, maybe, that he knew what he was doing.

I was so often lost in plays with Nikos! I remember in *St. Joan* he had me come out and take this stool and pound on it. It was the stool that Joan sat on at her trial. And I played a man that wanted her to be burned, to do away with her. She is burned, and then there's a scene where my character comes in and gets very upset and this stool was still out there on the stage. So Nikos gave me the task of taking this stool and trying to destroy it. Well, this became a running gag and I just dreaded it. I dreaded it because it was high emotion, and it came directly out of something that he gave me. It was nothing that happened organically! It was about an actor trying to make it organic. So I guess I used my fury at having to do this. I mean, this was the first time I'd ever worked with Nikos, so then it was a very simple relationship. I was an actor trying to do what a director asked me. There were no layers, that came later – the complications of getting mad at Nikos for being insensitive about this or that.

Eventually I had fun with the stool, but there was some kind of rage somewhere, perhaps at myself at not being able to really make the moment work, so I just gave it all I could give. I would come out on stage and see the stool and I would throw it down with such a fury that it usually broke into a thousand pieces. And I probably was overacting my fucking head off! But I did it. It was what the director said to do. And then the reviews came out and said I was ridiculous!

That it was like a child's temper tantrum. Nikos wasn't asking for a temper tantrum, but because I didn't know how to do it, I suppose it became, in my fury at him, a temper tantrum.

JEAN Blythe talked, too, about Nikos giving her a frame to fill in a scene in *Three Sisters*, a frame for a big emotional moment. She said he had a vision of how it should be filled, but the actor was left with egg on his face if he couldn't fill it. But, instead of saying, "this doesn't work, I'm not doing it," you tried to go for it.

JOHN I think by watching the other actors, a lot of us saw that when these big moments did work how exciting and wonderful they were. We got that from watching each other. That's why most of us tried to do what Nikos wanted. Plus the fact that I think good actors like to be directed. Of course, there's arrogant ones who don't. But there's nothing that feels better than trusting your director.

JEAN Yes, I think when Nikos and the actor made those moments work, those were the great moments at Williamstown.

JOHN Because they were filled with so much passion. And that's what's exciting about theater. That high passion. That theatricality and high sense of drama. And that's what he was full of. I mean, he filled his life with it.

It's quite a skillful art, directing. To me, it seems that a good director honestly gives actors the feeling that they're coming up with the goods. And that every now and then they make a suggestion, give seeds, keys to unlock doors. But a good director always makes it feel like it's coming from us, the actors. And he guides a little. And then there's other directors who you can't please; nothing you do is what they had in mind, and that's a terrible feeling. They don't trust, they sort of pick when they direct. And I find that working with that kind of director, you start losing your instincts.

One of the first films I made was with Fred Zinnemann, *Julia*. He gave me some little seeds when I first met him about playing the role and basically he just left. And I'd only been in two movies before. One scene in a movie called *Shamus*, and one scene in *Annie Hall*. And still he trusted me. Which gave me confidence.

Nikos was like that too, but not with everyone. Marian Mercer – who played Masha in *The Sea Gull*? She could never please him. It's interesting that, on one hand, there were people who got that unconditional love, like from daddy, and on the other side there were people who got just the opposite, whose lives were made rather miserable for a period of time. *Cherry Orchard* was sort of like that for me.

JEAN What happened?

JOHN I'm not sure. I just know that, during *The Cherry Orchard*, I got upset with him. I thought he was playing with me, doing things purposely to provoke me. I remember I called him one day into the little prop closet across from the Ex and said something like, "It's getting too personal, you're using too many personal references." And he said, "Oh, no, Johnny, really I'm not, you musn't take these things personally." It may not have been personal, but the truth was by that time he knew me, he knew my weaknesses and strengths.

As I said, during *Cherry Orchard*, one day I would come in to rehearsal and Nikos would say, "do it this way." And I'd do it that way. And then the next day he'd say, "do it this way." And I'd do it another way. Again, it was almost as if he was testing me. But for some reason there was one day I came into rehearsal, and I did what he wanted with ease, my mind was clear. I didn't get upset about it. I just did it any which way he said. And it felt so good! I felt like a fool but I felt good.

JEAN I'm so impressed with your ability to express so honestly and openly all these feelings I think we as actors often have – and aren't all that honest and open about. Feeling at sea, feeling like a fool, the feeling of not knowing what we're doing! There's the tendency, I know for myself, to try to appear less lost than I actually feel. To not be so up front about it.

JOHN I mean, I think that's really all part of the process. And it is a rehearsal process. I think actors have to make fools of themselves. I think good actors are willing to make fools of themselves, because that means taking chances, risking. And if you risk, that means you risk failing. It's not really so important if you feel foolish or lost, or

148

all those things I often felt when I worked with Nikos. If you fail you fail, but you're out there. I think it's important to be out there.

Tony Capodilupo (Kulygin), Laurie Kennedy (Irina), William Hansen (Chebutykin) in "The Three Sisters," 1965

"Imagine things. Imagine many more things. Imagine that the water you drink is awful, that the house is hot, imagine that the sheets are smelly, imagine that the house has an echo, imagine there's a big nail, your mother put it underneath, so that you can be stepping on nails all the time. You know? Deal sufficiently with the underlying imaginary circumstances. It's kind of interesting. In life, some people do it, they believe they're always persecuted. I think you should get persecuted on stage, or you should be wooed when you're on stage. It has to be the sense of exaggeration, the sense of something totally inappropriate one way or another. It's kind of fascinating that a lot of the actors we see and that we like are always a little bit more – in a good sense – neurotic – than we would like to be dealing with. Not that directors are not! But there is a whole sense of fantasy. Sometimes I'll ask an actor, say at rehearsal, 'How are you?' and he says, 'Well! You didn't ask me yesterday!' That's par for the course. Really. People carry a certain temperament with them and it colors everything they do.

"I think you have to allow that paranoia and program for paranoia! Create problems for yourself. Unless they're natural. For everyone that Woody Allen works with it comes naturally. But for a lot of actors it doesn't come naturally. So make your own blocks. If you put a chair in front of the door, there will be something so interesting about opening that goddamn door. Have your props messed up so you can't really reach them. Get something on your hands and have nothing to wipe them with. Find enough problems which will involve you in one way or another, and being involved in them will require you to stretch your emotional equipment the way people stretch their vocal equipment by trying to reach certain notes, or their physical equipment by working out. You do this by finding a series of physical objects which tie you to the emotional work."

Nikos Psacharopoulos

A REPERTORY OF BEHAVIOR
Interview with Laurie Kennedy

Ms. Kennedy played Irina in three productions of *The Three Sisters* at Williamstown – the first when she was an apprentice at age 17, and again in 1970 and 1976. She played Anya in the 1969 production of *The Cherry Orchard* and Sonya in 1972's *Uncle Vanya*. Laurie and I started out at an Upper East Side coffee shop in New York City; then continued our conversation walking through Central Park.

JEAN What a coup to land the role of Irina while an apprentice. Was that your first experience with Chekhov?

LAURIE First was hearing my mother talk about playing Masha at Carnegie Tech – or Carnegie Mellon, as it is now called. Her eyes would mist over remembering. And then in college – my teacher at Sarah Lawrence, Charles Carshon, was mad about Chekhov, and always assigned scenes. Then, the summer after my freshman year, I apprenticed at Williamstown and auditioned for Irina. In those days, Nikos and the Equity company would audition all the apprentices to see if there were any casting possibilities. I remember I did a piece from Thornton Wilder's *Pullman Car Hiawatha*. Well, a bell must have rung because after that Nikos auditioned me four times for Irina. But I still didn't know if I had the part! Rex Robbins said, "Keep asking him to audition you." So I did. I auditioned maybe six times, and finally, he gave me the role – oh, it was all very exciting for a young kid! So my real experience with Chekhov began then – watching all the actors and Nikos. Joyce Ebert did Masha, Carolyn Coates did Olga and Janet Sarno did Natasha. Bill Hansen played Chebutykin and was just incredible. He's always been the ideal for that role in my mind. I've acted opposite some wonderful Chebutykins but he was perfect.

JEAN What about your process, playing that part three times?

LAURIE Actually I played Irina four times. I did it at the Mark Taper Forum in 1976, before coming east to do it again for Nikos the same year. At the Taper, I finally solved the part to my satisfaction. It took me all those years to understand the fourth act, the scene where Irina says: "My heart is like a grand piano and I've lost the key." Irina, I think, is the most complex of the sisters – she goes from A to Z. Olga's journey is more confined, Masha's is very dramatic, but Irina completely changes. In the first act, she's a young girl on her birthday, full of hopes and dreams, and, by the last act, she's settling for what life brings her. She becomes like Olga.

There's so many theories about her. I think Nikos always worked under the assumption that Irina was Chebutykin's daughter by the dead mother. Rosemary Harris worked with the assumption that Irina was *Vershinin's* daughter by the dead mother! Well, that's fascinating! I loved working with these secrets. And the more I played Irina the more vertical and enriched the work became.

I had a lot of trouble, needless to say, when I was 17. I solved maybe the first act. Poor Nikos! The third act breakdown – I didn't have a clue. I didn't understand it. My father, the actor Arthur Kennedy, came to see one of the performances and said very gently, "You know, Laurie, an actor's life is very uncertain. It's a good idea to always have a secondary occupation!" Nikos tried to help me, but it took learning and life experience to be able to fill in the nooks and crannies of the role. By the third time I did Irina, at the Mark Taper, I understood a little more about loss and compromise, the erosion of one's dreams made more sense to me. My mother had passed away the year before; so the fourth act was more attainable to me. I began to comprehend Irina's decision to marry Tusenbach, a man she didn't love. Before, when I came to the fourth act, I'd always heard a little voice saying "Oh come on, Laurie, get on with it." It just wasn't organic.

Nikos loved the role of Tusenbach. He was very specific what he wanted. I have a feeling that role had a lot of reverberations for him personally.

JEAN How do you mean?

LAURIE He was very protective of that role. In the 1970 production, Yusef Bulos played the part and Nikos drove Yusef nuts with it. He wanted a quality with Tusenbach – he wanted him to be silly but not aware that he's silly. He wanted him to be in pain but not aware of the pain. He wanted something – unconscious. Not an easy task. Yusef worked very hard, I remember, to get that. But once you found your way with Nikos, as Yusef eventually did, and as I did, it was incredible. I've seen some turgid Chekhov in my day, but with Nikos the characters became very active and sparky. He brought such a joie de vive, he gave them a zest for life that brought out Chekhov's innate humor. Our productions were always very funny. I think that would have pleased Chekhov.

JEAN How did Nikos get there? Did you see a lot of changes or growth in each subsequent production?

LAURIE Well, they all were different. I have my favorite moments from each. But, yes, Nikos was growing, as we all were. Maturing and gaining wisdom. By the third one, he knew what worked and what didn't. And as you worked, you had the knowledge that you were part of a company, not just a group of actors thrown together arbitrarily, but people with past, a history with each other. It wasn't an effort for us to find the family relationships in the play – all that work had been done already.

JEAN What was the rehearsal process like? What was Nikos stressing in rehearsal on a day to day basis?

LAURIE What Nikos accomplished so well was opening up the "event" of each act. The name-day party in the first act, the Carnival in the second, the fire in the third, the departure in the fourth. These events were uppermost and very clearly delineated by Nikos directorially. Through that you found your character's specific reaction to the event. Natasha, for instance, didn't like the Carnival – it interrupted her plans to go out with Protopopov. Whereas Masha loved the carnival because it gave her a legitimate excuse to be away from home late into the night.

My favorite act in *Three Sisters* was and is the third – the confessional. The fire has so disoriented everyone that they say and do things they never would normally. Andrei confesses he's mortgaged the house. Masha confesses she's in love with Vershinin.

Olga confesses she would marry anybody who asked her. Chebutykin, the doctor, drunk for the first time in years, confesses to an empty room that he has killed someone while operating on them. I'll never forget Bill Hansen – he came stumbling into the room and started washing his hands at the sink and ever so slowly, the washing turned into a surgeon's washing, prepping for an operation. Which led him right into the speech. A great moment.

And Fedotik in that act – Nikos was very insistent that he be hysterical. He enters with his guitar which has been destroyed in the fire – evidently, his whole house has burned down and he comes in cradling this burnt out shell of a guitar – and in our production Nikos had him laughing hysterically. I heard a story once, either from Nikos himself or Carrie Nye, that as a young boy, Nikos' family had a lot of money. His mother was so wealthy, she had gold bracelets all up and down her arms. Then, during the war, in order to make ends meet and pay for food, she gradually removed and sold bracelet after bracelet until there were none. I think the loss of tangible *things* was very specific for Nikos. His experience during the war paralleled Fedotik's.

JEAN Yes, that's a wonderful story – even though I'm not sure it's myth or reality! Act III is a real turning point for Irina, isn't it?

LAURIE Oh yes. Irina starts by talking about her brother's failed life. And then zeros in on herself, the failure of her own life. There's that wonderful line, "I can't remember the Italian for window or ceiling anymore." But she's still fighting. At the end of the act she says, "I'll accept anything, but please, can't we go to Moscow?" By the fourth act she's not fighting anymore. She has grown up, she accepts that life must be taken on its own terms, that she can't have it the way she thought.

Irina's always learning from both her sisters throughout the play. She watches Masha, unhappily married to Kulygin, having an affair; and Olga, unhappy without a man, always headachy from her work. In the first act Irina's solution is work – and going to Moscow to meet her knight in shining armor. She cries, "Work, work, we must work!" But by Act II she realizes work isn't the solution. I always loved it when the audience laughed at her disillusionment. I remember thinking, "Isn't it wonderful, they understand!" The third

155

act is despair. And in the fourth, she's resigned.

JEAN   And yet isn't there also some movement beyond the resignation, isn't there a sort of rebirth at the very end?

LAURIE   Yes, that's quite true. Those three last speeches of the sisters at the end of the play – God, what a difficult section! Nikos and Olympia came up with something new the last time we did it. I think Olympia felt she didn't want to just stand there making a speech. Nikos must have been tired of that, too! Anyway, Masha and I were on a bench with Olga behind, standing. In the distance you could hear the military band leaving town for good. And Olga has the lines – let me find it – [As Olga.]

> "How happy the music is...It makes me want to live! Oh, God! The years will pass, and we shall all be gone. We shall be forgotten... Our faces, our voices will be forgotten and people will even forget that there were once three of us here... But our sufferings will mean happiness for those who come after us... Then peace and happiness will reign on earth and we shall be remembered kindly and blessed. No, my dear sisters, our lives aren't finished yet. We shall live! The band is playing and soon we shall know why we live, why we suffer... Oh, if we only knew, if we only knew!"*

And Olympia dragged me off the bench and started to dance with me! Well, Tusenbach had just died, I didn't want to dance! But she pulled and pulled and then Masha, who had just lost her lover, somehow got into it too and we all ended up dancing! We were not just going to curl up and live just waiting to die. And I don't mean to make it sound like it was all victorious; Irina's going to go and teach, she's not going to Moscow. Life is not going to be all that they hoped it would, but – the dancing was about courage and bravery, really, in the face of disappointments. These were the kind of choices Nikos loved and encouraged. And what had been such a hard moment to solve became fun in the playing of it. And yes, renewing. A beginning. A resurrection.

JEAN   It's the same for Nina in the fourth act of *The Sea Gull*, both an ending and a beginning in the same moment.

Reprinted by permission of the Nikos Psacharopoulos estate.

LAURIE "Endure" is the word she uses. "Endure."

Now that I think about it, it's amazing to have done the same part three times with the same director. Nikos was always so generous with giving actors the chance to try something new. I remember finding something, that third time, that changed the way I reacted to the news of Tusenbach's death. I'd never been satisfied with my work in that scene. When I heard that he'd died, I just crawled into Olga's arms and wept a little and then said my speech. It felt flat. John Glover, who played Solyony in that production, told me a story about Geraldine Fitzgerald – how she, in *Juno and the Paycock*, started cleaning the house when she heard that her son had been shot. She went about her chores and his death hit her much later in the scene. I thought, "Well, that's the way life is – a shock like that doesn't penetrate right away." So that gave me a clue about how to play the moment when Irina finds out that Tusenbach has been killed in the duel with Solyony. It came to me that the whole direction of her life is changed in that moment. So, one day in rehearsal, when I heard that Tusenbach has died, I just nodded and walked over to my suitcase and slowly put my gloves on, picked up my suitcase and started to leave. Not until then did I let it hit me – I no longer had anywhere to go. The first time I tried it, it took too much time. I'm not sure the rest of the cast wanted to wait. But Nikos gave me such space, he never said, "Come on Laurie, hurry up." He let me experiment and change and what grew was a very alive, very organic moment.

JEAN It seems to constantly come back to finding the behavior, finding the physical life.

LAURIE Yes, and ultimately that encourages the emotional life. Nikos went for that, particularly with his actresses. I often ran the light-board as an apprentice so I'd watch every night of a run of a play. And these stunning emotional moments would pour over the footlights at me. I grew up on that kind of work, watching Joyce Ebert, who had one hell of an emotional instrument, and Olympia, taking so many risks. And, of course, Bill Hansen.

I remember a wonderful moment Joycie had in the fourth act of *Three Sisters*. Masha is talking to Chebutykin, waiting to say goodbye to Vershinin. She's very upset and she says – here it is –

"When you take your happiness in snatches and little pieces and then lose it again as I have, little by little, you harden up, you become bitter. I am burning inside. Look at our brother Andrei, all his hopes are gone. Once upon a time thousands of people were hoisting a bell. It took a great deal of money and then suddenly the bell fell to the ground and broke in pieces – all of a sudden without any reason, and that's what happened to Andrei, too..." When Joyce said the word "broke" she snapped a twig she was carrying, she broke this dried up old stick. She had half a stick in her hands and when she saw some birds flying south a moment later, and her hands went up in the air with the stick, saying, "So free, so free!" As if she were blessing the birds and telling them goodbye, be well, be safe! It was a beautiful moment.

JEAN Blythe said she also found something very resonant in that moment.

LAURIE Yes. There were certain conventions, certain things that would be held onto and passed down. Austin Pendleton told me that that moment with the stick actually began with Kim Stanley's Masha at The Actor's Studio. She also had a stick, and, as the story goes, evidently this was something Lee Strasberg, who directed that production, had seen in the Moscow Art Theater production! Stanley did something else with the stick, too, that Austin told me about. Andrei spends most of Act IV wheeling around his little baby Sophia in the baby carriage. And of course Andrei's wife Natasha, and her brood have taken over the place by this time. And apparently at one point, when Andrei passed by, Stanley (as Masha) made a sort of stabbing motion with the stick, into the pram! Isn't that wonderful, poking a stick into a pram?

JEAN I love things like that because it's the way great moments in the theater stay alive, passed down through the generations, as it were. There must have been a lot of that at Williamstown, too.

LAURIE Nikos didn't try, ever, to recreate the last production of the play, but he would sometimes try to hold onto something exceptional. Of course, some great moments couldn't be repeated because they were so specific to the actor. Firs in the fourth act of

Cherry Orchard had a supreme moment with Bill Hansen. Firs is left by everyone, indeed locked inside during their rush to leave. All alone, Bill would go and sit on a chest and say, "They've left without me." Well, Bill had a bone disease that made it difficult for him to walk and sit. And in order for him to sit on the chest he had to pull his leg up with his hands. Something in the way he did that just took your breath away. No one else could have had that kind of private moment.

Yes, in working with Nikos over and over, and in working over and over again with each other, there were many things that got passed down. There grew up among all of us a repertory of behavior for the Chekhovs, that was very much our own. Williamstown was our Moscow Art Theater. And perhaps some of the things we did will be passed down, too.

Joel Grey (Platonov), Carrie Nye (Anna Petrovna) in "Platonov," 1977

"It's never really interesting to see somebody as Blanche in 'A Streetcar Named Desire.' It's never interesting to see four apples. It is only interesting to see Cezanne's apples. Or somebody else's apples. With Blanche, it's interesting to see Diane Wiest's Blanche versus, let's say, Carrie Nye's. Because Carrie Nye's Blanche is her own Blanche, not an archetype of Blanche. One bad thing about acting is that people assume there is somehow, somewhere, an archetype, a goal for each character in a play. That's not interesting. That's why we don't watch much theater nowadays...In an ideal world we should all see six actors' Hamlets."

Nikos Psacharopoulos

GOING TO ZERO
Interview with Carrie Nye

Ms. Nye studied with Nikos at Yale; one of her earliest WTF roles was playing, at age 18, Blanche du Bois in *A Streetcar Named Desire*. In 1977, she played Anna Petrovna in Nikos' production of *Platonov*. At the time of our interview she was preparing to go into rehearsals for *The Sea Gull*, to be directed by Bonnie Monte at New Jersey Shakespeare Festival. Our interview took place in the living room of Carrie Nye's Upper East Side apartment in New York City – replete with dogs, champagne and occasional asides from husband (and WTF company member) Dick Cavett.

JEAN Why do you think *Platonov* is so rarely done? How is it different from the other plays?

CARRIE It isn't a great, finished play like *The Cherry Orchard* and *The Three Sisters*. It's written quite clumsily. And Nikos did have a literal, line by line, literal translation from the Russian. It's a much longer play in the original so, every time it's translated, the translator chooses certain things and leaves out other things. That's why every time you see it, you get a different title and completely different take on it. It's a sketch, not a play, I think. Chekhov just spills out sketches of characters that turn up in other plays. He's working on the character of Anya, who will emerge again and again, as with other characters. They are characters in transition, who are going to show up in other plays as really finished works of art. But in *Platonov*, they're not.

There's no catharsis in this one either, except, of course, that Platonov dies. And it ends with that ironic line, "Didn't you know that love is a dangerous game at best?" It doesn't sound like Chekhov, it sounds like Schnitzler.

JEAN Or like a line from *Les Liaisons* –

CARRIE Well, there is a little liaisons dangerous being played by

162

all of these people with this man, Platonov, who is playing with them, and who holds the trump card. Probably Anna does, because she's knows things aren't going to get better, because she accepts things as they are.

JEAN On reading it again I was surprised by what a very modern play it is.

CARRIE Very modern play, sexy little number. Is there a Platonov character who turns up in any of the other plays?

JEAN Well, Ivanov is sort of the same character, and that's another early play. Vershinin, Trigorin, Astrov – those men aren't as nebulous.

CARRIE Those are men that have some substance. Maybe Platonov is an early sketch for a giddy girl, I mean, he's such a fool! At least I perceive him that way. Angst ridden, in the chicken coop, trying to rise above his station and struggling like a fly in amber. Essentially a worthless person. There are no depths to Platonov, and he doesn't achieve them with his suffering. He only annoys you. "Platonov, please go home, please leave!" The only person who's taken in is the ingenue, and at the end she comes to kill him and misses. It's a play about people who are incompetent.

There were some problems with the production at Williamstown, but actually they fed my character. Anna has a problem that she never speaks of. In her irony and her wit and her humor, which is hiding a secret life, she has a hidden agenda and the production sort of had a hidden agenda too! And these things aided each other. Quite unconsciously they just happened. This was a wonderful company production and the casting fell into place perfectly, as it often did at Williamstown. I personally thought that everyone was very well cast, except for Joel Grey as Platonov. What Nikos wanted from him was not what other people have wanted from the character of Platonov. I questioned the casting, but Nikos said, "I want this little, Chaplinesque, puppet-like figure, who everyone manipulates." That really isn't the text of the play, but the play is so full of things it could go in any direction. I think Joel saw himself as a romantic leading man, which is kind of the problem in the play in a way, Platonov sees himself as a romantic leading man.

But everything seemed to fall into place in that production despite the problems. The audience actually liked it. They were enraged at Platonov, which is what I think you want in that production. I don't know what Nikos would say, except that it was an extremely funny experience, funny while we were having it. It was the sort of fun that comes out of desperation. We were all in a helpless and hopeless situation and we were working as one. We were all in the same lifeboat together, we weren't jumping out and swimming for shore in different directions. We were pulling together. We were interested in each other, we were interested in how Nikos would deal with the situation and deal with it he did. Isn't that an acting exercise: whatever you're given, you use?

JEAN It's what Nikos tried to get students to do in classes all the time.

CARRIE Perhaps he learned that in *Platonov*. Perhaps it was a hard lesson to learn, but he learned it there. *Platonov* was an extremely complicated text and we had a leading man who seemed at odds with the rest of the cast. But we all just went with it. No one said, "This is ludicrous, we can't go on any longer!" The more I talk, the more it sounds like that situation in *Platonov*, "It's ludicrous, we can't go on any longer!" Somehow that gave the whole thing an incredible, desperate energy. And you know, the hardest thing to do is stage laughter and silly songs, and you have to be merry; we were merry! We were terribly merry. The peculiar circumstances of the production fed us. We had no idea what anyone was going to do next, ever. From second to second.

One of the most fun moments for me was at the very end. At the end of the play Platonov dies of a heart attack but no one knows that he's died! Everyone says, "Oh, Platonov, get up and go home, for God's sake." I had a pitcher in my hand supposedly containing vodka and I'd poured a glass of vodka and was trying to give it to Platonov, and the doctor said the last line, "He's dead, poor Platonov..." The vodka glass was in mid air going towards him, but when I heard he was dead, I shrugged and drank it instead! That moment gave me the character.

JEAN Even though the play has limitations, the Anna Petrovna is really a tour de force role – with the same kind of passion and black humor of Masha in *Three Sisters*.

CARRIE Anna's actually more like Arkadina and Raveneskaya, I think. I don't know if I would have been a good Masha. Something too exotic. I could've gotten to Moscow.

JEAN Was Anna a satisfying role to play?

CARRIE Well, it was enormous fun. You have everything. You have the wit, the humor, the irony, the slapstick and then the great revelation that comes in out of left field. That underneath all that hauteur and irony and bon homie, she's lonely. She drinks alone in her room at night. And it isn't Bertie's lament, it's just simply a flat statement and nothing will help. This is the way it is and will always be. Which is wonderful, I call it going to zero. It had all that high energy and all those flashing fireworks, and then suddenly nothing, the abyss in the soul, nothing. I think I found that in that part and have used it since. I've always called it going to zero. You find it in the moments in the character and then you can duplicate it. It's complete relaxation, just total relaxation. Of course, acting is relaxing, it's the thing we've always known from the beginning. Go to zero. Nothing is hidden, everything is exposed, and it's very calm, very quiet, open but empty, almost like a hallway with doors at either end that sort of swing open to the wind, and the wind goes through.

JEAN You're talking about the scene where Anna's secrets come out. The scene between Anna and Platonov in Act III where she reveals her drinking and her private desperation. Here's the monologue – would you read it?

CARRIE [As Anna.]
   "One last drink... One more – To sadness! Damn it, I can't stand doing things halfway!...Either we drink or we don't. When you drink, you die. If you don't drink, you die. So we might as well die drinking... I'll tell you something, Platonov... I've been a secret drinker for a long time. You're

surprised? I started when the general was dying and I've never stopped... Another drink? No, I'll get tongue-tied and won't be able to talk to you... Nothing is worse than an independent woman. An independent woman has nothing to do... What good am I? What's my purpose in life? Why do I go on living? ...Oh, I'm immoral... I'm on the edge of the abyss... I'll die; people like me always do...if only I were a teacher, or a director...or a diplomat. Then I'd have been a power in this world! ...It's terrible to be an independent woman... Horses, cows, dogs – they're all useful, but not me. Nobody needs me, nobody needs an independent woman... Did you say something?" *

JEAN This scene isn't until Act III. Does any of that despair show beforehand?

CARRIE I think if you play her desperation from the beginning you're dead in the water. I don't think it ever shows, that's why it's an enormous challenge. I don't feel that you have to seed the part. Somehow, in all of the rollicking scenes in the first act, all of those party scenes, in which she is indeed toying with others as if they are large cats, it comes through. But I don't think the role should ever be seeded with desperation. I think you have to take her exactly as you find her, as given to you by the playwright. If you start out having hidden agendas, you've tipped your hand for that wonderful revelatory speech, the go to zero, the empty, the yawning, the black night of the soul. If you do that, you've thrown red herrings into people's laps. It should be a – breath-catching – moment! I mean, I'm talking like a director now.

JEAN As an actress, you can't know that that moment's coming.

CARRIE No, you don't know that moment's coming, although, as the character, she goes deliberately to see Platonov. But what does she go there for? I don't think she knows she's going to talk about her unhappiness, her drinking. I certainly didn't know where I was going with it. I'm talking now like a director and not like an actor, but I do think it would be crime to tip your hand and say, "Oh, yes, I

Reprinted by permission of the Nikos Psacharopoulos estate.

want to play this wonderful part because I have this big, revelatory speech in the end of the play." That speech always caught me unaware.

JEAN Nikos would often talk in class about just playing the circumstances in Chekhov. For example, the fire in the third act of *The Three Sisters*. Waiting for the train in the last act of *The Cherry Orchard* –

CARRIE – That's also a wonderful device for energizing a play. You have the metronome ticking, I mean Hitchcock did it too – Quick, quick, we're going to miss the train, something about a missed train, we're going to miss it, we're going to miss life, hurry, hurry, hurry. Missed trains, missed opportunities.

JEAN – Yes, and, for the actor, using that. Using circumstances like that as "springboards" for the acting. That when the circumstances are fully realized, the acting takes care of itself.

CARRIE Well, that's true but it's a terribly hard lesson to learn, for him and for actors. All this searching has given Chekhov a bad name, has given Chekhov dullness, and he's the opposite of dullness. If you just play it caught unaware, moment to moment, it becomes very active.

JEAN Yes, a theme of these interviews is how active Nikos felt the plays were.

CARRIE Well, Nikos was not a patient man himself, as you know. Just sitting there, doing nothing is something I never associated with Nikos. His brain was so active, the emotions were always right below the surface, this was something he could identify with in Chekhov. That activity is actually happening even when it's not perceptible to the naked eye. But it's happening, it's happening in the mind, there's a great deal of inner activity. Represented by trains or fire or the storm or something happening someplace else, in Moscow, let's say, that you're trying to get to. But Nikos never intellectualized the work. It was all there on the printed page, and you took the lines and you did it and the revelations happened to you

167

at the moment. We never discussed the "meaning" of it. He would sometimes say, "don't do anything." Or he would say to me, having worked with me for so long: "Technicolor." It meant he just wanted more color in the voice, or less color in the voice. We would use color terms. We'd gotten to the point that we'd communicate without communication, there would just be a few odd words. It was almost like throwing a switch. I would know immediately what he meant and try it.

I think there's something in the Greek and Russian and American Southern temperaments that's similar. That sense of: "If you don't stop screaming I will scream!" I think that's something that Nikos and I had in common. I don't think of myself as particularly American in my attitudes or temperament. An American Southerner is not like anybody else in America. Life in the South resembles opera buffa more than it does the average cross section of American life. My house in Montauk is Chekhovian, full of people doing precisely nothing in highly energized ways, getting ticks off of dogs and going fishing and looking for lost clothes. The wrong laundry is returned to the house and we all just wear it. It just seems to just go on that way, at a fairly high energy level, although no one's actually doing anything, they're usually talking about doing something. Packing a picnic, finding a fishing-rod, "Where are the dogs, they've been kidnapped!" "No they're just lost." "It's your fault." "It's my fault." "No, it's no one's fault, I've lost my mind, please shut up." That constant high energy and no one's ever doing anything! Chekhov is not a dry study of a certain culture, it's very dramatic, high energy stuff. And the unimportant things and the important things are happening absolutely simultaneously and you cannot tell the difference.

It goes too fast to make judgments. You're not sitting there listening to the clock tick. The pace of Chekhov, I think that's what Nikos hit. Chekhov has always been paced wrong in this country, slow and weepy and sentimental. A lot of suffering and a lot of pauses. The reason it's such fascinating stuff for actors to play is because it turns on a dime, in the midst of laughter – suddenly – tears! And then laughter again, as it happens in life, except it's better written than life. Actually, you know, the messiness of all the translations helps. Maybe he wrote in Russian rather messily. I've never felt that I've had to stick to the text absolutely word by word, when I'm playing it. I know the plot, I know where I am as the character. Why are there no great translators of Chekhov as there are of Brecht or Moliere?

JEAN I don't know, that's a good question. Most of the Chekhovs at Williamstown were Nikos' translations, translations he culled from existing versions and by going back to the original Russian with a translator.

CARRIE He did that when I did *Hedda Gabler*, too. We sat down with every available translation and went over every single line and decided which one we wanted to use, or a combination of the above. We did that as early as *Legend of Lovers*. He really chose it word by word. And he would go over and over it with the actors for the right rhythm.

JEAN You used the word "messy." That's often a word he used when giving direction in class.

CARRIE It was always, "Mess it up, mess it up." That's what he'd say to me, because I'm really very precise about when I pick up a prop and when I put it down. I don't plot it out, but once it's in the rhythm of the character, it gets very precise, having done a lot of precise comedy – Wilde, Coward. And a lot of Shakespeare which requires a certain amount of precision. And Williams. Blanche duBois is so perfectly phrased, it's as precise as Shakespeare; you change one syllable of that and you're wrecked. But because of my own tendencies as an actress, Nikos would say, "mess it up, mess it up." And I knew what he meant, he didn't have to explain it to me. Maybe I'm the one he said it to originally, I'm the one who needed the note the most. Also, the actual words that Chekhov used, since we're not playing it in Russian, can go any which way. The language is messy. It's not about *how* Irina says something, it's about *what* she means, that's what you need to find. The words themselves are not memorable. That's why if you knew the plot and knew the character, the words become somewhat incidental and can be played around with. Although it's still not given to everyone to do this, I think you still have to have a sense of your character and the period.

JEAN Were there any moments in *Platonov* when you and Nikos clashed?

CARRIE We never clashed in that play; never, ever clashed in that play. He had such energy and such force that, why resist it?

That's what we always want in the theater. What fool would say, "No, I don't want to do that," when what he gave you to work on was so patently interesting? It was very relaxed. He didn't worry, I think, about anybody. He knew that these actors would find something, and if it was the wrong thing he would steer them in the other direction. I think he was as interested in the hateful word "process" as we were, before we used the word "process."

Certainly, in both Russian plays I did with Nikos, Gorky's *Children of the Sun* and *Platonov*, it seemed apparent that you had a gang of actors who had all worked together for a very long time, who trusted their director implicitly and who were taking a real leap into space with these two plays. The Gorky I think has never been in English, and seldom done in any language, possibly for very good reason, I thought, after I read the literal translation! And the *Platonov* was completely new to all of us. And he had this coterie of actors who were willing to completely trust him with these very odd plays. You had no preconceived notions about these plays, you'd never seen them before, you didn't know about them. You weren't aiming toward anybody else's production except Nikos'. He was somehow able to make it clear – or we were willing to trust him if it was not clear – where it would go. As a group. They were both group efforts. I really felt that we were a team and nothing – bad – could happen to us. It was a constant exploration and revelation. There was a great bon homie which you need for the text, it's in the text of the play, but also among the actors. We had a very good time.

JEAN Olympia talked about that, too, that she trusted that Nikos would never let her look or let her be "bad" on stage.

CARRIE Yes, I always felt that about Nikos, I always felt that he would stop me before I kill again.

JEAN Austin said that a different kind of intelligence was required to work with Nikos, that Nikos believed the actor's intelligence is in the body, in the nerve endings.

CARRIE I'm completely anti-intellectual. I mean, the plays are *there*, great scholars have written a great deal about the meaning of the moments of resurrection, and the use of symbolism, ad nauseam. None of this is useful when you're doing it. I don't even think it's particularly interesting to read about.

It's like saying, "Why do you like red?" You just like red! What we're talking about now is really after the fact. I hadn't a clue about any of this when I was actually doing it. Or if I did, it didn't seem to be important. It was completely in and of the moment. And what was marvelous and fun and thrilling was to see it all just sort of spill out unexpectedly like brilliant ribbons out of a basket. Just spilling out all over the place.

And actors, whose work you thought you knew, suddenly finding something, and their pleasure in finding it! It was never a tortured process, it just seemed to – happen! A lot of life, and juice, and color. Lots of color.

Frank Hamilton (Ferapont), Stephan Collins (Andrei)
in "The Three Sisters", 1987

"Your audience is very bright, they can read the play and get it. They don't need you to clarify it for them. They need you to filter it through whatever is maladjusted or unfinished or unsaid in you in order for the performance to be interesting and alive. Look, play that scene every day for three weeks instead of once and you'll be dying to entertain yourself. Forget the audience, you'll be dying to keep yourself interested! Actors only ever go wrong in long runs because they haven't found that unfinished part of themselves to filter through whatever role they're playing every night. Find that one unfinished thing in you, which is informed by the circumstances of the play, and you'll never go wrong."

Nikos Psacharopoulos

REMOVING THE COVER
Interview with Stephen Collins

Stephen Collins first came to Williamstown in 1979, to play
Christian in *Cyrano de Bergerac*, directed by Nikos with Frank
Langella in the title role. He returned to WTF regularly in a
variety of roles and, in 1987, played Andrei in *The Three Sisters*.
Steve, wife Faye Grant and daughter K.C. had just moved to an
Upper East Side apartment in New York; we talked there, sitting
on the floor as the furniture arrived.

JEAN What other Chekhov roles have you done besides –

STEPHEN Just Andrei, which I've done twice. First at the
Brooklyn Academy of Music in 1977, ten years before the
production at Williamstown. This was when Frank Dunlop was
making the first stab at creating a national theater there. Rosemary
Harris was Olga, Ellen Burstyn was Masha, Tovah Feldshuh was
Irina, Austin Pendleton was Tusenbach, Rene Auberjonois was
Solyony, Denholm Elliot was Vershinin, Margaret Hamilton was
Anfisa, Barney Hughes was the doctor, Rex Robbins was Kulygin.
An extraordinary cast, but it wasn't a very good production. I was
playing Andrei and I was about 28 or 29, and I felt completely at
sea, particularly in the last act when his life has sort of crumbled and
his dreams have crumbled and he's left alone with the baby carriage.
I didn't have a clue. I don't think I was ever unhappier doing a play.
I remember noting that Chekhov had one way or another
dramatically resolved the other characters, if only to have left them
behind, as the sisters have been left behind. There's a sense of
resolution. But not Andrei – he's just an open sore. If you graph his
life from the start of the play to the end it just goes straight down, it
doesn't explode, it doesn't finish, it just kind of – oozes. It was a
very short run, it only ran for about a month, and I remember
thinking that if it went a day longer I'd commit suicide, I hated
doing it so much.

174

JEAN You hated it because you couldn't get a handle on the part, or because the character was so depressing for you?

STEPHEN Both, both. So cut to ten or eleven years later and Nikos asked me to do it at Williamstown, I had absolutely no interest. And I was very disappointed. I seem to remember putting in a request for Vershinin, which Nikos politely listened to. And then he said, "I really want you to play Andrei." And I just said, "Oh, Nikos, really, I *did* it, I was terrible, I hated doing it, I didn't solve it, and I don't know how I could solve it any better today." But as Nikos was wont to do, he persuaded me. And he put together his own extraordinary cast – Chris Walken, John Heard, Kate Burton, Amy Irving, Roberta Maxwell, Frank Hamilton – and so I just thought, "what the hell." Sometimes I think that's what happened at Williamstown – you give those little grudging "yeses" and they end up changing your life.

So I went in rehearsal and I discovered what I'm pretty sure Nikos knew, and why he'd been persistent in asking me to do it – that I was now ten years older and the difference between being in my late twenties and my late thirties meant that I had a lot more experience with loss and sadness and pain and a sense of my own mortality and all the things which Andrei is struggling with at the end of the play. So that this time around, I did feel I solved it, I feel that it was one of the best things I ever did on stage. And I remember being astonished about halfway into rehearsals that this was no longer strange, unfamiliar territory. I got to those final scenes with the baby carriage, which had completely mystified me, and whereas before I'd felt like a horribly bad actor ranting and raving on the stage at BAM, I now felt frighteningly at home! I understood Andrei's sense of loss at the end of the play. He has lost his own potential, thrown away his own future. This seemingly limitless, wide-open future that everyone feels for him at the beginning of the play has now been used up, spent. And he's reduced to pushing a baby carriage around for a loud, irritating, domineering woman who's having an affair under his nose. His sense of loss became for me a metaphor for whatever it is we've lost in our lives. Indeed, to a great extent, I had to grapple with my own sense of where I felt I'd let myself down – you can't help confronting these things when you're doing Chekhov, and Nikos would, of course, push one to do it anyway. So now the role made all the sense in the world and the last

175

scene made all the sense in the world and it felt very complete.

JEAN Most of that last scene is with Ferapont, isn't it?

STEPHEN Ferapont is there – it's not what we would call dynamic interaction, but he's there, and his presence there is both a comfort and an irritant to Andrei. I suppose almost like Hamm and Clov in *Endgame*, the person who's your nurse and takes care of you; the one you both can't do without and are constantly irritated by because they remind you of how vulnerable you are and how much you need them. And Ferapont is there with the papers to sign and he's just a reminder of the boring, endless work that Andrei is doing that doesn't fulfill him and never goes away.

The other scene that was tremendously difficult both times but which Nikos helped me through was the fire scene. Andrei comes in, and he's pretty broken at this point and just so pathetic in his own eyes and in his sisters'. And he does a bit of ranting about his need for forgiveness. And again, I felt completely flummoxed by that the first time I did it. At Williamstown I found that I had to do a pretty intense emotional preparation. I had to make my entrance completely broken inside.

The thing about Nikos and Chekhov that I found was that – as in everything that Nikos directed – he urged you to be brave emotionally. What Nikos wanted to see on stage was people with their guts hanging out, one way or another. It didn't have to be obvious, they didn't have to be crying and ranting and raving, but they had to be out there with big problems that they didn't know how to solve. And God knows, in Chekhov, all the characters have big problems that they don't know how to solve. But also Chekhov is pretty much devoid of histrionics. It doesn't call for big, theatrical, "style" acting. So in a way it was perfectly suited to what I think Nikos liked: work that was emotionally very rich, very complicated, very layered, but at the same time not just people chewing the scenery. The thing that I can remember him saying over and over in different ways during rehearsals for that play – whether it was to me during the final scene, or any of the sort of set-pieces of which there are many – he would say variations on this: "That's wonderful, but now I need you to mess it up. Because you're presenting it to me, it's very laid out, I understand it all, but you're too much in control of what you're saying. This character couldn't possibly be that much in control of the words that are coming out of his mouth. They're falling out of his mouth, he doesn't know what he's saying, he's searching for the truth, he doesn't really know how he feels."

The other thing I remember, my favorite thing that came out of those rehearsals, was actually a rule that I discovered through Nikos. He was giving a note to an actor – whoever it was was a good actor because there was nothing but good actors in this cast – and he stopped the scene and said, "You're lying." And the actor said, "Well, yeah, right, I'm lying here, this is the moment my character is lying." And Nikos said, "Yeah, but I can see that you're lying." And the actor said, "Yeah, okay." and Nikos said, "No it's not okay, if I can see that you're lying then so can this other character and so can the audience." And the actor said, "Well, yeah, you know, I'm fooling them, but I don't want to fool the audience, I want the audience to kind of know I'm lying." And Nikos said, "No, no, no, we'll find out later. Chekhov will tell us later in a different way that you're lying when you say this, we will then all have been fooled by you, all of us." The point is that Nikos was saying the play will solve that problem for you. And ever since that moment, when I watch movies and plays and television programs, I realize often that I'm watching very good actors show me that they're lying. It's a thing actors love to do. You see it all the time. But in life we're very good liars when we lie, otherwise we wouldn't get away with it! It's so simple that you wonder how any actor could make the mistake. And it makes you so much more powerful when you're willing in the short run to lie and have the audience not know, so that later they say, "Oh, my God, that son of a bitch, he was lying!" And of course, it's what the playwright intended.

JEAN Many of the actors in the 1976 *Three Sisters* talked about having extraordinary breakthroughs in their work at that time. Austin, Olympia, and Blythe all said something to the effect that in the rehearsal room there was an encouragement to work from very primitive, inner places – of loss, sexuality, aggression – for Blythe in working on Masha, it was connecting to a place in the body, she called it the place where inspiration comes from. Olympia talked about her responding from her essential self, Austin talked about finding a release in his work that had eluded him before.

STEPHEN That's very interesting to hear those words in the same space – to hear of loss and pain mingled with being oneself and mingled with sexuality. There's no logic to that connection but it's absolutely true and real. Nikos was completely aware of it – in the bigger sense it was one of the reasons why Nikos always had around him actors, singularly and in groups, with a tremendous amount of sexuality. Williamstown was a sexy place and that wasn't an accident. Nikos wanted people around who didn't leave their sexuality at the door when they started acting. And, strangely enough, two things I've learned over the years that most actors unconsciously check at the door when they start acting: their sexuality and their humor. Not necessarily their comedy, but their humor. I think what really tickles us down deep is also what turns us on and Nikos loved that kind of vibrancy of people dealing honestly from their sexuality. He knew that it infused a play with a special kind of energy that was irresistible to an audience and essential to bringing the play to life. And I think that part of the reason his productions of Chekhov were so successful was that there was always a strong sense of sexuality.

Since Nikos is gone, I think so much about all the things that I know now that he knew then. He didn't ever tell us in so many words that he knew them, he just knew them, and he set about ways to introduce us to getting closer to them. I had a wonderful experience in the *Three Sisters* I did with Nikos, for all those same reasons. I felt alive on stage, I felt in touch with my humor – I got a lot of laughs with Andrei, and it's not considered a funny part. I wasn't trying to get the laughs, they were just there. I felt very in tune with who I am, with my own sexuality. And that's a lot a part of Andrei's loss. Andrei's driven sexually, that's why he marries Natasha, she just drives him wild. And that sexual longing for her blinds him to all the things he should see, namely that she's not a very good match for him.

It's strange that doing Andrei, who is often regarded as the perennial loser, that doing a part like that could make me feel so alive and so satisfied, once I felt that I cracked the nut of the part –

JEAN What was that nut?

STEPHEN I think it was getting to that place where I could come to grips with using my own sense of loss and despair, using it as the underlying truth of who Andrei is. I mean, that's what you do as an actor, you take your own emotional reality and you throw it up through someone else's life and character and words. And you have to be careful not to make it just about you but nonetheless to use your instrument. And what Nikos knew then that I didn't know was that I was carrying with me a great deal of – loss, that I was no longer the bright, golden kid I'd been when I did that production at BAM. He knew, better than I knew at the time, that I could now relate. He knew what I'd been through, he knew the disappointments I'd had. He actually seemed to know every secret thing about most everybody who ever worked with him! He knew what our strengths were, our weaknesses. And mind you, we never discussed these things.

He was a seer, he could just see that about people, with a very minimum of contact, he saw down to people's core, if he cared about them or liked them. That's why I think it felt like such a treat to work with Nikos. You felt – by definition, you felt – taken care of, because to the extent that we are children and the director is the daddy or the mommy, you want a daddy who definitely sees what you really are, not who's guessing, not who's using a lot of wishful thinking, not who's projecting his own neurosis onto you. None of that. And Nikos really could tell the truth about people – in an intuitive way – you don't know how he knew these things, he just did. He just knew what made people tick.

JEAN I think this is what Blythe meant about feeling permission to use all aspects of herself.

STEPHEN Yes, and it's only in the great plays that you really can because they ask of you the complicated layers of emotion that we all carry around with us. And the reason it's frustrating to do thin material or bad material is that is doesn't get into real, layered, textured emotion, it just stays on one level, and we long to play the complicated –

JEAN To be well used, to be ourselves.

STEPHEN Yes, to be ourselves! So, the bliss of doing Chekhov is that you're in a moment on stage of great pain, and then you start laughing, which is so much like life. Or you're at the most pained moment your character has in the play and the audience is laughing. Now, they're not laughing because you're asking them to laugh, or because you're playing for a laugh, it's just that they recognize themselves and laugh at themselves! And that's why Chekhov called his plays comedies.

I remember making Andrei's first entrance when the sisters call him out to meet Vershinin, and he's terribly shy and he doesn't really want to and he's madly in love and he's sort of been sitting in his room dreaming of Natasha and playing the violin. I was very, very awkward and shy as a kid – very. And people don't know that about me because they seem to think that if you look a certain way, that you've always been confident. I've never been confident. That scene was very painful, and I related to it strongly. I remembered I felt like I wanted to die when I was dragged out by my parents to be introduced to guests. So I used that in that first scene. And the more I contacted that experience within me, the more the audience laughed. They all remembered being dragged out by the family to meet people, too! It's an amazing kind of comedy because it's not the comedy of gags and it's not the comedy of wisecracks and it's not the comedy of punchlines. It's just behavior. And recognition. And people laugh with relief to see that, 'Oh goodness, other people go through this too!'

The joy of doing Chekhov is the joy of solving millions of little puzzles. It's like when you crack the crossword puzzle, and you say, "Oh my God!" At first, you read a scene and you think, "What are they talking about, they're not really talking about anything, what are they saying?" And then all of a sudden you realize they're saying, "I love you," but they're not saying the words I love you, they're saying something else. Or they're saying "I want to die, I hate my life," but they're never saying those words, they are instead saying, "Oh, don't believe me, don't believe a word I've said." At that moment, at the end of Act III, Andrei's really saying, "I'm a fool, I've thrown my life away, I don't even know what I'm saying when I say it. I'm not worth listening to, you know that I love you, I wish that you could just say that you love me." And the joy of doing Chekhov is solving all those little puzzles.

JEAN And discovering the specific moments from your own life –

STPEHEN Yes. In order to get there you have to be so emotionally available. Nikos never said, "be vulnerable," but he would urge people to embrace their confusion and vulnerability – when an actor would stop and say, "I just don't know what I'm doing!" and Nikos would say, "Good, fine, that's okay." And they'd say, "What?" Actors in that moment always think that what they want to hear is for the director to say, "Ah, well, here's the answer: it's A,B,C and D." And Nikos would just let you sit there and be in that place of not knowing. That's where characters on stage, especially Chekhov's, always are! And we as actors, as artists, somehow want to come out and control it and prepare it such that we can offer it up to the audience like a perfectly gift-wrapped box. But we can't. It has to be a box that maybe the wrapping isn't so great and maybe the tissue paper is ripped, and who knows what's inside of it. You don't ever quite know.

And he wanted the mess. He always wanted the emotional mess to be seen. He didn't want it to be seen in cliched ways, you know, with gnashing of teeth and wringing of hands and wailing, but he wanted always to see the mess underneath the control. So it became about people *trying* to stay in control rather than *being* in control. He was much more interested in the ways they weren't in control rather than the way they were. That acting is about maladjustment. That you couldn't ever have it quite together on stage. And if the words seemed to be quite together and quite logical, then Nikos always wanted you to find between the words, and between the period at the end of a sentence and the beginning of the next sentence, that gap, that not knowing what to say next, that searching for how to say it, as opposed to just the smooth transition to the next line. He wanted to see confusion, bewilderment. So that you were searching for the words, discovering them, and they were coming out so that you never knew what you were going to say.

So I found that, to work with Nikos, I had to always offer some of the performance up to the gods. That is to say, I had to be willing not to know exactly what was going to happen when I went on stage to a certain extent. Obviously I knew I was going to go out and say these words and be on certain parts of the stage, but beyond that, I had to "not know." Maybe it's ten percent, maybe it's twenty percent maybe it's fifty percent, I don't know, but to some extent, what he wanted to see was – he *loved* desperation. In all it's guises. Nikos could recognize a desperate person who seems totally cool, completely collected – and what interested him was the desperation.

And I think he had such a love for actors – he loved many particularly neurotic actors. Because as long as they could come up with it, he loved the fact that they were always uncertain and not knowing if they could do it. He loved the sense of actors not thinking they could do it, because he got to do two things, he got to use that feeling onstage, which was very powerful. And he got also, in the best teaching sense, to usher them through the process by which they learned they could do it. You always felt very grateful to Nikos afterwards. I remember how grateful I felt once *Three Sisters* was up on its feet that he had talked me into it. I thought, "Oh, my God, what if I hadn't done this!" And, of course, my reasons for not doing it were all ego. They were all, "Oh, it's not that great a part, I've done it before, I'd rather be playing the big romantic lead, blah, blah blah." And actors do it all the time, we make choices for roles out of our image of what we think we should be playing rather than what might in fact be the most appropriate for us to learn. Nikos was so brilliant and so intuitive that I don't think he stopped and said, "Stephen needs to play this part right now." He just knew.

He's the only person I've ever had in my life who kind of looked out for me in that way. The way he cast parts with actors that he liked in plays that he liked, he just was automatically doing people favors! In the way that the best teachers do. They don't have to stop and think about it. Their intuition is just so great. And his intuition about who should play what, was astounding. God, I miss that. It's that relationship to an artistic director that actors virtually don't have in this country, because we don't have theaters that revolve around the same people producing, directing and acting. Where people aren't just jobbed in.

JEAN The actors I interviewed said that in order to really get to these breakthroughs in their work, they had to come to a point where enough trust had been built from working extensively with Nikos and each other. I know that, for me, when I'm working with a new director, I spend so much of the time trying to determine whether or not I'm going to give him or her my trust. Am I going to give it up or not?

STEPHEN Well, Nikos created a safe place to give it up. I mean, as an actor, you want to reach down into the depths of yourself and work from that place which is truly who you are, but a director has to make it safe for you to do it. There's a million different ways to do that. One of the ways Nikos did it was by somehow just sending out to you with his eyes that it was okay, it was safe, he wasn't going to abuse that. I always felt that around Nikos: he wasn't going to abuse it. If you would go very far emotionally, he'd be there to catch you somehow, with his very presence. And he surrounded you with other actors who would also understand. And catch you, too, and be there for you and give you the space to do it. I really think so much of directing is making it safe for people to go down as deep as they want to, and he knew just how to do that. Most directors are simply trying to get the play on so that it can be successful, so that they can be successful and so they can have a hit and that's all fine – they really want to do the play, they love the play – but they don't have an investment, really, in the actors. Nikos had an investment in the actors.

JEAN Actors were a longterm commitment for him, yes.

STEPHEN If he liked you, he wanted you around. Also, I'm sure that we made it safe for him. I know that he felt comforted by the presence of certain actors, it made it safe for him to go as far as he needed to go. If he had an actor around who just didn't get him, then it constricted him too. It's like a big sandbox and you all have to play in this sandbox together, and you all have to go through all the horrors of the first days of school. That's what the rehearsal of a deep, difficult play is like. And you've got to be willing to get in the sandbox with the other kids and know that they're not going to kick you in the teeth and laugh at you and point at you, otherwise you're not going to play. So he always made a wonderful sandbox. It didn't mean that you were automatically comfortable with everything, but somehow there was just enough safety there to go to the unsafe places. That's really what it's all about. If you don't have safety you can't go to the unsafe emotional places. You just won't. Your survival things will stop you from doing it. And since Nikos was always pushing you to go farther into the darkest forests of your psyche, you couldn't unless you felt safe. Williamstown itself was safe. But, more important, Nikos in a rehearsal hall made it safe and the other actors that he chose made it safe. You were finally up against yourself and you had no excuses not to go where you had to go. And so I was amazed that I could find, in *Three Sisters*, those depths of despair that absolutely had eluded me ten years before.

JEAN There was also, at least for me, always a sort of Pavlovian response when one arrived in Williamstown –

STEPHEN The whole architecture, inside and out, of the town, the theater, the trees, the whole placement of it. And the people are part of that architecture. It's like when you go into a home that makes you feel comfortable and safe, you can be yourself. That's why people always refer to Williamstown as a family, as a home. Therefore it was safe to just be yourself in the work. To use the deepest parts of yourself in the work. It's true – the whole architecture – and Nikos was part of that architecture. You take Nikos away from that architecture, and it doesn't feel like home to me anymore. To me it's now a place. Maybe it's a wonderful place sometimes, maybe it isn't. But if you remove any of those essentials, it's not the same place.

JEAN It just this moment hit me, that when you really connect with it, how scary it must be to play that role, to play Andrei.

STEPHEN Since that's the only part in Chekhov I've played, I can't really comment on the others, but it's always scary to play a great role and they're all great roles.

JEAN I mean in terms of the journey of loss in that part.

STEPHEN Yes, all about loss. And I think what Nikos knew – Nikos knew that I was at a time in my life where I was coming to grips with not being – this is hard stuff to talk about, but ten years before, when I was at BAM, everybody was saying, "this is the next Robert Redford," I mean that's the kind of press I was getting. And then – I mean, I've had a wonderful career, but I was not the next

Robert Redford. And I think some part of him knew that, all of that, because when I first worked at Williamstown a lot of that heat was on me. And he didn't care about it at all in terms of who I was as an actor, but he knew that that was a truth, a thing that I was grappling with in my life, coming to terms with not being a huge star. And as successful as I ever am, and I've been very fortunate – but in my own eyes, I will never be as successful as I should have been. And it was that that I had to use as Andrei. And it was very dangerous, because who wants to look at that? You spend enough time thinking about it! But also, of course, it's wildly therapeutic, and then, when you do it, you discover it's very healthy and it helps you just look right at it and see that it's not the end of the world.

I mean, also, just to encounter and live with the pain. I guess the other thing – maybe Greeks know it better than most people, but we in the west don't accept pain as a part of life, we just try not to deal with that. And God knows, the Russians do. I know as I get older the more that I accept that life, on any given moment, on any given day, week, month, year, whatever, is alternately joyous and painful, that the pain is part of it, then the more it is okay to go on. I spent many years of my life just trying to keep pain away and you just can't do it, it simply can't be done. And I think Andrei is all about that, all about a person coming to grips with pain in life, who I think thought for some reason or other that he might not have to.

Any good therapist will tell you that you don't live, you don't start living until you start living with pain. Until you start seeing it for what it is, naming it, and allowing it to be there. Tolerating it without trying to get rid of it. Learning to live with it. I don't think one can act Chekhov until one has done that. And that's what I had started to do in the ten years between my first journey with Andrei and my second. Without it, my first one was so incomplete. With it, then it's very comforting. That's why I could happily do Chekhov for the rest of my life. Because it's more like life. It makes it okay for there to be pain, it helps that. I think that's why audiences respond to it when it's good. They're reminded that life goes on, even though there's pain.

JEAN I think, also, we're dying to connect to that, even when we try desperately to push it away – what's that quote – "no matter what else, we long for reality."

STEPHEN We try desperately to push it away but it can't be done. In the west particularly. All television advertising is about pushing away the pain, whether it's emotional pain or physical pain.

JEAN Nikos also talks about, when dealing with someone else's emotion, the tendency in American plays is to say, "don't be dramatic, stop it." Whereas in the Russian plays –

STEPHEN It's about taking the other person's pain seriously. Well, that's how you make people feel safe. You make people feel safe by accepting all their feelings, not just the positive ones, but the negative ones, at least by allowing them to be in your presence, and that's what he was great at. It was okay to be whatever you had to be. If you were confused and bewildered and hurt and frightened and anxious in rehearsal that was all fine. He didn't want to see you walk in all confident every second. He knew that that wasn't real. He wanted to see the other, he wanted to see what was underneath our cover. We all have our elegant forms of covers. And then we went to Nikos, and we worked on Chekhov in order to have those covers removed, at least for a while. I think that's why we act, anyway. We want to get to what's real for us.

Kate Burton (Anya), Maria Tucci (Varya)
in "The Cherry Orchard", 1980

"I don't really think about how to do Chekhov anymore. I guess, subconsciously, there's a sense of each one of them as an instrument – this person is the violin, this person is the piano, this person is the cello, I think it comes out that way. But that is obviously a subconscious judgement that one makes – somebody's serving, somebody's wanting, someone is dealing with this or dealing with that. It's difficult to tell because now I've done these plays so many times that it has become subconscious. I know what the characters are supposed to do but I don't know why they're doing it. I mean, if I'm pinned down, if an actor asks me "why" I will find a reason for it, but it's best if I don't get pinned down."

Nikos Psacharopoulos

ORGANIC MATTER
Interview with Maria Tucci

Ms. Tucci played Yelena in 1972's *Uncle Vanya* directed by
Austin Pendleton. She first worked with Nikos in 1980, playing
Varya in *The Cherry Orchard*. A Williamstown "regular"
throughout the eighties, Maria most notably played Serafina in
The Rose Tattoo, a role she first worked on for the six-hour
Tennessee Williams: A Celebration. Maria and I talked over a long
lunch at Sarabeth's Kitchen in New York City.

MARIA Nikos was a Chekhovian director even when he wasn't
directing Chekhov. I didn't do much Chekhov with Nikos, but I
learned about playing Chekhov with him through other insights he
gave me on other plays. I feel he approached all plays as if they were
Chekhov – it's not as if he made the Greeks into Chekhov, but the
passion he brought to Chekhov was the same passion he brought to
any play. What keeps coming to mind about Nikos, is his love and
generosity, but the love was his making you take risks. Every
character's needs were to be so clear and to the limit. And nothing
gets in the way. I mean, there's that funny line he once said to me,
"Don't do business, Maria. When you do business you just look
busy." I knew what he meant right away. As an actress I've often
felt, if it's true, I have to find something to do here, I have to be
washing the dishes, I have to have some activity, but what Nikos
was saying was, "No. You can actually feel as if you ought to be
washing the dishes but stay still at this moment. So that you have the
two things going on." He was wonderful at keeping you simple
while complications were going on inside you.

Nikos had an extraordinary sense of humor, which is not just
about being funny, but to me, humor – and the humor that is often in
Chekhov – is somebody doing two things at the same time. They
think they're talking about one thing but they're really talking about
something else. Or they think they're merely folding up the baby
blankets and their life is falling apart in front of their eyes. As Nikos
grew to trust the actor more, he gave you these little – quick –

statements. People say sometimes that he seemed unintelligible but that was a mask he developed, I believe, on purpose. Because to be intelligible means to *give* the actor the performance. But to make little sounds and suggestions, it means that the actor will find it through innuendo and therefore find something much more interesting. The actor will then have found it himself. It doesn't mean that Nikos was playing a trick, saying, "You find it, I know the answer." He's saying we, together, trust each other like two animals – like the way the deer nudges the fawn with her nose, or the cat licks the ears of her kittens – and you'll get it more from the nudge and the lick of the ear than from the statements. Because the statement dies within a few days. You know, if you try to play: "Aha, Nikos said that's what this scene is about," you've already gone past the scene and into a concept, and you can't play a concept.

JEAN I found, working with Nikos, that sometimes he'd give just one direction, one very simple sentence, but that one sentence informed everything.

MARIA Yes, exactly. In *The Rose Tattoo* I was dealing with Serafina talking to the Virgin Mary all the time and it wasn't working. And he said to me, "No, Maria, you have a *personal* relationship with the Virgin Mary." That opened everything up for me. Of course, she's not up there! I was placing her up in the sky. She's right here in the room, she's with me! Now that was a much better direction than, "Don't look up at the sky." It's one sentence that instantly connects you and gives you *miles* to go – you can go very far with that one sentence, because a personal relationship with the Virgin Mary, is – she sits down to dinner with you perhaps, she sits next to you on the sofa, she comes when you need her. He gave you things you could run with. He just wasn't interested in the words of talking about it. He would say, "And then you just – Ahh!" And you'd say, "Yeah, I get it!" Because there was – organic matter – flowing between you and him. Austin works this way too.

The other wonderful attitude that Nikos also gave me is hard to put into words, but I knew that Nikos never wanted an actor to be – ugly. [Slowly.] Now how can I specify this? It doesn't mean that he didn't want you to be dangerous, frightening, raw or any of those things. But the small, petty feelings he usually discouraged. In other words, it's almost as if the neurotic reaction didn't interest him, only the deeply passionate reactions. Actually, the example I remember is from *The Crucible*, not from Chekhov, but I feel this infused all of his Chekhov, too. I was playing Elizabeth Proctor, and her husband comes home, and there's a question of her husband having an affair. He comes home and she doesn't want to say, "Where have you been," but what slips out is, "You're home quite late." There again I was playing two things but they were the wrong two things: a sort of self-pitying thing, a sort of nastiness about her. Nikos didn't like that, and I know exactly why. Because it limited me as an actor. It made it neurotic or tiny. I was playing sort of small, petty emotions. What he wanted was to see what happened if the emotion was larger, to see what happens if you're unafraid of it. Not to play it larger but to know it in a deeper way. To own it.

He found the innate attractiveness of every character, even if the character was an unpleasant person. I like to push myself to the limit and I don't feel I have to be loved on stage, it wasn't about that. But he gave me the realization that unless you went on a dangerous and long journey with the audience, the audience isn't going to care. Unless you could show the deeper and truer needs, underneath the cover, he wasn't interested. So it was very "up" working with Nikos, one felt very elevated. He forced you to elevate the character, in a way. Again, it helped me in *A Lesson From Aloes* because – neurosis is only interesting up to a point on stage. Pain, profound pain, is really interesting. Gigantic rage is really interesting. But pettiness – all right, you might have to add an ingredient of that, but let's see how long you can avoid the pettiness, and avoiding this will expose so much more. I have a feeling that all of Nikos' direction, in the end, aimed at exposing and simplifying and therefore elevating.

JEAN How did you both develop the trust that's required for that kind of work?

MARIA *The Cherry Orchard* was the first play I did with Nikos and when I arrived he hardly knew me. And I totally agree with you, trust is a requirement for important work to happen. I just had this experience with Athol Fugard [The playwright and recent director of a production Ms. Tucci did of *A Lesson From Aloes*.]. We got to a point where we understood each other so well and we went to places that we never dreamt that one could continue to go to, and go to every night. And Nikos worked the same way – but not when he didn't know you. So, when I first arrived, Nikos basically came up to me and told me what Varya was about. "She's like my sister," he said, and began using this mournful, whining voice, "Eat something, sit down." And I began to panic inside thinking, "Wait a minute, that's the *result* of the character, I can't play her like that." And he wanted me all in black. And I thought, eventually this may be how she turns out, but I can't know this now. So I quietly went into the costume designer and said, "Dunya, do you think there might be some little color in the first scene? I happen to have this blue blouse at home that I think would work..." And she got excited and wanted to try it. And here I must give Nikos total credit: this is the way he's wonderful. I came on stage in the first tech rehearsal thinking he was going to scream at me because I'm not wearing the costume he asked for. And I also was playing some things differently from what he'd been telling me. I thought, he's going to kill me. But he didn't say a word! End of the rehearsal, he comes up to me and says, with astonishment, "I didn't know Varya could be played like that!" It was so generous. You see, his ego wasn't involved in it. I mean surely, Varya is, at the end, in black, she becomes the woman with the keys. But in the beginning you've got to see her hopefulness. And when I showed him this, Nikos totally agreed. From then on, we were soulmates.

His greatest talent came after the first week of rehearsal. The beginning, the blocking, what did it matter? The process while the actors were stumbling around and learning the lines, that wasn't interesting for him. You realized that he was bored at that point. He couldn't bear the bitsy little things, like the little acting doodles in between the lines. [She imitates his impatience.] "If you say something, say it." This gave the actor such strength and clarity. Which in a way was why he couldn't bear early rehearsals because early rehearsals, the actors have the book, they don't know what they're doing, they're apologizing, they're breaking for coffee, they don't know where to stand. None of that interested him. But the moment he had something tangible to work with, then he'd hang your performance, so to speak. I used to say to people that Nikos could call you into his office right before you went on stage and in five minutes give you twelve coat hangers on which to hang your entire performance.

Once you got to know him, you felt you were in the hands of somebody who was going to tell you what he didn't like right away. You didn't have to figure out what he was thinking, or guess, "Does this man like this or not like this?" "Am I doing something wrong?" Which to me is a great relief. There wasn't all that – mystery. You were in on it with him, because he gave us the feeling that we were all equals in this process, that we were in this together. He wasn't afraid to be impatient, to say, "Oh, don't be silly, don't do that, it's awful!" I thought it was refreshing that he wasn't afraid to say, "I don't like that." He didn't dance around it, he wasn't afraid of hurting your feelings and you weren't afraid of hurting his, either. That was silly, why should your feelings get involved in it? It wasn't personal. You already knew he liked you as an actor, so you'd just shrug and say, "Okay, I won't try that." During *The Greeks* – the marathon two night condensation of the war of Troy – I used to say working with Nikos was like going to the doctor. You do your scene and he'd say, "Good. Take two speeches, work on them like this and call me in the morning."

JEAN You've talked a little about Varya's journey, where she starts from. What happens by the end? What happens in the scene where Lopakhin comes to propose to her?

MARIA The reason that Varya's so difficult is that she has to believe that this proposal will happen throughout the scene, so that when it doesn't happen, she has no idea that she's crying until after she's begun crying. He leaves at the end of the scene and the inner monologue for me was something like, "It will be all right, it will be all right, no, no, it's over! What do you mean it's over?" It's like bad news. There's such a temptation on stage to prepare yourself for bad news. When people get terrible news very often they don't have any reaction at all. It's three minutes later. Or three hours later.

When I played Irina Kate Reid said something wonderful to me. I was about twenty at that time and I was full of feelings. And Kate said to me, "Maria, she's not kidding when she says, my heart is like a grand piano that nobody plays. That the key *is* lost. There's no emotion in her. She is emotionless at that moment." Irina's been so passionate throughout the play, and then, finally, there's nothing, the little piano is *locked* away. There's no need to embellish it, there's no need to feel a moment of self pity, it's just acceptance. And that was very helpful to me as a young actress. Because I didn't believe I could stand on a stage and not have feelings. Nothing. That doesn't mean anger, it means nothing. A locked piano. You know – the possibilities of beautiful sounds but they are locked away!

Certainly, for me, the trick about acting is to surprise myself. All the rehearsals are about getting to the point that you don't know what the play is about, not getting to the point where you know what the play is about. In life I know that I often speak first and then I hear what I've said. The lines pour out and only *later* do I examine it. In *Lesson from Aloes* – I'm only thinking of that because it's the last thing I played, a revival of a performance I did ten years ago – but I certainly had no idea what I was going to say. This woman's had these terrible episodes but there are moments of great lucidity. I remember walking into my bedroom on the stage, and what I played was, "What did I say, did I say something bad? Oh, dear."

JEAN Is that what you mean about the end of the *Cherry Orchard* scene, after Lopakhin leaves?

MARIA Yes, he leaves and, you know, she's a very practical woman, so that for her – even in that scene – even then, to sit still for Varya is rather difficult. Hard for her to have idle hands. She knows everything that's going on inside him and yet she doesn't. I remember that scene being over before it began. Suddenly we were having a little conversation and then it was over for both of us. He found he had left and I found that my life was over. And then the practical took over. I was looking for Trofimov's rubbers, I had found one, and then I found the other after the scene was over. I remember the feeling of standing there as if he'd been sucked into a void. And then, "Oh, I see, there's my life. Stretching out in front of me."

JEAN Varya keeps saying to everyone, "What can I do, he hasn't proposed." And then the moment comes and she's so awkward in a sense that she can't salvage it, another woman might have helped him propose to her, but she can't.

195

MARIA That's where she's funny and pathetic and maddening –
she's already taken on the role of the caretaker sister. Like what
happens with a lot of children who become older than their parents,
who take on the role of parent to their parents. There's resentment,
there's humor, there's pathos. The important thing was that I can't
know, as the character, how maddening Varya is. Let the audience
think those things, not me.

I just suddenly remembered, out of the blue, something that
happened in *Rose Tattoo*. Nikos said to me, "Maria, she's a practical
woman, she cries, she cries, she cries, but then she sees his jacket is
torn. She stops crying long enough to say, 'Your jacket is torn. I'll
sew it up for you, I do sewing.' – and then she goes back to crying."
It's the same with Varya. My life is over and now I have to find the
boots. And never wallow. Never settle in that moment. Because
there's the next moment to get to. Where are you going next?

It's strange how they interchange for me, Williams and
Chekhov. Not that they're similar writers, but Nikos' style of
direction for both of them was similar. Well, they're both about
people who go on. Tennessee's characters go on. In *Night of the
Iguana* – Shannon asks Hannah what she will do when her
grandfather dies, "stop?" "Stop or go on, probably go on." That's
Hannah's answer, and Tennessee's answer, because those characters
are parts of Tennessee. And that's the same as the end of *Three
Sisters*, "The band is playing so joyfully, Oh, my dear sisters." They
go on. Sonya sits down and begins to work again at the end of *Vanya*
– oh, that glorious last scene. Nikos, Chekhov, Tennessee – it's that
– enobling – thing about going on.

Some of the WTF "family" : Austin Pendleton; Frank Langella with Blythe's children, Gwyneth and Jake; Blythe Danner; Laurie Kennedy; Peter Hunt with son Max, and Nikos.

"A painter paints a sky red because he sees it that way. And if somebody says, 'that's a red sky,' the painter says, 'sure it's a red sky!' But he didn't make it red in order not to paint it blue. He painted it red because he sees it red. It's not at all peculiar to him, and he didn't paint it that way in order to be strange. It's perfectly normal for him. In the same way, your acting must be just as organic, even if the form of the material isn't quite as naturalistic.

"I go back to Greece to look at a Greek play and I can't even hear what they're saying, I really can't. Because there's just too much of an awareness, in the way they do it there, that it is a Greek play. So the man who is the head of the Greek national theater goes, [Atonally, in a declamatory, unnatural way.] 'And now I will go and tell all my friends –' and you just say, 'What? What?' You really cannot hear what he's saying, which has nothing to do with audibility. You have no way of hearing this because there is an assumption that because it is poetic language or Greek language or exaggerated language, it should be delivered only in one way.

"The same thing with Shakespeare. I mean, everyone is just bending backwards to do those damn plays in a poetic way, and consequently you don't know what they're saying! You do not know what people are saying, because they're so aware of how they're saying it. It's just like the way people do the Chekhovs, there is that: [In a mournful, breathy, melancholic tone.] 'Oh, yeah. No. Why. Uh. Ee. Ah.' And you say, 'What is going on?' And somebody says, 'Well, I did it that way because the play's about the inactivity or the melancholia' or something like that. That's why there's so much bad Chekhov going on, because people try to play those things. Never allow the form of the material to stop the life of the material."

Nikos Psacharopoulos

BACK INTO THE FLAMES
Interview with Peter Hunt

Peter Hunt, who became Executive and Artistic Director of the Williamstown Theater Festival the autumn after Nikos' death, has been with WTF almost since its inception. Peter did the lighting design for several of the Chekhovs and played the role of the Stranger in the 1963 production of *The Cherry Orchard*. Peter and I talked at my home in Los Angeles, just before he left to oversee the 37th season of the Festival.

JEAN You're probably the WTF family member with the longest history, and now the Festival seems destined to be a large part of your future. What kept you going back to Williamstown year after year? There were certainly other choices for you.

PETER I never knew the other choices because I went right from Yale to Williamstown. At that time my interest was in lighting. I mean, it wasn't, really. I got into lighting because my father refused to send me to Yale if I remained an actor. I wanted to be an actor/director. But then Abe Feder, a famous lighting designer who also did industrial work for my father, made my father think it was all right if I got into lighting because I would blow off this theater thing and make money lighting gas stations and supermarkets! So I just sort of plunged into lighting and pretended that it was as exciting as acting or directing, and low and behold, it was. And then Nikos let me design *Skin of our Teeth*, which was the first show I ever lit. John Conklin did the sets and I did the lighting and it was pretty awful lighting, I'll tell you! But that didn't stop Nikos. He still said, "Come on up to Williamstown and be the electrician." Well, we worked so hard that the designer could never stay awake to do the lights! So I ended up sort of designing the lights that first year. And after that, I just didn't consider any other options besides Williamstown. I was working in a beautiful plant, not just a barn with three lights, and I was working for a boss who cared about what I did and inspired me to do better than you thought I could do. And with people like John Conklin and Santo Loquasto – at that point, of course, who realized what they were going to become? But I think a lot of the reasons they became the top designers in the country is because of what happened to them in those years at Williamstown.

In the early days there was no place for me outside Williamstown, where I had the equipment combined with a kind of protective envelope and a caring environment. Where somebody wasn't saying, "Just make it brighter and go home!" What I'm saying about myself as a young lighting designer was very similar to what happened to actors and actresses later – the feeling of being challenged in a good way rather than in a bad way. And at Williamstown, one year leads to another and you're still there.

Nikos was always willing to bring people along. If he didn't think you had it you were just dismissed, but if he did, you were brought along. And you were not only encouraged but you were given responsibilities. And so, fortunately for me, he brought me along. One year I was production stage manager, and one year I was company manager, for several years I was his associate director. I was a director, I was an actor, lighting designer, it didn't really matter. He wanted me there.

I don't know how many years I ran the light board, but that became another education, because the light board was about four feet away from the stage, in the orchestra pit. And I was there every night in that pit watching all these superb actors. That was, indeed, a classroom. Seeing these performers over and over again and being sort of a part of the performance.

JEAN So, you were there for the first Chekhov. What was that like?

PETER The first one, *Sea Gull*, was a wonderful discovery on everybody's part because it was a new frontier for us. Nikos spent a lot of time working on the adaptation, it was something that he obviously had a great affinity for. I don't think he realized it at the time just how great it was. But by opening night it was clear. I remember going to the run-through in the Ex and just being blown away, it had this quality that was unlike anything I'd ever worked on. We'd done some Chekhov at Yale and of course I'd read all the plays, but the productions I saw were always very dry and bloodless. What Nikos had done and continued to do more and more and better and better, was to somehow tap into that incredible balance of humor and pathos. You would laugh and your heart hurt at the same time.

At that time I was still doing lighting. Now, Nikos was always very inventive with lights, always wanted lights to dance around the stage and focus here and focus there and be very dramatic and supportive of the moments in the play. But when I went to the rehearsal of *The Sea Gull*, something dawned on me. I don't know if you can call it naturalism, but – Chekhov tells you what the lighting is at any given moment. It all has to do with the time of day. There are very, very clear reasons why the sun goes down here and why the moon comes up here, that whole natural atmosphere is intrinsic to the scene – Chekhov uses times of day and seasons to a faretheewell. So after seeing the run-through I went up to Nikos' office and I said that I thought this was going to be quite different from anything we'd every done. And if he would allow me, I wanted to experiment a little and not have lots of little cues. I didn't want it to be, for example, somebody goes here: the light comes up, someone then goes away: the light goes down. Instead, I thought that it was like a great symphony. An act begins as the playwright has described it and then throughout the act the inevitable change of light is just one long, moving cue. It's especially true in the first act of *The Sea Gull*, the whole movement into night with the moon rising. It's the undercurrent of what the act is about. And when we got to the tech rehearsal, Nikos was great, he just let me experiment with this idea I had about the sort of gradual movement of light.

For the Chekhovs, I never wrote any cue sheets. In the old days . we didn't have a new fancy light board like we have now, with computers and all that stuff. I think it had about 40 dimmers. It was like playing a piano, I would just piano the lights all through the act as whatever was happening in nature was happening. When all was said and done, it was quite different, quite fun, and, I think, created a wonderful look.

That was something you could do with the old light board. When I graduated from lighting to directing it was about the same time that lightboard was graduated to the scrap heap! But it was a sad day because there was something wonderful about that, you weren't just a button pusher. I felt every night when it was show-time – I always felt that I was putting on a show too, and that I was part of it and that the lights were just moving along with the actors.

Again, that kind of thinking was something that Nikos encouraged. Both of us were a little dumbfounded when we got all the modern equipment in there and had to try to figure out new ways – in some ways it was better and faster, but we sacrificed. We lost a little.

There's a footnote to this lighting story that is very funny. The year after we did the first Chekhov, I was acting in *The Cherry Orchard*. I played the Stranger, who just has that one moment in Act II. I had to spend an eternity in this graveyard at the back of the stage, waiting to make this entrance – and then I had to come out and say something wonderful, I forget what it was. Supposedly I was Chekhov, or at least Nikos told me that's who I was! I was very proud to be Chekhov, although I was bored as hell sitting in this graveyard on stage, waiting to make my entrance! But during that scene in Act II, once I came out, the sun sets. That's another one of those moments. It's done on purpose, there's some kind of symbolism about the Stranger coming out, and then the sunset. My lighting associate, Billy Mintzer, was running the board because I was onstage. But from on stage, you could see him in the orchestra pit. He was attempting to make this sunset happen in this daring new way where it's all pianoed and you just play it like a piano and don't necessarily follow specific cues. But one night Billy had trouble with this particular thing, and everything but a sunset happened. I was trying my best to concentrate on playing my part, but out of the corner of my eye, all I could see was the wrong lights going on and that's all I could think about! I don't think anybody on stage or in the audience knew, but I was a basket case by the time I got to the wings. Then Bill Hansen, who was in the scene with me, came to me in the dressing room that night and said: "You were wonderful tonight!" He then described things I found in the scene! I certainly wasn't aware of any of it, I was just trying to make sure that Bill Mintzer got the lights right!

Other than being stuck in the graveyard, my dealings with Nikos in terms of Chekhov were almost entirely visual. It very much had to do with how to support a certain mood that he was going for, and creating that mood on stage. I was never a party to the early creative process in the rehearsals. I only know what I saw – and more importantly what I felt – when I worked on it. When I stood back and had a chance to watch the end result with an audience in a theater, to watch this chord being struck with an audience because of

Nikos' incredible affinity to the life, the rhythm, the people. I mean, that wonderful letter he wrote when he was 17 – that's it exactly, it's so very Chekhovian. He really found the joy underneath it all, the joy of humanity, the joy of human endeavor. I look back on the discovery of Chekhov as a turning point for the festival. There were several – one of those was *Our Town* which Nikos directed with Thornton Wilder playing the Stage Manager – which was really our first big time success. People literally camping out on the front lawn trying to get tickets. *The Sea Gull* was another big turning point for the festival. Obviously the Festival and, most importantly, Nikos embarked on a journey.

JEAN What kind of growth or changes in the Chekhov productions did you see over the years? Did Nikos immediately hook into it, or was it something more gradual?

PETER I think he immediately hooked into it but – which is not to say he didn't grow, because he did – and there were also some productions that were setbacks, but there's a funny thing in this business. Which is not quite the way to put it, since "business" is more of a Hollywood term, but there's a thing that happens, a magic that happens when you're at the beginning. You can grow as an artist, you can obviously approach the next piece of work with the knowledge from the one before and build on that and push the envelope that way or this way. Indeed, you're always growing and you're always maturing. But then there's also this other side which is the sort of youthful – flash – when you first embrace something so passionately and it's so fresh, and sometimes that's what it's all about.

And it was that way with *The Sea Gull*. I'd seen scenes from Chekhov at Yale, but to me it was just something you talked about in class and got through. I mean, some guy in Russia and who cares? And then to turn around and see this thing speaking to us and moving people to tears and to laughter and just totally taking over that theater was remarkable. Did Nikos grow? Sure he did. Was each show better than the one before? I can't answer that, I don't know. Maybe they were but – it's like your first kiss, or your first – whatever! Love affair! There'd also always been that connection to Tennessee but we'd done Tennessee by then very nicely. There was an early *Streetcar* with Carrie Nye that was a very memorable production. Both these writers spoke to him and he had a passion for them and just, frankly, knew how to do them. There was no two ways about it. And now that I'm in this odd situation of being the successor, if you will, I feel a great burden of the success of those plays. In terms of when and how we go back to Chekhov. But we will. I'm now in the process of trying to do a Chekhov Festival for the 40th Anniversary, dedicated to Nikos. I really somehow don't want to just do it casually, one production lost in the middle of a season. It's too special an area. Somehow I want to do it in a way that is a celebration.

JEAN At one point Nikos wanted to do a Chekhov rep – a whole summer of the plays in repertory.

PETER Yes. I'm thinking about that for the 40th . I know that so many members of our family, and I hope you, too, would want to be a part of it. I'm not sure who would direct, though!

JEAN I'm finding out in the process of doing this book that Nikos' approach or style of doing Chekhov now resides with a large group of people. As Austin said, there evolved a way of doing Chekhov at Williamstown that came into play even when Nikos wasn't directing.

PETER That's a very good point. That's a very astute thing. The sum of all the parts is going to overpower any single person, especially a director. I mean, by this time, what do you do? Sit there and just add water!

JEAN For yourself, as a director, are there things you learned from Nikos that you've used over the years in your work?

PETER   Well, there's so many things, it's very hard. Directing is sometimes doing nothing, sometimes doing more than you ever thought you could do, every case is different. But what you just said about there being a way of doing Chekhov at Williamstown – that struck me, because I am Nikos' offspring. I mean he was my teacher at Yale, my mentor at Williamstown, it all rubbed off. Now obviously I do certain things my own way, but still I'm an extension of that. So, what is that? Part of it is caring and having a commitment to all the elements of the theater – a lot of directors don't know how to incorporate a set, how to run a tech rehearsal, don't have a visual sense. At the same time caring about the rehearsal environment so that there is an emotional sense in the room that's correct for the play you're doing. I mean, are you having fun doing a comedy? When do you break tension with a joke, when do you allow it to become very serious? He knew how to play all that. Those are lessons I learned just watching him work. Also honesty. When you hit your head on a wall, back up and go another direction. Don't be afraid to say you're wrong.

My favorite example of that is the *Our Town* story. Thornton Wilder, as I said, was playing the Stage Manager. For some reason he and I struck up a friendship, and one day we were standing and talking outside the Ex, and Nikos burst out of the rehearsal room and came up to Thornton and said, "The scene isn't working." And Thornton Wilder said, "What? The scene isn't working?" Nikos said, "Yeah, George and Emily, they're on the ladder, doing the homework scene." And Thornton said, "What's wrong with it?" And Nikos said, "It doesn't work." And Thornton said, "What are you talking about, it's a Pulitzer Prize-winning play, it works!" And Nikos said, "It's not working. They're up there, I'm playing all the values, they're in love, he's in love with her, they want to get married – but it's not working." Thornton's jaw drops to the floor and he says, "My lord, what are you doing? It's very simple! He's stupid and she's smart, and if he doesn't get the algebra questions for tomorrow's homework, he's going to flunk. THAT'S IT!" And Nikos said, "But Thornton, it's a love scene!" And Thornton said, "That's for the audience to decide." And Nikos said, "Got it!" And he rips open the door to the Ex and yells, "Everything we worked on is off! You're dumb, you're smart! Play it!" And people were grabbing their handkerchiefs and sobbing during the scene. But the beauty of this story, was just – Nikos' willingness to completely drop it. There was no ego. I mean, this was a man who had a considerable ego, but an ego strong enough to put the work and not himself first. That was something that I think every actor and actress who ever worked with him knew.

Nikos also understood the priorities of how you put a play on. How you do it fast. Because he always had to work with no time. He knew when it was time, in rehearsal, to allow a twenty or forty-five minute discussion with Bill Hansen, or Blythe, or you, about, say, motivation. But then when it came time to do the tech rehearsal on stage, it was "You go here, you go here, sit there, criss-cross. Next!" He would never throw a rehearsal or a tech by losing track of what the priorities were at any given time. He knew how to go back and forth without sacrificing anything. Many directors blow their techs because they don't know how to move back and forth between these things. They blow their rehearsal period because they spend the first week on the wrong thing. And these were techniques that I absorbed and learned from him and I apply them in television and everywhere else. Basically it has to do with the clock. He taught me how to work fast because at Williamstown you never had time. If you could do what he did in two weeks, which was what we did in the old days, you can do anything. And he did it year in and year out. Of course, gradually he added more rehearsal time.

I've always said that what people consider the liability of Williamstown is our asset. That it's a pressure cooker. That you'd better come up with the goods fast. Anybody can direct a feature if you have seventeen months to do it in! A gorilla can! You just keep shooting until one shot works! "Let's put the camera here." "Let's put the camera here." "Let's try it this way." "Let's try it loud." "Let's try it soft." "Your dog died." "Your dog lived." And then we'll print everything and six years from now we'll figure out how to put the picture together. How about the way they used to do it? *Casablanca* was made in three weeks! But nobody does that anymore and then they wonder why the business is costing so much money. And Nikos was that master of how to do that. I mean, here was a man who knew how to sit and talk to an actor or an actress on a very fundamental, emotional and inspiring level. And at the same time he was a technician. And at the same time, outside of all that, he was also a businessman, he understood the business of running a theater.

There was a great sense of professionalism, too, of course, many things. But most of it was the absolute passion. I also, frankly, was with him many times when he was despondent. We had our ups and downs, there were years where suddenly he wanted out of

Williamstown, "This is not what I want to do with my life," I remember him saying, "and I've done this and this is boring." That's only human. I went through several of those with him. There was a big one at the end of the sixties – I think that's the closest he came to leaving the Festival, he wanted to move on and he was burnt out. Then, something happened, new people arrived, and he was off and running again. His commitment to make Williamstown what it was was so great that it was very hard for him to go off and do anything else. Obviously I've thought about this a lot, especially in the last few years.

JEAN Even as an actress at WTF, there was always a sense of an enormous amount being demanded of you. The highs and lows somehow were more extreme than other places I've worked.

PETER Almost every year, at the end of the season, I would say, "I'm never coming back to this place, it's too much work, it's awful, I can't stand it." And then I would have anxiety dreams for the entire month of September. I would dream wildly, the subconscious was having a field day. I never understood why that was, but there was a post-partum disaster leaving Williamstown where so much had been required of you and worked at such a feverish pitch and you were on tap 24 hours a day or at least 20 hours a day, and then suddenly it stopped! Whatever part of your brain that was trying to keep everything sorted out and working was just going crazy. Finally I'd get the month of September behind me, and then I'd try to settle down and do whatever I was trying to do – in the early years it was getting through school and later on it was just getting through a cold winter in the east. And then, of course, what still happens, sometime in January you start to think about that theater and whatever was completely burnt out somehow disappears and you began to feel ready to go back into the flames again .

The highs and lows, yes, my God! Nikos and I – our fights were apocryphal! People used to talk all the time about our screaming and yelling at each other. In later years I would come back to light a show of Nikos' – I never lit anybody else's shows anymore, at that time I was directing, but I would come and light for him. And then he'd play what I call torture time. Where he just beat the hell out of me. One time I even quit on a show.

JEAN What happened?

PETER Same as always. I would set up the first cues and he would come up and yell, "Petro! It looks terrible, this is not what I wanted!" This happened just about every time. And one time, I think it was *Cyrano*, I just walked out. I think I yelled something like, "I'm too old to be treated this way, I'm out of here, I'm never again setting foot in this toilet!" Of course the next day it was patched up. When he called me back to do *The Crucible* I ran up the first cue and I start fiddling around a little with the lighting and Jimmy Naughton, who was playing the lead, was sitting right behind me in the house because he didn't enter for a while. Nikos was down front talking to people and he suddenly backs up four steps, looks at the stage, turns around and he starts up the aisle. I just muttered under my breath, "Oh no, here he comes! And he cries out, "Now, Petro! The lights!" And before he could say anything, Naughton said, "It looks like a Rembrandt!" Nikos sort of stopped in his tracks and looked around and said, "Oh, yeah?" And I turned around to Naughton and almost cried, "YOU DON'T KNOW WHAT YOU SAVED ME!"

Now, you have to ask, why would Nikos and I put each other through this? Because we loved each other. Nikos and I loved to yell at each other just to get the blood going. Just to know that you're alive. If it were ever for a minute taken seriously, he never would have hired me and I never would've gone back ! You know?

JEAN My impression was that no matter what, the two of you were having an awful lot of fun working together. Olympia said that Nikos told her during the 1976 *Three Sisters* that what finally mattered for him wasn't so much the play or even having the perfect actors for the roles; the most important thing for him about doing a play was having a rehearsal room full of people he loved.

PETER I agree with that. The more you direct the more important that is.

JEAN What productions of Nikos' did you feel most strongly about?

PETER I still cherish *The Play of Daniel* and *The Play of Herod*.

The most extraordinary work I've seen. This was a formidable partnership between Nikos and Noah Greenburg, who was the Director of the New York Pro Musica. It was an absolutely religious experience. I ran that light board all over the world, and I lit it year in and year out every Christmas in New York. People flocked from all over the world to see it. I feel sorry for all the people who never saw Nikos' work on that.

And the Chekhovs. He understood those people, their homes, their told lives merging with what's to come. It was all very personal for him. I look around your home, I see some of the things that were his – you can even see it in this room. It was just very close to him. He didn't have to say that in rehearsal, it was just part of him.

We all work in a sort of code, I think. There really has not been fashioned a language for what we do. Words do not really do it. I found this out when I did a movie in Austria and half my cast didn't speak English and I don't speak German. And I realize that I didn't need the language. That mostly what we do is with a very different type of communication, it's a language that happens on an instinctual, or some kind of – weird – level, and Nikos was a genius at that. Because he fractured the English language it didn't matter anyway. So he would say something that you didn't quite understand literally because it wasn't understandable – but it was. But it was. On a much deeper level. And the fact that it was all twisted around helped it. One of the greatest movie directors ever is Michael Curtiz. Directed *Casablanca*, among a thousand others. Michael Curtiz was Hungarian. Fractured the English language. He's the one who said, "Next time I send an idiot out for something, I go myself!" Many times the language got in the way for him. It was like, "I can't say what I mean but you know what I mean!" Nikos was the same. People would ask me, "What the hell did he say?" And I would say, "I don't know, but I know." With Nikos, what he wanted was always deeper than the words.

So much of what we do is intuitive. We just pick up vibrations from each other. As an actress, you know, you walk on a set and you know –

JEAN If you can work –

PETER You walk in a rehearsal room and suddenly – I can work here. I can make some mistakes and make a fool of myself and try something and they're not going to whip me and put me in a cage. Something's going on. I can maybe have a chance here.

Frank Langella (Treplev) and company of "The Sea Gull," 1974

212

"When Frank Langella came to audition for me, he did four lines, and I cut him off and said, "Great." He said, "What do you mean? I prepared —" And I said, "Listen, I'm going to hire you." At that time he hadn't done anything but after his four lines from Richard II, I knew I wanted to use him. Olympia Dukakis did the same, a very brief audition. I was very impressed with the way they were using themselves. I hired Blythe Danner on that basis, too — I saw a clip from a movie that was maybe only a minute long or less. That's all I saw of her. But what I saw was an honesty, an honest use of her wonderful instrument. What else do you need? Someone sings five notes for you and you take a chance."

Nikos Psacharopoulos

STRIVING FOR GREATNESS
Interview with Frank Langella

Mr. Langella first came to Williamstown in 1964 and returned in 1965 to play Solyony in the *The Three Sisters*. In 1974, he played Treplev in *The Sea Gull* (onstage and for PBS). Standing out from the many roles he played at WTF over the years is Cyrano de Bergerac, which he did twice. Frank and I talked over lunch at a restaurant in Los Angeles that reminded us both of a favorite Williamstown restaurant, the British Maid.

JEAN Was *The Sea Gull* a play you were eager to do?

FRANK No! Not at all! It was a production that I fought doing up until the last second, literally.

JEAN Why?

FRANK I didn't think I had an affinity for Chekhov. I didn't find it as exciting on the page as I did other playwrights. I like epic acting and I like size and I like scale and I didn't see that on the page when I read Chekhov. I saw it as these – little family dramas that unfold, you know? It was Nikos who taught me about Chekhov. I didn't know how funny it was. It wasn't until I began to play it that I saw how funny it was.

JEAN It's true what you just said about the difficulty of getting it off the page. I think a lot of young actors have trouble with that.

FRANK It's different than what you expect. You know, life is a Chekhov play. It's probably why we don't get attracted to it initially because Chekhov plays are like life and we act and go on the stage to get away from life. You want something different. So we get tied into the so called well-made play, the one where there's the exposition scene and then the discovery scene and then the recognition scene and then the climax and then the denouement.

214

Well, Chekhov doesn't follow that arc. Chekhov just sort of goes up and down: little hills, little valleys. And when you read it, you think, "I don't know, lovely stuff to say, but –." It doesn't have quite the – thrill on the page that other plays do. But then you start to play it and you realize that it's the best. I would compare it to Shakespeare.

JEAN But at first you fought it.

FRANK Yes. At Williamstown and other places I had played a series of men very much in control and with a lot of authority. And that summer Nikos kept calling me for about a month, saying, "You're going to play Treplev in *The Sea Gull*." And I kept saying, "No I am not." And he said, "Yes, you are, I'm not going to cast it, I just won't cast it." And I thought, of course he's going to cast it, he has to go into rehearsal! And he got Blythe and he called me with that. And I kept saying, "I don't want to play it, I don't like it." And I also thought I was too old, I was thirty-four then, and I thought he should be played by a boy. Little did I know that you can't play it when you're a boy, you have to play it when you're older.

JEAN That's what Blythe said about Nina, too.

FRANK You just have to be grown-up. Anyway, I had a house in Connecticut and the night before rehearsals started for *The Sea Gull* in Williamstown, Nikos called me and said, "Rehearsal's at ten o'clock tomorrow morning." This is really true. I said, "Who's your Treplev?" He said, "You are." I said, "Nikos, I'm in my house in Connecticut, I'm not going anywhere." He said, "I'll see you tomorrow morning at ten o'clock." And I hung up the phone utterly determined not to go. I hung up the phone and then I walked to my closet and pulled out suitcase and threw some stuff in it and got in my car and drove to Williamstown the next morning. And I arrived and walked into the rehearsal room and there were Lee and Blythe and Kevin McCarthy and Olympia and Louis and I just sat down. I mean I hadn't even looked at the script, I was so angry with him. But yet I was there. That was about the only time that he muscled me into anything.

The first week of rehearsal I regretted my decision. And I went to Nikos, and told him that I still thought it was wrong. But obviously there was something unconscious working. I mean, he said exactly the right thing to me. He said, "I want you to play this part because I want you to be vulnerable to somebody on stage. I want you, actually, to be chasing somebody for a change." And I understood what he meant, about not using my vulnerability enough as an actor. [With laughter.] I actually think he said, "I don't think you *can* be vulnerable."

JEAN Like a challenge.

FRANK Right. So I memorized it with a kind of ho-hum air, and somewhere, somewhere at the beginning of the second week I began to see – I began to feel the material. And I was very inspired by what other actors were doing. It was the first time Blythe and I worked together, and we had an instant connection, an instant rapport. And I had a very dicey and difficult relationship with Lee on and off stage, which fed our roles. And then I fell in love with being a juvenile, I had never been a juvenile. I had never played the traditional juvenile roles. So, Nikos was right, it was good for me to find myself being the boy, racing after his mother's love, racing after Nina's love, being very intimidated by Trigorin, all these things.

JEAN Did you feel pleased, eventually, with your work in it?

FRANK Pleased is a dangerous word, but playing Treplev set me off on a new path. I was always happy that I did it and I was always grateful to Nikos that he sensed I should do it.

JEAN Do you have a sense of what made Nikos so simpatico with Chekhov?

FRANK Chekhov's scenes and stories and character relationships and plots are complicated, mixed-up, funny, sad, tragic, not at all obvious, unfolding in complexity, and that was Nikos' personality. And I think that he responded to Chekhov because there is no easy answer in a Chekhov play, you just have to go through what you have to go through to come to those great moments at the end. You just go through a myriad of complicated human relationships. And I think Nikos' complications as a man suited the material. I think his duplicity and his truth, his vulnerability and his strength, his manipulativeness and his directness, his pettiness and his largess – all the things about him that were so volatile and contradictory were very well suited to taking twelve or fourteen characters and blending them together and watching them interact and watching them break each other's hearts and hurt each other and love each other. And there is never any clear leader in a Chekhov play, there is never any designated star. He liked ensemble plays and Chekhov plays are ensemble plays. Maybe that's another reason I resisted it. In my youth, I was not an easy ensemble actor. I tended to race after the central position, tended to be a lead horse. So all those things made that material perfectly right for that man. Both *The Sea Gull* and *The Three Sisters* are two very strong memories for me. I did a lot of plays with Nikos, fifteen or so, and I don't remember a lot of them as much as I remember those two.

JEAN You were one of his favorite actors to work with – how did that relationship happen, how did it develop?

FRANK I think that he cottoned to me on sight. I think he just said, "That's my kind of actor," on sight. That was the feeling I got from him. I don't know why. I was an obstreperous, volatile and extremely difficult actor as you, who worked with me, know! I was willful and stubborn. And I wasn't seduced by Nikos. I was too much in my own willfulness to become a "Nikos worshipper." I sort of met him toe-to-toe, even as a kid. He was very fond of telling people that when he invited me to come to Williamstown and told me what roles I was to play, that I said, "But I only play leading roles!" And I was twenty-four. He wrote me a letter about it at the end of the summer, he said, "I'm sorry there are no more leading roles!" But I wasn't ever in awe of him. We had a long conversation in a car once, where we said we both felt that each of us understood the worst about the other. And somebody once said, and this may sound self serving but I don't mean it to be, that I was Nikos' Christian.* That in my work with Nikos I was able to express in my acting the things he felt that he wanted in his direction. Because we did have an extraordinary rapport, where I was able to give him

*The young man in *Cyrano de Bergerac* who uses words written by Cyrano to express his love for Roxanne.

217

everything he asked for. Because nothing he said ever seemed wrong. It seemed absolutely right to me. I never disagreed with him.

When Nikos and I worked together, it was always clear to me, when I would look at him in a rehearsal room, watching, that I was emotionally fulfilling what he actually, truly believed the character should be. That I somehow was a walking emotional example of his idea of it. It just happens sometimes with a director that you are his vision as an actor. So that's what I think happened between us and it happened very quickly.

I think that one of Nikos' gifts was that he had an extraordinary eye for talent. He brought along some of the finest actors in this country and he appreciated them and understood them. And if you *weren't*, he was a talent snob. If you weren't talented he wasn't interested in you. He would often use untalented people, but he would treat them badly. And this is a very important point about Nikos. How can I say it? I'm a firm believer in the necessary - cruelty it takes to run a theater. Every good artistic director of a theater I know has a cruel streak, and I know why. It's necessary! It's important. If you didn't have it, if you were sentimental or sloppy with your feelings or not cold-hearted about what you needed to keep your theater going, you couldn't run it. And Nikos had it in spades. Peter Hunt has it, Arvin Brown has it, Gordon Davidson* has it. You need it. So, Nikos adored and worshiped and coveted and protected talent. If you didn't have it, he just didn't care about you.

When he would do a Chekhov and put this incredible group of actors into a production, I'm sure he felt like some kind of wonderful lion tamer! He could actually stand there and manipulate all these exotic, dangerous animals going about their own search for their own truth. And he would help guide them. The actor relationships in *The Sea Gull* were extremely volatile. Lee and Kevin had an extremely difficult time. And then Kevin and Blythe had a bad time. I don't know whether Blythe and I had a bad time on that show, I think not. And as I said, my relationship with Lee was also dicey. And Olympia had a very bad time in that show, a very bad time. From my own experience, twice, when you did a Chekhov play with Nikos, everybody was very emotional all the time. We were emotional rehearsing it. We were emotional performing it, and we were emotional after we did it. We stayed up all night and we

*Artistic Director, Mark Taper Forum

talked about it. Partly because the play does it to you, but also because Nikos plugged the right actor into the right thing. He knew, very, very cleverly, most peoples' Achilles' heals. And he knew how to get to them, he knew how to attack and he knew how to make people feel insecure and worried and how to get people to want to be with him and how to get people to toady after him. And all of that is necessary because great plays need that.

JEAN Can we talk a little more specifically about what you plugged into with that role? About your process of approaching the part?

FRANK It's funny but I don't think – you'd think by now I would know – but I don't think I have a process. For me, acting is – a wilderness! I brush my teeth, I shave, I shower, I learn the lines, and I plunge into a kind of wilderness and I'm never certain that I'll ever get out of it. I'm never certain that I'll ever find civilization, I just become immersed in it and I begin to think the way the character thinks when I'm playing it. I don't carry it home at night very much. And one day, something happens. What I call – I often call it a lucky accident. I'll pick up a certain prop, or a certain actor will look at me in a certain way, or suddenly one speech will catch fire in my head, and from that one speech the character will begin to fall into place. And I think, "Oh, what a surprise!" I'm not sure I'm really a good interview because I'm really a seat-of-the-pants actor. I just learn my lines, I get up and I go with my instincts. I try to get out of my own way. Whenever I louse up as an actor it's because I'm in my way. I have learned over the years that my initial instincts are the right ones, they're just the right ones. I mean, I can refine it and change it, but – I think you just have to do it, you know? And do it badly. And from doing it badly in a rehearsal maybe you'll find the right road. But you can't intellectualize it and you can't theorize it, you just can't. I think that I trust myself – a lot, and I trust that one day something will come out.

JEAN Did that happen with *Sea Gull*? Was there turning point when the character began to fall into place?

FRANK Yes. It was with Bill Swetland. There was a kind of ramp, remember? There was some kind of walkway down to the water, and

I was leading Bill Swetland, whom I adored and fell in love with in that production – I became his puppy. I was leading him in, and we were rehearsing in the – "L" – is that what it was called?

JEAN The "Ex"

FRANK [Laughing.] Obviously I thought it was "L" for Langella! Anyway, we came down and Billy sat down and put his head to the side on his cane, and he said the line where he asks me to tell him something, and I just – caught it! I just felt the magic of that speech, I understood what that boy was about. Acting for me is always a surprise. I really think you just learn it and you *allow* yourself to just be there, you even *allow* yourself the frustration, you *allow* yourself your own bad-ness as an actor, you *allow* yourself the pain, you *allow* yourself the I-don't-know-what-I'm-doing. I see so many actors ruin themselves in rehearsal by trying so hard to get it right! There isn't any "right." You just get up there and you keep doing it. And one day you do it like this and one day you do it like that, and then, if you're lucky and you have ability and you have a good director, something happens and you take off. That happened in that moment with Billy. And then in the television version of it, many, many of those moments happened for me. On camera. Many happened like revelations, on camera. Nikos had never seen me on film before. I'd already made two or three movies, but that didn't count. You know, if you didn't work at Williamstown, in Nikos' mind you hadn't worked!

JEAN Did the performances for the camera change very much from what you were doing on stage?

FRANK Something incredible happened that I now remember. We played it for two weeks and it was immensely successful and then we lost it, around the middle of the second week, something happened that productions often do when they build to a crescendo. And this one kind of lost it's center, or maybe it only did so for me, I don't know, you'll have to ask the other actors. But I felt that we had somehow not quite risen to it, we just sort of lost our way with it. And we all knew that we were going to put it on tape. At that point, Great Performances was there, negotiating with everybody. I think we went right from the final performance into the taping, the next day, and we shot it in five days. There was something about the atmosphere of that little house up on a hill in Williamstown. It rained a lot, it was cold, and something about the atmosphere of that place where we taped reawakened the play in a different way to all of us. It got much more real and much more simple because we had come down from the stage.

Blythe and I did the last scene two times or three times and we did at it two o'clock in the morning, instead of taping it till one or two in the morning, we taped until four or five. And we taped it before we taped other scenes. And I remember feeling very, very, very alive in front of the camera, in a way I don't think I had been in my other film work. Partly because we had no time, partly because there was this tremendous energy from the stage production that was still with us. There was a lot of rivalry in the company as there always is in Nikos' companies and also a lot of genuine love. So it was this charged atmosphere! We were all off in corners, preparing, arguing – I remember the scene when they all go off in the troika and we had to get that right before the light went and we got it all in one take as we were counting down the moments we had left, things like that. Now it makes me want to see it.

JEAN There's so much pain in Trepleff, in just about every moment he seems so – tortured. Is that the pitfall of playing this part?

FRANK Yes, the pitfall is to miss the humor. You know, I have a ten-year-old son, and sometimes he comes at me with the most passionate commitment and care about something so funny to me. And I sit there trying to keep the corners of my mouth from twitching because it's very important to him. Whatever it is, you know, "She took the bird and she said something to the bird and I was going to say it to the bird!" And I say, very seriously, "Yes, you're right, you should've said that to the bird." And I think of Treplev, and I think that's what he was. He's always *there*, always ready to be something for someone, loving his mother very much, loving Nina very much, hating Trigorin. Like all young men with immortal yearnings, he's wrapped up totally in his view of the world.

JEAN Let's look at this last scene between Nina and Treplev. Let's just sort of go through it line by line and just see what strikes you. First of all there are the given circumstances. It's two years after the end of Act III, Nina's left, Treplev has begun to have some success, he's been published...

FRANK [Slowly.] It's funny, I used so little of that. I usually try to find the essence of what's going on in that person, in that moment, in his life. What I may be, right now at this table talking to you, is a result of my fifty years on earth and what I've accomplished, what I haven't, and my successes and my failures, but I'm not aware of that when I'm talking to you. When I'm talking to you I'm just being me in this room, at this table, at this time. [As if going through an inner monologue.] Is the tape recorder working? I have an appointment later, do we have enough time? Etcetera, etcetera. And that gives me a kind of immediacy about things when I play them. I try not to burden myself with too much history or too much research, it seems to get in the way. It gets in the way. Sometimes I do, but for the most part, I think, well, I'm him, I'm sitting at a table and I'm trying to write. And it's very frustrating, I don't write well. What he's saying is, I wish I were this kind of writer, a commercial writer, but I'm not. So that's what this speech was for me.

JEAN Would you read it for me?

FRANK [As Treplev.]
"I've talked so much about new forms, but now I feel that little by little I am slipping into mere routine myself. 'The placard on the wall proclaimed' – 'pale face in a frame of dark hair' – frame – that's flat. I'll begin again where the hero is awakened by the rain, and throw out all the rest. This description of a moonlit night is too long and too precious. Trigorin has worked out his own method, it's easy for him. With him a broken bottleneck lying on the dam glitters in the moonlight and the mill wheel casts a black shadow – and there before you is the moonlit night; but with me it's the shimmering far-off sound of a piano dying away in the still, sweet-scented air. It's painful. Yes, I'm coming more and more to the conclusion that it isn't a matter of old

222

forms or new forms, but that a man writes, not thinking at all of what form to choose, writes because it comes pouring out from his soul." *

Actually, when we did it on camera, this moment in the play was totally Nikos'. It's one of the best things I think I do in this show. Treplev is sitting at his desk and he's writing the story. Well, Nikos was behind the camera and I did the speech once and he came out and said, "You haven't got it, it's all wrong, you had it in the play, but –" And he just said three or four short sentences. And the television director wanted to go ahead. You know, "We got it, it's on camera, let's go." And Nikos said, "No, no, no, I want to do it one more time." And everything I proceeded to do in the speech, the second time, came directly out of something Nikos said to me.

JEAN Do you remember what that was?

FRANK It was something very simple, but the way he said it connected me to something extremely personal, I related to it in a big way. The gist of it was something like, "don't play a defeated man, play a man searching, trying very hard to work his way out." Which is what the creative urge is all about. And that's what I think I did with Treplev through the whole show. I tried to play somebody whose energy was trying to *find* something, rather than somebody who just decided to give up, someone defeated.

[Following the text.] And when Nina comes in, I think that he's just completely overwhelmed. My feeling about it, looking at the words again, is that when he sees her he's like a kid at Christmas, someone lit the tree and suddenly he sees all these presents. "I had a feeling, all day I was restless, oh, my sweet, oh my darling, you've come, let's not cry, let's not." He's just so happy.

JEAN So happy that – he's almost missing where she's coming from.

FRANK Absolutely. Totally, totally involved – as people who are obsessive are. They're in love with their love, they're not in love with the person. And she says, "There's someone here." She's

Reprinted by permission of the Nikos Psacharopoulos estate.

completely wrapped up in the reality of coming back to this place and he's just so happy to see her.

JEAN When she says, "I am a sea gull" what does that do to him? What does he think about that?

FRANK He doesn't understand. I mean, when I look at this – my God, it makes you want to play the scene! But Nina's in a very bad way. [Laughing.] Nina's far more complicated at this moment than he is! He's crazy about his girl, he's crazy about her, he has to be with her. She says "What was I saying about Turgenev?" And he says, "Not again, please Nina." Because he doesn't want anything to get in the way of what he feels. He doesn't want the bad stuff to come out. He says, "Nina, I cursed you and I hated you. I tore up all your photographs." To me this is what it's all about. "My heart is bound to you forever. It's not in my power to stop loving you." It's very simple. This is an obsessive young boy, madly in love with somebody, a boy whose mother rejected him always in favor of somebody else. Never could get his mother's attention. Nina showed some attention to him and he becomes crazy about her, but then she falls in love with somebody else.

He says, "You found your way, you know where you're going but I still move in a chaos of images and dreams, not knowing why. I have no faith and I don't know where my calling is." People who don't have a center, who don't have a true anchor inside themselves fall in love all the time, get into trouble all the time, because they're always looking for someone else to shore up the hole, the emptiness. And the reason Treplev is so appealing to so many young actors is because he is quintessentially that. And then it becomes pretty clear that Nina's not going to serve that function for him anymore. And long ago his mother has rejected him in favor of Trigorin, so that when Nina finally leaves, I think there's like a little psychic break for him. I've read enough about people who commit suicide to know that a great many people who shoot themselves don't do it in a moment of high exaggerated emotion. They kind of very quietly, in the moment, just decide to do it. They've just decided it's not for them anymore. I think that's what Treplev does. "I hope no one meets her in the garden and tells Mother. That might upset Mother." That's his last line before he goes off and shoots himself. "My mother's going to listen," he probably thinks. "Well, I hope Nina doesn't make any noise, I don't want my mother to yell at me."

JEAN So there's that wonderful incongruity of what's going on in his mind as opposed to the decision he makes to shoot himself.

FRANK And we often make decisions like that about so many things! Movies and plays would have us believe that when we sit down and make a decision to do something, we have a revelation or a strong idea, but I don't think that's true. I think you're walking around the house, as I did that day, saying "I'm not going to Williamstown to do *The Sea Gull*," and at the same time you're packing your bag. Because you have a certain body truth and your body spells it out for you, fulfilling that which it knows is destiny. Your brain is getting in the way but your body is saying, this is your destiny, this is where you're going. And I think maybe Treplev is one of those people who couldn't and can't face the everyday, real world. And often those people die young, they just don't make it to an older age because they can't handle the vicissitudes, they can't handle the onset of reality that comes with age. And with the onset of that reality comes a kind of – frightening cynicism or frightening – brutalism which, as an artist, you have to fight every day of your life. When you get older it gets harder and harder to wake up everyday and find that – wild passion – it just gets harder to do. Because life corrupts that in a sense. Treplev just got out. There's only one way to recover it, there's only one way to maintain it: that is, in your work, you find it over and over again, if you choose the right kind of work. And if Treplev were able to take it all and pour it into his work, it might have been his salvation, but he wasn't.

JEAN What you were just saying about walking around the house determined not to go and packing your bag at the same time – I think that's the essence of the humor in Chekhov. The absurdity of somebody doing two completely contradictory things in the same moment.

FRANK Some of the biggest laughs I can remember ever hearing on the stage would be in those two Chekhov plays. These incredible laughs of recognition. For example, the moment when Olympia tore apart the flowers. That's where Chekhov gets missed, people who

225

play it wrong, play it for deep dark tragedy. Life isn't that way. Life is funny in it's ludicrousness.

JEAN You're talking about what I think was central to the WTF experience. I think audiences came to expect in a "Nikos" production those incredibly funny moments of recognition, or those powerful emotional moments. There seemed to be a propensity for that, on a regular basis. I think Nikos enabled actors to find an abundance of those moments.

FRANK I hope you can find a way to make that tribute to Nikos because it's very true. It's no small thing to be the man who prepares the ground for the seeds, who creates the atmosphere for that. And that's the chief thing Nikos did, with a lot of controversy and a lot of difficulty and a lot of sturm and drang and drama which is what it should be. You did walk on the stage in that theater *knowing* that you could fly and soar. And knowing there would be somebody back there to appreciate it, wanting you to fly and soar. On the nights when I felt I had come to something really good in my work, he'd be in my dressing room when I got downstairs, he'd be waiting for me to tell me that he'd seen it. I always felt that Nikos – *saw* what I did. I mean, I was admittedly an actor probably in more need of attention than any actor I've ever seen or worked with! And that drove me to such – extraordinary – kinds of behavior that could be, I know, difficult for a lot of people. But Nikos understood it in me and didn't judge it at all. Liked it, I think! So that when I was able to take it and harness it – which is what acting is about anyway, it's acting in spite of your neurosis, not because of your neurosis – when you get out there and you're able to take it and shape it and make it into an art form, it's great to know that there's somebody that you're working with who gets it. Who comes back and says specifically, "You did *that* tonight, and you actually in that speech were able to do such and such." Nikos was able to do that for me, and very often when I would go off, I'd come to him and say "I've lost that speech." And he would say, "Yes, you have. It's because of X, Y, and Z." And he was always right, always. I can't say in any play I did with Nikos that he ever really steered me wrong.

JEAN I was very moved about what you were saying a moment ago about how he would come backstage and recognize specific things in your work. Because I think there's such a longing to have people in our lives who really *get* who we are, what we're trying to do in our work.

FRANK Someone who has the sense of the arc of your life in your work. And have somebody notice, just notice. I think that's why we all get so caught up in awards, too. It's just somebody saying, "Here, take this, we liked what you did." It doesn't last very long, but for those few moments someone says, "I appreciate what you do, I honor what you do." And when you were really, really cooking and good, he saw it and he appreciated it. Certainly, in *Cyrano,* I could feel him, I could literally feel him in certain speeches. I could feel him in the rehearsal room and I could feel him in the back of the theater. More happy and more moved and more excited than anyone else if I was getting a speech the way he wanted it or the way we had agreed on, or even if I was just off on a flight of fancy.

I want to tell you about something that happened the first time we did *Cyrano.* We were in rehearsal for the last scene, the scene where *Cyrano* dies, and it was Laurie Kennedy and Yusef Bulos and maybe one or two others. It was the first time we were off the book, and something just – happened. I started to cry and Laurie started to cry and Nikos started to cry and I remember at the very end of the gazette speech, I remember Nikos just getting up and coming into my arms and Laurie's arms and the three of us just stood there weeping. Well, I don't tell that story because I'm sentimental about it, or because, [In a gushy voice.] "Oh yes, we all loved each other –" because certainly that wasn't always the case!

But, where else, where else, but in that theater and in the wrestling with emotions and parts and tasks as great and as powerful as the things Chekhov offers you and a play like *Cyrano* offers you; where else can you get that kind of open rapport that will enable three human beings, who didn't know each other all that well at that time, to wrap their arms around each other and weep together? What usually happens is that when you finish shooting a scene someone says, you know, "nice work" or "good scene" or "that was great, we got it on the second take." But – if you can actually work in a little room in the summertime and actually come together and cry with each other – not for the sticky, silly, sentimental reasons that most people talk about Williamstown that annoy me. Not for those reasons. You stand there and cry with each other because you did – great work. Because your work was honest and full, and Nikos' was, and Laurie's was, and we knew we – we made something. We knew we – made a baby, an artistic baby. And most of the time that doesn't happen.

I guess what I'm saying is if one wants to applaud Nikos for anything, then one wants to applaud him for his creating a place in which – striving for greatness was the order of the day. And there's hardly any place left where anybody wants you to do that anymore. Most of the time people just want you to be the going thing or the current thing or they want to fit into the demographics of the profession.

I look at what Nikos did as a monumental achievement, really. The pulling together of so many extraordinarily gifted people in so many various plays. It had about it a feeling of real, true, comradeship. There was always this wonderful sense of that when I was there. I remember just extraordinary things. I have nothing but great memories.

Part Two
THE ACTING NOTEBOOK

"Some tie, invisible yet significant and essential,
existed between the two of them...and among all,
all in this life, even in these wilds, nothing is accidental,
everything is filled with one common idea,
everything has one soul, one aim; and to understand it,
it is not enough to think, to reason, perhaps one must
also have the gift of insight into life..."

from Chekhov's short story, "On Official Business"

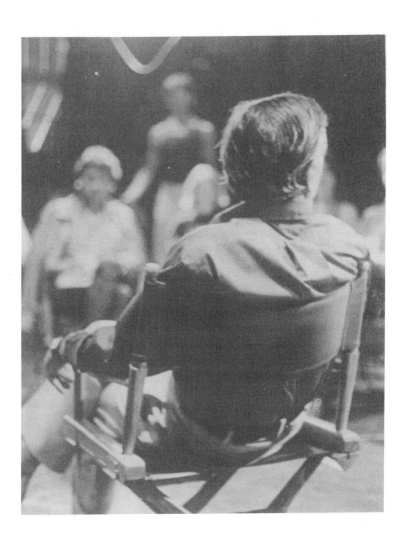

Nikos, in the directors chair.

INTRODUCTION
To The Acting Notebook

"...I found with Chekhov that slowly I got to like many more characters than I did at first. At the beginning, I felt I was dealing with an almost black and white statement. Eventually it turned out to be various shades which makes it more and more fascinating because it means that each of the characters defies classification and that is great. Although they are part of a world, it is a world that cannot be pinned down.

"That is really what has saved Shakespeare, Euripedes and Chekhov. These playwrights have become great and survived because they are dealing with the human problem which continues to be interesting and alive no matter what the temporary sociological conditions are. What makes Chekhov exciting is that it deals with the richness of the human experience which has been, and will continue to be, with us."

Nikos Psacharopoulos

When Chekhov was asked by his wife, in the year before his death, what he thought the meaning of life was, Chekhov replied: "You ask me what life is? It is like asking what a carrot is. A carrot is a carrot, and nothing more is known."

Directing or teaching Chekhov, Nikos adamantly resisted making interpretative comments about meaning or analyzing what Chekhov's plays were "about." Nikos' directorial handwriting on the stage could be read in what he didn't do as much as what he did — the negative space eloquent with the absence of an overlay of "concept" or polemical point of view. The closest he came to putting forth an interpretation was in refuting an interpretation. For example, from a newspaper article in 1980: "It's a lot of nonsense to say that Chekhov is an 'inactive' playwright. His people are making a passionate commitment to attempting actions which might be

233

crushed by circumstances or antagonists or other things. The important thing is, they are *attempting* to do it."

And yet, if anything, what they are "attempting to do" serves as a loose credo. In the critiques ahead from the class notes, Nikos' take on acting Chekhov shows up most in his specific suggestions as to what the characters physically *do* on stage. His direction builds moments of behavior, behavior that he suggests gives rise to the "life" of the material; behavior that piles up to open up the world of the play. Any interpretation of what this string of moments of "life" added up to, when eventually put together, was left up to the audience, and was meant to be different for everyone. When asked, in a 1976 interview, why his production of *The Three Sisters* was so successful, Nikos was brief: "The play became a piece of life and, like life, it interpreted itself."

The introductions to the translations of Chekhov plays I used in college unfortunately abound with the kind of value judgments Nikos eschewed. To take just one example, Robert Corrigan, in talking about the "symbols" in *The Three Sisters*, gives this interpretation: "...Moscow is the symbol of the three sisters' dream of happiness. This we know is an illusion and their belief in this illusion shows how *out of touch with reality they are.* And yet the play is filled with less obvious symbols that make it clear *that everyone in the play – with the exception of Natasha – has, to some degree, lost touch with reality.*" (Emphasis mine.)

Surely it could also be argued that Natasha is the character most *out* of touch with reality, but I think Nikos would have felt either perception antithetical to Chekhov. In the third act of *The Cherry Orchard*, Chekhov sets up a similar conflict in point of view in a scene between Ranevskaya, who owns the estate, and the "perpetual student," Trofimov. Ranevskaya, waiting for word the estate, becomes emotional about the possible loss of it, and expresses her wishes for another outcome. She also speaks of her love for the man she's left behind in Paris, a man who, at one point, left her for another woman. Trofimov urges Ranevskaya to face up to "the truth" about the sale of the estate and the character of the lover she's left behind in Paris. Ranevskaya responds by saying, "What truth? *You* can see what's true or untrue, but I seem to have lost my sight, I see nothing." She goes on to suggest that Trofimov's vision of "the truth" is colored by the fact that he has not yet suffered, that after

234

experiencing suffering and loss, it's less possible to pass judgement.

In other words, reality, in reality, is up for grabs; and who's to say, in Ranevskaya's or in our own lives, exactly whose perception of it *is* it? Corrigan's judgment that the sisters' belief in their dream of happiness in Moscow makes them "out of touch with reality" is rather like Trofimov's judgment of Ranevskaya – and no more or less "true" than the extent that any one of us is "out of touch with reality" in our beliefs in our own personal symbols for happiness.

An implied distance between "us" – the reader/audience – and "them" – Chekhov's characters – prevails in quite a few analyses of the plays. Ronald Hingly suggests: "Chekhov supplies...the spectacle of characters palpably less vital, less heroic, less significant than the average theatergoer, however inclined to self-disparagement, might reasonably suppose himself to be." Robert Brustein states that Chekhov "...qualifies our sympathy for the victims. In most cases, they seem largely responsible for whatever happens to them. This is not to say, as some have said, that we do not sympathize with their unhappy lot; we do. But since Chekhov highlights their inertia, irresponsibility, and waste, we also deplore their helpless inability to resist their fate." Nikos clearly disagreed. In exhorting a group of student actors who played the collection of characters in the second act of *Uncle Vanya* at a rather "hysterical" and "suicidal" level, Nikos says: "Why do you think these characters are so problematic?!... It was not *life* that was creating your problems, *you* were creating your problems. Theoretically, you all should be perfectly normal, fun-loving people – who care, who have relationships, who are just fine – except life creates problems for you." In other words, characters no more or less vital, heroic, significant, irresponsible or inert than any one of us.

To insure that both he and the actors resisted temptation to pass judgment or underline meaning, Nikos eventually opted to rehearse scenes completely out of order, even to break even the scenes themselves into pieces that were rehearsed non-sequentially, in ten-minute chunks scattered throughout the rehearsal day. His reasons for this were simple. "I...do that just to get people to play little moments here and there; to just assume that there are all these little pieces of life that exist all on their own," he says in the critique of *Uncle Vanya*. "Each moment has to have some kind of interest and fascination, but no judgment, about what it means in the overall scheme of the play." This non-judgmental-ness, combined with a focus on what the characters are "attempting to *do*," encourages the actor to ever-increasing degrees of apprehension of the text and characters unmediated by "thinking" – and seems to elicit a similar, unmediated apprehension in the spectator. "All good art is a way of living rather than a way of thinking," Nikos said in an interview in 1976 – a philosophy evident in his productions: watching a Chekhov at Williamstown, you didn't *think* about life, you were giddy with life.

In the interviews in Part One, the actors focus on *The Three Sisters, The Cherry Orchard, Uncle Vanya* and *Platonov*. Part Two, The Acting Notebook, is a gathering of notes, critiques and interviews Nikos gave on Chekhov over the years. Serendipitously, his most extensive critiques in The Acting Notebook are on *Uncle Vanya* and *Ivanov*. I've given a synopsis of each scene before the notes and critiques but they obviously will make the most sense when read after the related scenes from the plays. I've also included, in this section, additional chunks from the actor interviews that relate specifically to Nikos' direction of certain scenes.

The shorter critiques in this section are drawn from Nikos' rehearsal notes, my own and others' notes, and interviews. The longer critiques are from the class tapes, recorded in 1987 and 1988. Nikos often moves in the critiques from the particular to the general, especially in the long critique of Act II of *Uncle Vanya*. Here, guideposts and an overall approach for acting Chekhov emerge from the particular circumstances of each individual scene, and so gives applicable values not just for *Uncle Vanya*, but for the kind of acting Nikos encouraged in all of Chekhov's plays.

Jean Hackett

Nikos, directing

"Don't assume that because you have a play where the sentence structure is slightly peculiar for you, that you have to sound like you're really underwater! Don't ever assume that you have to really change from an organic acting base in order to get something out of a scene. When the language of the text is different from the language you are using, you must find a way to make it just as natural for you, not similar, but just as natural. It's the way good singers approach a song. For a great singer, it's just like talk. They approach a song like talk, rather than enhancing the artificiality of the form of singing.

"I think the more exaggerated the form of an art is, the more organic the acting has to be. That's why, for instance, the best people to work with when you're doing a play are those people who have a tough time with lines and therefore they put in their own words and they try to make sense with the lines as they speak the lines. So it is the line that is active, rather than the feeling about the line. If you try, for example, to make your acting expressionistic, when you do Brecht, it's as if you are assuming that the interesting thing in the material is the form and it is not. It is the life which necessitates that kind of form.

"In a Greek play it's not that there is a peculiar kind of delivery, it is that somebody's pain is so great that they cry out: 'Oooooooooooh!' rather than 'Oh!' But it doesn't mean because it is a Greek play the 'Oh' should be done in a stylistic way, in a Greek way, whatever that may be. It means that the feeling should be exaggerated in order to meet the form. Forms are repeated only because there's some kind of essence to it. So that no matter what the form is – it might be that it is some kind of ritual, it might be that it is poetic – it comes from something organic. Do not try to 'show' what you think the play is all about by doing something with your acting that comments on the 'form' of the material. Do not try to be poetic with Shakespeare, do not try to be lyrical with Williams, do not try to be expressionistic with Brecht and, please, do not try to be moody with Chekhov!"

Nikos Psacharopoulos

239

Cast of "Uncle Vanya," 1984

Notes on
UNCLE VANYA

*"The demand is made that the hero and the heroine should
be dramatically effective. But in life people do not shoot
themselves, or hang themselves, or fall in love, or deliver
themselves of clever sayings every minute. They spend most
of their time eating, drinking or running after women or
men, or talking nonsense. It is therefore necessary that this
should be shown on the stage."*

Chekhov (Letters)

Class Critique on ACT II

This critique of the whole of Act II of Uncle Vanya touches on a
variety of precepts Nikos felt were central to acting Chekhov. For
the sake of clarity, I have substituted character names from the play
for the names of the student actors playing the rolls.

Synopsis of scenes in Act II

Act II begins late on a stormy night in the dining room of the
Professor's (Serebryakov) country house. Serebryakov, ill, has
trouble sleeping and the rest of the household has been staying up to
attend to him. Yelena, his younger wife, sits up with him and tries to
comfort him but he rails against the difficulty of growing old and the
pain he has from the gout. Eventually Sonya, Serebryakov's
daughter, and Vanya, the brother of his first wife, come in to take
their turns with him. The Professor remains discomfited and
irascible, refusing to see Astrov, the doctor he requested Sonya send
for. Finally Marina, the old servant, sympathetically convinces him
to go to bed.

Yelena and Vanya are left alone in the room. Yelena voices her
frustration about the way the family lives; Vanya, who has been
drinking, pours out his love for her. Exasperated, Yelena leaves the
room. Left alone on stage, Vanya speaks of his longing for love and
the mistakes he feels he's made in his life, especially in idolizing and
working for his brother-in-law, Serebryakov.

Astrov, who has also been drinking, comes in. He and Vanya
talk circumspectly about their attraction to Yelena, as Telyegin plays

the guitar. Astrov goes to get another drink; Sonya reappears and as she chastises her Uncle for drinking he is struck with her resemblance to his late sister, Sonya's mother. He leaves the room in tears.

Sonya calls Astrov to the room and begs him not to let her Uncle drink. She gives Astrov some food and he begins talking to her about his disgust with Russian life, his lack of satisfaction with his private life, the rigors of his duties as a country doctor – and Yelena's beauty. Sonya implores him to stop drinking, extols his virtues and then speaks covertly of her love for him. He suggests he cannot return her love and quickly exits.

Alone on stage, Sonya expresses both her happiness in loving Astrov and her despair that she is not beautiful. Yelena comes in, acknowledges the unease between her and Sonya and insists they become friends. Sonya agrees and they drink a toast to their friendship. Sonya, crying, confesses her love for Astrov. Yelena speaks at some length about Astrov's talents and the hardships of his life as a country doctor, and admits to Sonya that she is "very, very unhappy." At the end of the scene Yelena wants to play the piano, something she hasn't done in a long while. She sends Sonya to go to Serebryakov and find out if the music would disturb him. The act ends with Sonya reappearing and telling Yelena, "He says no."

NIKOS Okay, guys, I will talk initially about the overall picture and then I'll move to each specific scene.

First of all, I think all of you kept score of what you were doing on stage. You were like children in a sandbox, saying, "This is a moment about laughter." "This is a moment about a piano." "This is a moment about grapes." All of which is true, but, in effect, we were getting the detail before we were getting the life of the detail. Like the way medieval painters have someone like St. Nicholas carrying a little ball. You look at the ball and say, 'Aha! He loves sailors!' You don't get to see it from the faces, you don't get to see it from the deeds, you see it from the *attributes* they gave.

In the same way, your behavior many times turned into attributes. The behavior turned into attributes because it was bound up with such a sense of invention, either on the part of the actor or director. It was very clearly pointed up that: this moment is about two people getting drunk; this is a moment about somebody holding a bottle. It's like you were all constantly saying, "This is something important." "This is something precious." "This is something telling." The details become "telling" rather than casually thrown in.

So it became a scene about people inventing rather than about people discovering.

In essence, it's what I've been saying about Picasso. Picasso could paint with a stick in the sand, as well as with a brush on a canvas. Sometime or another the work has to become accidental. So that all those things that either the director or the actors put in disappear – how they happen disappears and they happen accidentally. So you do not remember the moments of behavior in their exactness or in sequence but you remember their essence, you remember them in your imagination.

It's really wonderful when someone comes up to me about a play that I've directed and says, "Oh, how wonderful she was! She did this and this, and the way she comes down the staircase!" And a little while later, you think "Wait – there was not a staircase!" Or, "there were a lot of staircases, but she never came down one!" That is what imagination has to do in the theater. With the good actors that you trust, you almost think they did something that they did not. Moments in the theater have become legendary that never really happened! You never want to say, "Sweetheart, you never did that! Everybody just *assumes* you did that in a performance!" In Williamstown, we keep doing shows that we've done before and the new actor will come to me and say, "Oh, I hear the last time you did this play so and so did this and that." And everyone agrees and then I think back and say, "No, she never did that!" It's because something in the performance led to certain assumptions. What's that line about – education is what remains known of what remains of education – it's that kind of thing.

What really happens is that once the details become forgotten they become much more interesting. Because then you find out that your activity becomes an *inevitable* way for you to behave rather than coming out of a conscious decision about how you will behave up there. So the sixty-three little things that one puts in a scene become one, and the actor and the director and the audience never know where the one begins and the other ends.

Now, when you make your behavior into "symbols" or "attributes" that are so clearly defined, this not only causes the process to get lost but it also sterilizes you vocally. I thought that a lot of you were putting in very definite strokes with your voices. I would not have gotten what scenes were about if I'd just been listening to you and not able to see you. I got the scenes physically but not vocally. When we were doing Pinter's *Old Times*, Elizabeth Smith, who is a brilliant voice teacher, said, "Well, you're never going to solve it because all the lights are on." And somebody said,

"What?" She said, "All the lights are on." "Yeah?" She said, "Turn off the lights so the actors can't see each other, so they have to do the whole damn play by just using their voices. That's all they have to depend on. They can go through the moves, they can do all the behavior, but it's not in someone looking in the eyes, the play is in the voices."

You were shortchanging your voices many times. Your voices didn't have either the desperation or the enjoyment. They did not have the connection of: [Long, drawn out, plaintively.] "Why – ?" It is more interesting if it is: [Again, drawn out, longingly.] "Why – " than if it is: [Short, staccato.] "Why." Why is this? Because "why" is a *searching* word, right? And your voices should mirror that. This is why it's tough, occasionally, in translations, because people cannot find the equivalent sound to the original one. So the sound comes in as *text* rather than as a sound in a language. Which is wrong because many times the feeling of the word is the sound of the word. Language obviously is sounds as much as it is meaning. Somebody like Tennessee Williams picks up long sentences as much for the way they fall on the ear as for what they mean.

The things you pick up to do in Chekhov, your acting tasks, should never be as appropriate as they were now. Your behavior was really too appropriate. Your choices were absolutely right, absolutely literal, the sort of things which makes an audience kind of relax, because everybody "gets" everything. Then the things you do become like a simultaneous translation, really. And although sometimes these things were interesting and alive, although you were having a great deal of fun, even though the things the director gave you created a great deal of freedom, they were too appropriate.

Don't assume, consciously or subconsciously, that everything gets solved in every moment. When you have fourteen tasks up there, when you have fourteen things working for you, make them springboards for the life of the scene rather than guideposts. Make the tasks things that bounce you up and down and make you do other things that you don't know you are going to do. Rather than using the tasks as: "If I do that it means I'm happy," "If I do this it means I'm worried." In essence, sometimes some of you seemed dubbed in the scene, you seemed dubbed because a problem had been solved before the text came in, and the problem was solved by a very interesting and colorful visual image. As I said, it's like the painters who used attributes to tell the story. You invented behavior which then became symbolic of something else. And all this richness of detail sometimes became an end in itself instead of being used as possibilities to stimulate you. The ideal kind of work between a

244

director and an actor is not discovering that thing that tells the story, but discovering those things that cultivate the emotional world of the actor to become more open and more free. We've somehow got to be able to differentiate between these things.

ACTRESS So that it's not so literal?

NIKOS No, no, it's not necessarily that. I mean it's fascinating, a lot of times in movies a lot of the work is literal, the director puts in very literal things to tell the audience what it's all about. It's okay if it's literal as long as it's creating the conditions for the actor to respond. What I'm saying is that definition has it's virtues but it also has its drawbacks. I think the biggest drawback here was that moment "A" stood for moment "A" and moment "B" stood for moment "B" and so on. You were *manipulating* the life rather than allowing the life to *emerge*.

The danger of knowing, consciously or subconsciously, *why* you're doing what you're doing, and not forgetting why, is very interesting in the theater. The two or three people I work very well with always come up to me and say, "Why do you think I am dumb? I'm very bright." And I have to go out of my way to say, "I don't think you're dumb, let's just suspend intelligence for a while in order to do the work differently. The less we both know about what we're doing, the better off we are."

For example, [Yelena], when you have a line that is interesting, you stop and you tell us that you *know* it's interesting. And, by that time, it loses its suddenness, it loses it's – sense of jumping out and being – unprotected. It should just be unprotected and unfinished and then – on to the next moment! It's like the way people scratch their head or their knee or adjust their tie. The way people move their hands. It's – something! But it shouldn't be framed as an interesting moment. It just – is! It just exists without your comment on it, your knowledge that, as an actor or director, you are pointing something out about the text.

Now, let me move a little more specifically, scene by scene.

There's another problem I think that you all should be watching, which is, you were making decisions about values in this material and you were making judgments about the material. I think I suggested before, and this is one of the Chekhov lines, that there is no judgment made on the material. What is interesting is the fact that the *life* appears, and then somehow, you say, "Oh! that is what life is all about." Rather than making a plan: "This is what life is all about," and going on to show that.

Because of that, the scenes became a little too problematic, they became a little too definite, they became too much about: "This is what I have to talk about," or "This is what I have to do," or "This is what I really want to say." For example, it stretches credibility that you [Serebryakov] would be such an awful person in the very beginning, that you would be so upset. I don't mean this as an interpretation about the character. It's just that once you somehow pass judgment on this character's problems, once you make this man totally impossible as a human being, then the problem has been articulated. When the problems have been articulated, the problems are no longer great.   ND

[Nikos then proceeds to analyze and act out a portion of the scene.]

It's like:

[As Serebryakov.] "Who's here, who's here, Sonya? –"

[As Yelena, gently, lovingly.] "No, darling, that's me."

[As Serebryakov, eagerly, urgently.] "Oh it's you, good, let me talk to you, let me talk to you."

[Nikos speaks out Yelena's inner world with expectation and eagerness.] So, Yelena, you go closer to talk, you want to talk, but instead of him telling you about whatever is in his heart, he says:

[As Serebryakov.] "You know, I have a problem, I have gout, my leg hurts. You know what they say about Turgenev?"

And so you go closer, you think you'll hear something exciting about Turgenev. That's one of the reasons you married him, because he says exciting things about Turgenev! And instead he says:

[As Serebryakov, flatly.] "Turgenev got angina because of gout."

[After the laughter, Nikos continues.] So you see, it is not that these people's needs are different, it is that the world has changed for them. He is not an impossible person, he is in pain. It is the world, not the two of you, that breaks you apart.

The scene started with such a level of disgust on your part [Serebryakov] and, on your part [Yelena], at such a level of ignoring him. What is interesting about that? Ignoring him is not interesting, because you can get up and go to a corner, you can go even further and leave the room. Ignoring someone on stage is never interesting. What is obviously interesting for you, as an actress, is to have to sit next to him, to have to listen to all of it and say [Gently.]: "Yes, dear. No, dear," – and not being able really to express your feelings. Same thing with you [Serebryakov]. You say things like, [Vulnerably, openly.] "Listen, nobody's really paying any attention to me." But it's not interesting if you make it very interesting. Then you *deserve* for people to not pay attention to you and the fact that she does not

246

pay attention to you is nothing really new, but a kind of ordinary occurrence. And then we don't want to listen to you either, we dismiss you. What is interesting about a scene where a boring person is being ignored by someone?

You all had a tendency to come on stage only to deal with problems. You were very goal-directed towards the "problem" in the scene, rather than saying to yourself: "There are no problems, I am just really leading a life." Once you lead a life, then the problems develop. You were not taking the time in your acting to just lead your life.

For example, after this scene between Yelena and Serebryakov, Sonya enters. You entered and went directly to them, as if to solve a problem. Instead, if you had gone around the room as you're talking, thinking, "Now what should I do? Lights, we don't need lights, I'll blow out candles, I'll arrange something," then you would find that in the *middle* of this life, the other things come out. So it doesn't become about making pointed statements. You were making pointed statements in your acting about this or about that, rather than just saying, [As if with a shrug.] "Well, that's what life is: I hate, I love, I want to do this, I want to do that. I sit. I pay attention. I don't pay attention."

Connect to other people on stage with you, too. Look at them, establish that it's not always a relationship between the person who talks to the person he's talking to, but to the life that is going on. Remember that in this material important things come out of unimportant things, and the important and the unimportant have equal weight. You were all, really, on such a suicidal level of existence! You had no life, you only had problems! You can't really do that, because you'd never make it to the third act, let alone the rest of your life! I mean, it has to be: [In an off-hand, meandering way.] "I talk, I talk about this, I talk about the world," and somebody says, "Play the guitar," [With surprise.] "Ah! You ask me to play, I'll play." And someone else says, "Wait! I don't want to fight you now, I'm listening to the guitar." And someone else says, "So, oh well, I don't like the way you play the guitar, so let me tell you something." You know, if you go someplace and somebody makes a production number about playing the guitar, even if you have a problem, you suspend your problem for a little and you stop and listen to the guitar.

In essence, it's allowing the life to come in. Chekhov doesn't move from big crisis to big crisis. I mean, you were all so undone! I didn't think that you all could really survive another second up there. You were all suicidal, you were all hysterical, and it was not

247

life that was creating your problems, *you* were creating your problems! Theoretically, you should be perfectly normal, fun-loving people who care, who have relationships, who are just fine, except life creates problems for you. We begin to see that life has created certain problems because one of them has aged and one of them happens to be attractive, and one of them loves working but it gets too much for her, and one of them drinks.

Okay, Vanya's entrance. First of all, except for your words, I never knew that you have a world that you don't want to share with the other people, that you deal away from, and that makes you vulnerable. And then, all of a sudden, everyone but Yelena disappears and you start dealing with her from your secret world, [Urgently, pressured.] in a very important way, and you start talking to her and exposing yourself and becoming vulnerable to her and opening up. But your tone of talking to her was very similar to the way you talked to everyone else, only the words were different. Obviously, we talk one way to Sonya, one way to Yelena; to the nurse we talk a third way. Remember to deal with the adaptation, remember to shift the way that you talk to somebody, before the definite line, right? You don't have to wait for the line saying, "I love you," before it's clear that you really love that particular character.

And then, Vanya, it would be great for you to just let loose, because all of a sudden here's your chance. Remember how beautifully it's constructed. A lot of people, unimportant action, then suddenly you're all by yourself with only one person, *the* person, and you let loose and you don't know what to say! Find springboards to let loose, find ways that the material is so exciting to you, find things you want to do that are so exciting, that what you end up saying is never really calculated but just kind of pours out, and the words are far too few for all the things you have to say to her! Your acting was right on the money; very, very accurate, which is a similar problem, [Sonya], that you had in the last scene. Your words became measured rather than: "I have ten thousand words to say, but I'm not selecting them, ten of them just surface accidentally without me knowing which ones."

Don't go up there and do something until at the end you say, "Oh, boy, was that foolish!" You were never foolish enough and accidental enough with that scene [between Vanya and Yelena]. I don't know, I don't know if you should stutter. You don't know if you should trip over things, if you should try to sing to her. If it could just pour out, if it could have some sense of the privacy that creates foolishness, then I think the scene would've been more

248

interesting for you.

There was something very moving with the monologue. But you were only using the monologue to solve something on your mind, something you were preoccupied with. I just wish you would just let loose and not keep score. Remember, you're alone on stage. If someone is alone on stage, then they can be foolish, right? I mean that they can just say, [Eagerly, loosely.] "Oh, God, to be free of imposition of having someone else around here, [Chaotically.] and she says this, and she says that, and I wonder – [Yelling.] WHY!!!"

The playwright does not give you lines like, "Let me think about this, and let me think about that." He gives you a speech where you're frustrated because of something that you're not able to achieve. So, hit your head, sing it, pour the wine all over you, drink, stuff yourself with bread. Find things that allow a great deal of freedom for you rather than, [Pensively.] "My mind is involved with the subject, I'm trying to solve it, I'm trying to figure it out." You were mesmerized with your problems. Use the text much more, as I keep saying, as a springboard rather than an imposition. It was too much of an imposition for you and it became thoughtful rather than open and being about how when you're alone on stage you can do any kind of damn thing you want.

You know what it is, obviously? It's just much more interesting ᴺᐃ if we do not know _why_ we are saying things. That's what I mean about not making judgments. Vanya, Astrov, in the next scene, between the two of you, you both were very alive on the stage, which was wonderful, but, again, you were very problematic with things, you were too definite. Astrov comes in, and how much more exciting it would have been, on your part, if you did not _know_ this was a conversation. Somebody brings you in to tell you something and you say, [Pouring out, carelessly.] "Fine, fine, I don't know what to do, I mean, I do this, I do that..." Why? Because people allow themselves to open up when they are not pinned down. You see, if you assume that the other character will never really quote you or doesn't hold something against you, then the speeches will be more free for you. If you don't suspect that Vanya loves Yelena, then you can really go up to him and, basically, say, [Openly.] "She's a splendid woman. You know, isn't that interesting what people do? I mean, why do they do that?" And the same thing with you, [Yelena], it's, "Look, sweetheart, look Sonya, I don't know why you're asking me questions but, thank God, you're asking me things." Then it becomes much more frightening for you. It is frightening because you're not in control of it.

Chekhov always gives you the wrong person opening up to the

249

wrong person. I mean, you have Trofimov and Ranevskaya in *Cherry Orchard*, Andrei in *Three Sisters* talks at length to a man who can't hear, Ferapont. And the reason Chekhov does this is really very simple – so that you don't have to be careful. If the playwright is going to give you careless moments, moments where your soul comes out without manipulation, then you really have to allow yourself to part with information carelessly, freely.

How much more interesting if this conversation between Vanya and Astrov was really two interrupted monologues between the two of you. You don't know what he thinks, he doesn't know what you're thinking, so you can open up completely. I thought, [Vanya], it got kind of shy for you, it got all about one element of the character. Don't assume that character is something that's consistent on stage, especially in Chekhov. You could have been nasty, you could have been mean, you could have been temperamental, you could have been a lot of things if it all came out of the same kind of source. I thought that you found something wonderful but you hid behind it, you did not allow yourself to deal with all the other aspects that are also part of that whole strategy.

In the scene with Astrov and Sonya, Sonya says, "Look, I want to find out something. Suppose I had a sister and she loved you, what would you do?" Instead of taking your time and reflecting on this, instead of guarding your response, suppose Astrov is just caught completely off guard! So he says: [Mildly panicked, as if thrown off and suddenly on the run.] "Well, darling, I don't know what I would do, I really don't, I've got to go! Well, maybe I'd tell her this, I'd better go. [Upset.] How the hell do I know what I'd do? Well, bye, I'm out!"

What I'm saying is that then it becomes *life's* problem or *life's* virtue or *life's* glory, not *your* problem or *your* glory. Acting should obviously be in spite of yourself rather than because of yourself, and the best acting comes from finding and heightening those particular circumstances that allow you to be thrown off. I thought you [Astrov] played with definition, but you really played it as if you were aiming *directly* for this, and aiming *directly* for that, so it became functional rather than really caught by surprise.

[Sonya], I thought it was the best acting I've seen you do, really. But I wish you would get annoyed occasionally. I wish you would deal with some other elements of Sonya. For example it could be:

[With annoyance and frustration, Nikos says Sonya's line to Astrov, yelling it.] "Come on, I beg you, don't drink!"

[As Astrov, quickly, contritely.] "Okay, I won't drink, take the bottle."

250

[As Sonya, taken aback.] "Oh."

[As Astrov, chastened.] "Well, okay, I'll leave."

[As Sonya.] "Well, I mean, don't go. Have some cheese."

And then, Sonya, you are so happy that he stays, and you like to wait on him and make him happy, and all of a sudden you find yourself pouring the bottle and giving him a drink!

You are all laughing because that's exactly it. I wish you people were dealing more with the craziness and arbitrariness of life that comes naturally out of the circumstances and out of a certain kind of impact that you have on each other. *ND*

Now, the final scene between Sonya and Yelena. I thought that, once again, Yelena, you did not let it come out. You were very careful in parting with your information, rather than playing the circumstances, which are: that the two of you have become friends. So that you spin around, so that the one keeps pouring wine for the other, etc. You kept making decisions before you were doing something. You did not have that sense of life going on. It was almost as if life existed only in your short sentences, and in between you were both moving away and becoming distant. I wish the drinking would continue, I wish the hugging would continue, I wish the crying would continue, I wish you would throw things at each other. There were too many decisions before the event. Things were taken too literally. Don't be so careful.

Find the life of the scene, which obviously here is two people becoming friends and opening up. It's one woman who is really not dealing with the "man" issue because she is married. It's about these two women having a girl talk, you know what I mean? It's like a thirties movie where the two women go to the ladies' room and put lipstick on and exchange white furs! There is that kind of madness to it and I wish you'd find that in the scene.

Put scenes on the right track without judgment. Put them on track in terms of the particular situations that actually exist, which are: [Carelessly, easily.] two women all alone drinking and picking up plates and having some food and eating some of the cheese and cleaning up and lying down possibly, or going all over the stage, throwing things at each other. Why do you need that? You need these things in order to create continuity so that whatever lines you come out with don't become: "I am saying this to score a point, I am saying that to score a point." So that whatever scoring of points there is becomes accidental. It's just people who start talking, not knowing where they are going with it. Which is much more interesting than people who have a plan about how to score points and then speak. Yeah, Katherine?

251

ACTRESS PLAYING YELENA   Okay, say we get to this point where we are friends and we trust each other –

NIKOS Right.

ACTRESS And we start talking and suddenly I realize – I love the doctor. Can I show that to her? How do I –

NIKOS Well, I would say, if you suddenly make the realization that you love the doctor, what would you do?

ACTRESS I would hide it.

NIKOS How would you hide it? How would you do it? I mean, what do you think is the most interesting way of hiding it?

ACTRESS Ignoring it.

NIKOS Well, but you have a whole speech about him! You have all those lines about him, so you're not ignoring it! This is so-called script interpretation, dear, it's basic. Wait, wait. How can you make a choice to ignore it, to hide it? If the playwright gives you lines like: [Energetically] "No, no, no, the doctor, he plants trees, he does this, it's not the trees it's not the forest, it's – love! What does it matter if he drinks!" You're not hiding it if you say all these glorious things about what this man is, if the two of you exchange all those ideas, Yelena is not hiding it! Sonya asks you, "Are you happy?" And you say, "No." I mean, you do say [Heartfelt.] "No." Now! If you start calculating after she says "Are you happy?" If you think, [Pensively.] "Now wait, if I tell her I'm unhappy she'll assume it's the father, she'll assume it's Astrov," then you'll never be able to say the line that Chekhov has given you. The line that Chekhov has given you is: "No." That line is the truth! So it just has to come out.
   The same with the line: [In a way so self-evident that it's funny.] "Of course I wish I had married somebody else, but I didn't marry somebody else!" These things just kind of pour out. In the same way, it's just, [With abandon.] "I feel, I feel, like playing the piano, that's what I feel like doing. I feel like playing the piano!" And if you start doing things with your fingers, like cracking your knuckles [The description rises to a crescendo.] and you go out to the piano and open the piano and fling the music up in the air, then your body will start to interpret for you. [More and more an aria.] And you hear the watchman making noise outside, and you yell at him, "Shut up!

252

Get out of there! Don't knock! [Long, drawn out, recklessly.] I'm PLAYING!!! AHHHHH!"

You see? Now you are crying. That's what the scene is all about. And then Sonya comes back in and says you can't play. If you've done all these things, then you are free to just *react*. But it's not like, [In a measured, calculated way.] "Ah ha. I feel like playing the piano so I will because I want to demonstrate to you how good I feel." So that it becomes score 1, score 2, score 3 points.

Remember that between goals in any kind of game that you watch around, you know, this town, there's a lot of playing! But you go up on stage and you refuse to carry the ball! You only want to score points! You know what I mean? That's exactly what it is, you only care for scoring, and therefore you lose the gameness of it. Use that analogy in order to assume that what's interesting for you is playing. Because, really, it's the playwright who scores, not you. Chekhov takes you to the three moments or the five moments or the ten moments in each act where the points are scored. Any good playwright does that and, obviously, he's a very good playwright. So be sure that you don't stop the life of the scene to make a judgment about the importance of the scene, or the importance of a specific moment. Then you will find out how exhilarating, how effortless it is to just play. ɴᴏ

You know, [Vanya], if you just went into that monologue like, [With abandon.] "What the hell," he gets down on the floor, he hits the floor, he lies on the table; then *they*, the audience, will interpret for you. They will say, "Ah ha! He feels this way or that way." Don't do the audience's work for them. They are there to make the interpretations, not you. You know what I mean, [Astrov]? Everything you said had a purpose. People only do that in business, not on stage. When I go and try to raise money for the theatre, I have to be very careful about the things I say. Because those guys don't want to listen to emotional things about the work, they want specifics.

But if you're going to be up on that stage it has to be just the opposite, you have to deal with the whole life of it. The scene between the two of you [Yelena and Sonya] was so guarded that every statement was a cover for a cover for a cover rather than, "Boy, we have all these marvelous things to say to each other!"

I also think you should all be much more physical. Wouldn't it be wonderful if you fell on the floor and grabbed him, if the wine spilled and the candle dripped all over her? It's this kind of thing that would have given more immediacy and more life. What you really have to develop for this is a lack of reverence for each one of the

253

lines, and a feeling that each one of the lines represents another twenty-six things that you have underneath. So that the lines become much more accidental.

You've got to trust the playwright. And if you trust the playwright, you do not measure things, you're not careful with things. If you really trust the playwright, you assume that it is all going to happen without you doing it consciously. I remember the first time I did *Three Sisters* I found out that it was much better if I rehearsed all the scenes totally out of order. And the reason I continue to do that is just to get people to play little moments here and there, to just assume that there are all these little pieces of life that exist all on their own, and then eventually you put it all together. Each moment has to have some kind of interest and fascination but no judgment about what it means in the overall scheme of the play. Then it all comes out in a much more human way.

It's always wonderful if, every time you do a Chekhov play, if one of the actors is totally undisciplined. It's not that you want an undisciplined production, but it's interesting how electric something becomes with one person who is totally undisciplined. The first time I did *Three Sisters*, Olympia Dukakis, who played Olga, was such an undisciplined – wonderful actress – but undisciplined actress. So she'd just kind of move all over the stage and do all these things and everybody would have such a tough time! I mean in a good sense! Everybody would have such a tough time trying to find her! The same way with Austin Pendleton. He keeps thinking of different things all the time to do on the stage, intuitive and instinctive things, totally unrelated things. And Chris Walken, too. I mean, Walken never knows at all what he does, or why he does it, or what he's going to do next. That's what makes him so riveting.

So don't try to score points. That's what I'm saying. Because when you keep score, you only count those big moments, you only judge certain moments important rather than the whole fabric. That's why, [Vanya], although you were alive, you were aiming directly for the kill, rather than saying, [Nonchalantly.] "I don't know what's going on." Then you'd find out that all your crosses would've been much more interesting. I know you didn't rehearse it in this room, but, if you're going to come into a room, don't go directly for who you're going to talk to! Just come on in! [Rambling, expansive.] Come in, get behind the chair, look what is going on, and then realize, "Oh, God, I have to go to him," and then go to him. Don't open the door and immediately you're ready to deliver the line. Come in for something else: come in to pick up a book, come in to find a candle, and in between you say the line. The reason I'm

254

saying that is so you're constantly active and alive, rather than only active and alive in the big important moments in the play. Because then you have no life. Then, really, you go from headstep to headstep and you don't ever climb the staircase.

Don't sacrifice the process to deal with the obvious results that are pointed up in the play. I've said many times that, in Chekhov, getting there is *all* the fun. Not *half* of the fun, not *most* of the fun. Getting there is *all* the fun.

* * * * * * * * * * * * * * * * * * *

Notes on the characters of Yelena and Sonya

NIKOS   Chekhov often shows how funny people can be when they're emotional. It's Chekhov, the doctor, standing back from Chekhov, the poet. The scenes between Yelena and Astrov, Yelena and Vanya, Yelena and Sonya – are all about something Chekhov often deals with: misplaced love. There's the feeling of this play being a musical – play music underneath these scenes when you rehearse them.

Yelena might have some of any of these things: arrogance, the sense of everyone looking at her, the sense of an image of herself as reality, a sense of relying on her presence more than her intellect. She has moments where she almost accepts her superficiality but then starts worrying about it. She's bored, but she wants to *do* something – which is the Russian, rather than the French, sense of ennui. The nature of her character is that she makes very strong commitments to things in a very temporary way. Such as when she says to Sonya: "Let me talk to the doctor, find out if he loves you." She deals with the little things in a heightened way, making then very important. She magnifies the ordinary tasks in a way serious people wouldn't.

But if you imagine all the energy and commitment she gives to small incidents being channeled into the right thing, well, then you understand what makes Astrov love her. It's just the *circumstances* that limit her, not her character. Without this, actors tend to make a comment on the character. Don't judge her as someone who is superficial. Don't bask in the superficial because superficial people never really know what they are.

Remember, in a play like this, what part of Sonya is in Yelena and what part of Yelena is in Sonya. Two people on stage always have something of the other – they're not 100 percent Sonya and 100 percent Yelena – twenty percent of your character should be in her, twenty percent of hers should be in you. Otherwise the two of you would not be on stage together. There might be something about Sonya's intelligence that both attracts Yelena and upsets her, and there might be something about Yelena's beauty that both attracts and upsets Sonya. That's only natural. That's another area you must think of when you work on these roles. No good playwright ever has a scene where the two people are totally different.

* * * * * * * * * * * * * * * * * * * *

Maria Tucci on Playing Yelena

"Is Yelena Andreyevna, the professor's wife, an average intelligent woman, who is a thinking and decent person, or is she an apathetic, idle woman, incapable of thinking or even loving? I cannot reconcile myself to this second interpretation and I dare to hope that my understanding of her as a reasoning, thinking person who is made unhappy by her dissatisfaction with her present life is the correct one."

from a letter from an amateur performer,
Marianna Pobedinskaya to Chekhov,
Jan. 30, 1903

"Your opinion of Yelena Andreyevna is completely justified ... [She] may produce the impression of being incapable of thinking or even loving, but while I was writing "Uncle Vanya" I had something completely different in mind."

Chekhov, in a letter replying,
Feb. 5, 1903

JEAN What were the obstacles with Yelena?

MARIA I thought I'd have trouble playing that part. My joke in those days was that only Austin was myopic enough to cast me as Yelena in *Uncle Vanya*! I'd always played Sonya types. He offered me the role right before I went to Europe, so I was in Europe for a while thinking, how do I play a beautiful woman? And I remember seeing Antonia Fraser and I thought, well, Antonia knows she's beautiful, she carries her head as if it were on a platter, as if it were a

256

great gift she was offering, and it was. I had all these thoughts about how to be beautiful and then I got to rehearsals and I thought – beautiful – wait a minute! It bores her! People have told Yelena she's beautiful all her life, from the time she was four, she was told she was beautiful. And look what beauty got her. So beauty is the last thing she thinks about! It got her nowhere, it got her this professor she's unhappy with, it got her stuck.

What Austin talked about, which I loved, was her *active* boredom. She's not languishing in boredom. He put me on a swing and I would swing out into the middle of the audience, swinging with that tremendous energy that boredom can give you. Not the languishing, beautiful woman. And it was such a release to play her that way. Now, perhaps, she's always played that way, but I haven't seen her played that way the two other times I'd seen it. There are those lines about her, something like, "that woman, she staggers across the room," something like that. But again, that staggering is similar to the pent up passion that Masha has when she breaks up the card game. She's bored – like a lion is bored! Walking back and forth in a cage, looking for *something*.

One day Laurie and I were rehearsing the scene between Sonya and Yelena, and Austin said, "That's it, it's wonderful." And we thought we'd found the scene, we felt so full, so smug, and so pleased. So the next day, or three days later, we come to the scene. Maybe it was a few hours later, knowing the way rehearsals are at Williamstown! We do the scene again and Austin said, "No, come on!" He was saying, don't try to repeat what you just had. And then he said one of my favorite things, "Maria, don't play this the way you'd like to play it when you're a great actress. Go back to the beginning. There's been a storm." And I said, "Oh, Acting 1, I get it." You know, throw it all away. Which, now, is what I always try to do. Whatever you find, throw it out the window. Moment to moment: walk in the room, there's been a storm and she says, "What fine air," there's that wonderful smell, the ozone, and then find Sonya there and just see where the scene takes you. Which is, of course, what has to happen every night. It's so much easier not to know where a scene is going. But it's such a risk in that scene. Yelena certainly doesn't have a plot coming into the room, she doesn't come in manipulatively, hoping to find Sonya. And when she goes to talk to Astrov I believe she goes innocently and really hopes to do good for Sonya, but her own unconscious passion takes over. She doesn't know where the scene is going to go. Down she comes, and there she is and then the scene keeps expanding. It's such a wonderful scene for young actors to work on. It's on the run

257

like everything else in Chekhov.

I adored Yelena. At that time Mike Nichols was doing a *Vanya*, just afterwards, and he said to Austin, "Oh, you cast Tucci, I understand, it's got to be played by a European." And I know sort of what he meant. That sense of a woman who knows how to wear perfume, who knows how to dress incredibly well even though she doesn't mean to. She cannot get out of bed and put the wrong handkerchief with her dress. And to someone like Sonya this is absolutely mind boggling.

JEAN Those things are of another world to her.

MARIA Completely. Whereas with Yelena, they're not the interesting things, they just happen. But both these women are similar because they're both so longing for affection.

Both of them would like to exchange roles. Yelena wishes that she had more courage. Because, in the end, she does lack courage. It is her true laziness in a way, but also her intelligence. She also knows that she and Astrov would eat each other alive. No, perhaps not devour each other, merely burn each other out. Her logic tells her she can't go through with an affair with him, but at the same time she wishes she had the courage to.

* * * * * * * * * * * * * * * * * *

Laurie Kennedy on Playing Sonya

"...The whole meaning or drama of a person lies internally, not in outer manifestations. There was drama in Sonya's life prior to this moment, and there will be subsequently, but this [moment] is just an occurrence, a continuation of the pistol shot. And the pistol shot is not a drama either, but an occurrence."

Chekhov (Letters)

LAURIE *Uncle Vanya* was a special production. Santo Loquasto did a beautiful unit set – all wood with Vanya and Sonya's office slightly elevated. And there was a swing! Great set.

JEAN How did you approach Sonya?

LAURIE First of all, it was interesting, people kept saying to me, "You're too pretty to do Sonya."

JEAN Yes, it's unusual casting. In fact, I don't know many theaters that would cast the same actress as Irina, Anya and Sonya.

LAURIE Well, I think it has more to do with what you carry inside yourself. You can be beautiful and not feel it. Nikos must have seen something in me that he felt I could tap into – that made me right for Sonya. I was an attractive Sonya, what can I say? But how often is that true in life – don't we all know someone who is good-looking and bright and doesn't think so? It's not how Sonya appears, it's what she carries inside.

There's a Russian film of this play in which Sonya is quite beautiful. She's like a doe, very thin, beautiful face. The woman who played Yelena was large, lush, a woman! I remember she had roots growing out about an inch. Her hair was growing out from having been dyed. And I thought, how perfect. She was a sophisticated lady used to a city life with beauty salons. She goes to the country for a few months and can't get to the beauty parlor, so her roots are showing! Also it reflected what life with the Professor did to her self-esteem. Next to her zaftig, sexy femininity, Sonya looked like a little girl – more of a Vogue beauty. And Sonya's just a country girl. Seeing Yelena, this woman who's been around, interact with two country bumpkins – Astrov and Vanya – was very funny. She had something they had never seen before. She was a dame.

More than any of the other plays, *Uncle Vanya* moves into farce. After Vanya returns after having gone out to pick flowers for Yelena and finds her kissing his best friend, Astrov – it's a chase sequence right out of Keystone Cops! Vanya gets a gun and starts chasing the Professor all over the house. Lee Wallace, who was a great Vanya, kept hold of the flowers throughout the entire chase. It was so silly and yet moving. I thought Lee captured the essence of Chekhov in that choice. It is farce, you laugh at all these characters.

JEAN Even Sonya, who isn't the funniest woman in the world –

LAURIE Yes, there are laugh lines. Which aren't laugh lines in the sense of Kaufman and Hart. They're character laughs. Sonya says, "When a woman isn't pretty they tell her, 'You have beautiful eyes, you have beautiful hair.' " I remember getting a laugh on that and being surprised. The thing about Chekhov is, the laughs are always surprising.

* * * * * * * * * * * * * * * * * * *

Class Critique on Act II, a scene between Sonya and Yelena

This is a more expansive critique of the last scene in Act II between the two women that Nikos touches on in his longer critique of the entire act. For a synopsis of the scene, see the synopsis of the entire act, above.

NIKOS   I thought both of you made yourselves very available, and I thought, [Yelena], it was a great improvement from the last time. Unfortunately, though, it became a scene about lines rather than life. What Robert said was very right about something needing to be messed up in the scene.

To take a very obvious example, when you come in, and Sonya says, "The doctor was here." And you say "Let's drink wine, let's drink to our friendship." This moment could have many things: two people running toward the wine, one person trying to find a glass, the glass is dirty, the other person picks up the other glass, you try to pour, she takes it back, somebody's spilling the wine, somebody's wiping the other person with a napkin, etcetera, etcetera. The reason I'm saying that is not because I'm trying to add business, but it can't be a scene about people talking. There is nothing as dull as two people talking. Really. Unfortunately, it's considered a very interesting thing in the world right now for everyone to just, you know, talk. But this is not a very interesting thing to put up on stage.

For instance, take Sonya's first speech. You really didn't have to look at yourself in the mirror to deal with the line, "How awful it is that I'm not beautiful." If the playwright gives you a speech all by yourself, why would you deliver the speech in the same way you would've delivered it if there was someone else in the room? Right? I mean, here is your chance!

[Nikos acts it out:] "There's nobody watching me, I can just stuff myself with grapes, I can get fatter and fatter and fatter because he doesn't like me anyway. I can bang on the piano, I can run around." You know? "And then I come out of church and this awful woman says I look bad! I look bad! [Long, drawn out.] I don't!" If you're going to do something with the mirror, smash it or put the mirror down so that you don't have to look at yourself in the mirror.

260

But looking at yourself in the mirror and then saying that attractive – is stupid. You know what I mean?

Now, Yelena, you come in, and Sonya looks at you. And don't know what to say, you walk all around the room, and you think, Well, what do I say to her? Okay: "The storm is over, you know." And she doesn't say anything. And then you say, "Why are we enemies, I want us to be friends." And so, what should you do with that line, "I want us to be friends"? I mean, you did absolutely nothing except you stood there and said "I want to be friends"! A lot of people can stop you on 42and Street and say "I want to be friends," but you certainly are not going to follow them, dear. Are you? So there must be something else that you do, I mean, is it an embrace? Is it kneeling, is it sitting on the couch and calling her to you, is it wrapping a scarf around her? There are many things and it doesn't really matter what you pick. But the reason you need those physical things, at least for a while, is that they will make the scene much more informal for you.

I mean, you had that drink in your hand but you never drank it! How much more interesting if every time you were embarrassed you would be drinking a little bit more because you're upset because she's talking about Astrov. And [Sonya], you kept looking out the window! If I were her, I would grab your face and say, "Sweetheart, Sonya, stop looking out the window, it makes you appear crazy!" You kept looking out the window. Why, I don't know.

There are so many things! Why didn't you think about adjusting yourself on the sofa, why didn't you think of cuddling up, why didn't you think of just throwing your apron over your face while you talked, because you're blushing, why didn't you think of getting behind Yelena, and thinking, "you look so lovely I just wish I was as lovely as you are!" Why didn't you think of trying to start picking things up on a tray and running out with them? Now, what these things would do to you – they would not be gestures – they would give you constant activities. You could tickle each other, you could fix each other's hair, you can throw scarves around each other, you can pour more wine. You run to pour the wine because it's about to become exciting when [Sonya] says, "tell me something about him, would you please?"

Now, it is not for you, as an actress, to think that I want that line faster or slower, or with more this, or more that. To think about it that way makes it artificial. Instead, think of something that you want to *do* for her because she's going to tell you all the things about Astrov that you want to know. It'll make it more interesting for you if you run over here – run, pick up the bottle, and say, "Tell me

261

ɔmething about him." Do it right now.

[The actresses do a portion of the scene. Then Nikos stops the scene.] All right, this is good, but the last thing that somebody would do when they talk about the man they love, is an empty, little, pointing gesture to that sofa. I mean, the grabbing made sense because it requires the force, the vitality that is important. Now, do you see what you did, [Sonya]? You started that scene well, you ran on stage, but then you stopped and said your first line. If you had done it as you were running, rather than stopping – [Nikos acts this out.]

Our problem, always, is that we assume that we do not have demons to control, we really assume that we are there to talk and that we don't have to *earn* the right anew for somebody to be listening to us. And you earn that right only when you are creating situations on stage that deal with an overall life.

Even sitting on the sofa is not that interesting. I wish one of you was on the floor and the other on the sofa. I wish both of you would cuddle together, I wish both of you would start hitting each other. At the very end, Sonya, when you came back in to tell her she could not play the piano, you telegraphed it from the moment you came in, and then walked very slowly over to her. By the time you reached the piano, I said, "Oh, come on, please tell her, get it over with!" because I already knew a long time ago what you were going to say. Run to her, and then say the line! Or the two of you could've embraced each other, you could've started screaming, you could've shut the piano on your fingers.

Now, the reason we need those things is not to demonstrate visually what goes on emotionally, but because it is a scene about relationships, it's a scene about embraces, it's a scene about tears, it's a scene about handkerchiefs, where the words come in accidentally. So I'm not really saying, guys, in case of doubt, add props. What I'm really saying is that in case of doubt, find situations that make the conversations incidental and the life imperative. Well, look, it's really like the simple matter of singing in the shower. You know, I am told that people feel better singing in the shower. I don't really *know*, because I wouldn't do it! But people feel this, so they sing, and then the singing really becomes something else, because it's together with the water and the soap and whatever else, and it comes out in an accidental way.

It was very, very difficult, really, for the two of you, to make the scene exciting. You made the scene comfortable for yourselves, and I thought both of you were very appealing, as everybody said, and very attractive and honest with it. But you would not abdicate the rules, you would not give permission to yourself to get involved in a kind of situation where the lines would be incidental to the life.

So it became a discussion, rather than sharing secrets, complaining, crying, laughing, opening your souls. I don't know what your operative words were for the scene, but never make a scene about talking, make it always about something else. It would be wonderful if you made it a scene about two women getting drunk. You know what I mean? If you did that the scene would be wonderful because all the secrets would come out. Why do you think there are so many movies where two ladies go to the ladies room and put lipstick on together in front of the mirror? I mean, how many movies do you see about that? I just saw the play *The Women* in London, and that's all it was, they kept disappearing and gossiping, with a great sense of fun. Find, create for yourself the conditions where the lines are inevitable and possessed. They are inevitable, because silence is wrong for the situation, and possessed because they have a kind of a point of view that comes not from the text but from the situation.

The same thing when you went to play the piano, Yelena. You certainly could've looked through the music. Suppose the stool was too low, or you had to open the seat to find the old music that you didn't remember. Suppose you had to take off all your rings, your wedding rings, to play the piano and it became like taking off all your shackles, and your shawl comes off, as if you want to make yourself naked. Suppose the goddamn piano was dusty and you just kept dusting it and you thought you were taking all the dust from your soul! Because then you would create the conditions.

And you'll find out it happens all the time. In life it happens much, much more. I mean, I found out when I was doing *The Glass Menagerie*. I remember any time I would give notes, the first few days I started giving notes to Joanne Woodward she would go to a bouquet of flowers on the set and she would start cutting all the dead leaves, and after the fourth or fifth day, I realized what it was. I said, "Wait, don't get nervous now, don't play with the flowers, let me give you the notes." It was a kind of a thing she did that said, "Well I'm listening to the notes but it is not going to hurt me hearing the notes, because I can do this thing with the flowers." Everyone is constantly doing things in life that are connected to a whole psychological world, up to the time that you stop them and say, "Hey, wait, why are you doing that? Analyze yourself and tell me why you're doing this or that." But you must give yourself permission to do these things. In movies, where because the situations are often so drastic, you find out how much dialogue changes from the page to the screen. Because it is delivered in overblown situations. Add those things. Find the freedom to do those things.

When you say, "Let's become friends," let that play. That's a biggie. Let it play not as text, but in touching each other, embracing, dancing, sitting on the floor, throwing a couple of pillows at each other. I don't know, it can change every day, so don't think of these things as interpretive. And then the lines will come out fully. You see, what you don't want the audience to be able to do at the end of the scene is remember lines. Only in Shakespeare can you do that. The rest of the time, the more lines they forget from the text the better off you are. I mean the best thing would have been if the class had said, "Oh, the scene was about two women hugging each other." I mean even if a couple of people say it's a scene about two lesbians, that would be great, because that would mean you've done something that established another world. Or it can be that this is a scene about drinking, or two very silly, giggly people. But it should never be: "this is a scene about a woman who said this, and another woman who said that." You've got to forget the text in order to live it.

* * * * * * * * * * * * * * * * * *

Class Critique on Act III, a scene between Astrov and Yelena

Nikos talks here about the problem of making obvious choices that "underline" the text, resulting in behavior that is "symbolic" rather than organic. He encourages the actors to not "choreograph" their behavior, but to let it spring from the circumstances in the scene.

Synopsis of scene:
Sonya's unhappiness about her love for Astrov has led to Yelena's decision to confront him about his feelings for her step-daughter. She sends Sonya to fetch him. Left alone onstage, she talks about her own feelings for Astrov, her desire to escape from her marriage and her surroundings, and her guilt in knowing that Astrov has feelings for her rather than Sonya. Astrov comes in with some maps, thinking that Yelena has sent for him so that he can tell her about his hobby of charting the environmental decline of the region. But after holding forth on the subject at length he realizes Yelena has something else on her mind. Agitated, she starts her "little interrogation" and Astrov acknowledges that he has no romantic

feelings for Sonya. Yelena then asks him to stop coming to the house. He agrees, but confronts Yelena on the need for the "interrogation." Surely, he asks, she has already guessed his reasons for coming so often to their house – his love for her. He recklessly reveals this love now, begging her to meet him privately. She resists him, but they are on the verge of an embrace when Uncle Vanya, who has been out picking some flowers for Yelena, enters.

NIKOS I wish you [Astrov] were as carried away by the maps as you were carried away by the love for her. So that it becomes like, in *Candida*, when someone recites poetry to the person they love, or paints a picture for the person they love. His speech about the maps becomes the thing he does instead of saying, "I love you." It's not really avoidance, it's not really a substitution, it is a direct way of dealing energetically with loving her. It's the way great singers, like Frank Sinatra, sing. So that it becomes a kind of love-making through another medium. And I felt that was really needed because it would've given you something to hold onto, even though I felt your authority and simplicity was really wonderful.

Now, [Astrov] you have the line to her at the end of the speech, "You're not paying attention." You could've said this to her two or three times, and much, much earlier, because obviously she was going out of her way to tell us that she was not paying attention! [Yelena], you became a walking stage direction to justify his eventual line about your lack of interest in his maps. You don't have to be that obvious. And [Astrov], what I lost somehow was the sense that you are waiting for her to eventually get involved with this subject that you care about so much.

It's interesting how you both were not helping yourselves physically, by sitting back in the chairs. How much more interesting it would've been, when you say, [Yelena], "Now we have to talk," if you'd taken him to the couch because you really do want to talk rather than making it an interrogation. So that there would be an accessibility and an availability to it. You were leaning back, [Astrov] rather than leaning almost forward and saying, [with eagerness:] "Yeah," "Uh huh," "Yes." So from your physicality, I thought you both were holding yourselves back from dealing with the sort of things that control you, that overtake you. When the love came out all of a sudden, the grabbing and trying to kiss was interesting, but it was not as necessary as it should have been. As it would have been if you hadn't been so suspicious, if it had been – [Again, eagerly.] "You want to talk to me, what do you want to talk to me about, the maps? Oh, the maps," So that when you try to

265

describe these maps you get totally carried away by the sense of making love to her through your work.

There was such a cleanness to the scene in the beginning that was fascinating. But then you both, I think, really started getting very scared of the scene and going back to certain kinds of tricks you do. The tricks you do are really very peculiar because, for example, [Yelena], you gave yourself the freedom in the monologue at very beginning to do whatever you wanted to do with the speech. And yet you felt compelled to pick up the scarf that kept falling! So the fact that you have to maintain the scarf around your neck closes you in. You seem to have decided to lie across the table, but because that is very difficult acrobatically, it becomes choreographed, it becomes like a number. I mean, if you have to make decisions, don't decide *what* you're going to do, decide *why* you're going to do it. Decide to feel like running around, don't decide how you're going to run around, just run around! Roll all over the bed, jump up and down, decide things that would help your acting rather than things that tell us what your acting is. You block yourself emotionally that way, you were hurting yourself. You did one thing and then another and then you did something at the table and then the chair, and then the scarf – all these things were symbolic of freedom, rather than being the sort of things that come out of giving yourself permission, as an actress, actually to free yourself.

Now, you established four to five times, you made it clear that you were not interested in his material. That is not what she would do! What she would certainly do is try to be interested and find out she's not interested. That is the acting task. The acting task is not for you to make clear for us his line, "Oh, I can see you're not interested." It is justified. Since that line was coming up, you were trying from the very beginning to justify that line. The fact that he can see that you are not interested doesn't mean that we should all see it and should see it so far in advance, because then it becomes ludicrous.

Same thing with the chair, [Yelena]. You sat down to avoid him, and yet you kept turning your head away from him and not looking at him, but he could have come in closer to you and done whatever he wanted to do. You dealt with the idea of indignation rather than "Don't come closer to me!" Now, when someone says, "Don't come closer to me," they don't go and sit the way you did on that sofa! So, it was kind of coy – and also it's theatrical. You associate the business you come up with on stage with a certain theatrical elegance, with theatrical gestures, and that's not why people do business on stage. You do business up on the stage to make you feel closer to the kind of feeling you want to have when you're really living the scene. You kept contradicting yourself in the scene because you dealt with freedom, and then you would give yourself tasks that required regimentation. You dealt with danger, yet your behavior was theatrical, not frightening. You didn't go against a wall, you did not start backing up from him, you didn't allow this scene to be dangerous for yourself.

I guess I wish, [Yelena], that you would allow the speech to happen while you're talking. I mean, you are upset about Sonya, and you are worrying about your own life. Now you were dealing many times with what you were *realizing* in the speech rather than what you were trying to find out. And when you realize something and then state it emotionally or verbally, you're in trouble because then the words become idle. The words become idle because you're not trying to actually find something out with the text. When you were walking up and down it helped because –   *N.4*

ACTRESS That was the only part of that monologue that I felt comfortable with because it was the only thing that sort of came...

NIKOS That is because you gave yourself a chance to walk with no purpose, which gave you a feeling that "I'm trying to find out what it's all about." But the rest of it, you were like a text that is underlined. When you said the part about being a mermaid, you did something with your feet...then you went to the table on the next line...but that was a kind of difficult thing to do, it really was. You turned away in a very peculiar way, you were doing a lot things that were like, mildly theatrical, and I think you have to watch that. I thought the simplicity improved, but you're doing things that say you want us to know that you understand something about the script, rather than dealing with the openness of the text which is – [Loosely, inarticulately.] "I'd like to ask you something, I don't know how I'm going to ask it, it doesn't really matter, I'm just going to ask something." And then, you'll see, it becomes far more involving for you.

If we had a film of what you just did, you'd find out that you really love to do things when somebody else is talking. You know? Every time [Astrov] was doing anything you were registering little opinions: "Yes." "No." "Maybe." "This is what I feel about this." "This is what I feel about that." So it's as if you distrust the life of the scene. Because, let me tell you, nobody's going to look at you at that particular moment, you know? Or if they look at you they should really be thinking of him anyway which means that listening

267

is an extremely important part of your work. You seem to be programmed to be acting in your own way, independent of him. And I thought that because of that, you were eager to register your reaction to things before he even did them.

I think, once again, what we saw here today was just too much acting! A lot of acting. Divide it into blocks, divide it into units, divide it into chapters rather than into words. I thought it was good that your voice sounded much more real than I have heard it, and certain moments in the scene showed your progress as an actress. But in between you put in little things, little acting doodles, so I got lost. When actors put in little sounds in between the words, you know, sounds of laughter, sounds of tears, or even little words like, "huh" or "um" and you just say, "What's going on?" Because these little, parenthetical bits of acting are going on all over the place, we lose what's going on in the scene.

Be less reverent. Kind of try to say to yourself, "Oh, it's really not that great being up there and the sooner I do it the better I feel." I mean, you're just reluctant to stop acting, so you act all sorts of things between the acting that the playwright gives you.

ACTRESS When I first started to work on the monologue, I worked strictly on the emotional content of it – and then it was very bland. I mean, not bland, it was emotional, but then I also wanted to do certain business, so I felt like I also had to direct it. I tried to direct it and then stand back and get to the emotion...

NIKOS I'm not sure why you do that. You could have done the business or not done the business but the speech is not going to make it because of that! I guess what I'm saying is that if you're going to put in business, put in business that helps your feeling rather than that demonstrates your ability to understand the text. Do less. You really do two to three things in every moment rather than just one, and that hurts you. Do it more directly, deal with it more openly.

[Astrov] for you too, it would have been good if you'd found, physically, some position when you go to her, you know, throwing yourself on the couch, or on your knees, it would be great to find some ways to help you physically define the objective. And I suggest that you have the maps in three different places so it's not so regimented, so that you can move the speech with more freedom.

Louis Zorich (Lopakhin), Tom Brennan (Trofimov) and company of "The Cherry Orchard", 1963

Notes on
THE CHERRY ORCHARD

*"What's turned out isn't a drama, but a comedy, in places
even a farce..."*

Chekhov, letter to M.P. Alexeyeva,
Sept. 15, 1903

Notes on Act I, a scene between Anya and Varya

Synopsis of scene:
It is almost three o'clock in the morning when Anya, her mother
and their companions return to their home in Russia from a trip to
Paris. Anya tells her adopted sister Varya all about the trip, and
Varya tells Anya that since the debts of the estate have not been
paid, it is up for sale. In the middle of this, Lopakhin pokes his head
in the room, "moos" like a cow and exits. Varya tells Anya that the
proposal of marriage she was expecting from him still hasn't come.

NIKOS Just find things that, by reacting and responding to them,
you can create acting from. As I think I've said many times, you go
into the scene by having a portmanteau, you have a suitcase, and you
pick up certain things to wear and you wear them. I don't mean
literally, I mean figuratively. You pick up things like: "angry at this
person," "desperately in love with this person," "possessed by this
person." You pick up things that make you respond, and usually they
are in the text. Things like: "Everytime I see red, I get furious,"
"Everytime I hear loud music, I scream," "Everytime I eat this, I get
silly," "Everytime somebody mentions the word joy, I jump." You
take clues, you take things and you bring them with you on stage so
that when the other person does something, you get to respond.

Anya switches topics sixteen times in this scene – so the lines must
be incidental to something else. Deal with the circumstances: Anya
has been away for months in Paris, and when she comes home, her
clothes are different, her hair is different, the tea she drinks tastes
differently to her because she's become used to tea in Paris and not
at home! Don't deal with tiredness. To do something you must want
to do something, find all the things Anya wants to do, having not
been home for all this time. Find the things in the circumstances of
the scene that feed your acting... It is the set of particular

271

circumstances that gives you the character.

* * * * * * * * * * * * * * * * * *

Notes on Act III, a scene between Ranevskaya and Trofimov

Synopsis of scene:
It is evening on the day of the auction of the estate, and Ranevskaya is anxiously waiting for Lopakhin and her brother to return with news of whether or not the estate has been sold. Guests fill the house for a party and a little band is playing off-stage. In this scene with Trofimov, the tutor of her dead son, Ranevskaya expresses both her desperation about the sale of the cherry orchard and her longing and need to be with the man she left behind in Paris. Trofimov bluntly denigrates the man she loves and encourages her to face the truth about him. Ranevskaya responds by attacking Trofimov's lack of direction and manliness, calling him a prig and a nincompoop. As Ranevskaya tries to apologize, Trofimov becomes agitated, runs out of the room and falls down the steps.

NIKOS Don't ask for just one thing in Chekhov, ask for so much more than the other person can give. If you adapt yourself so totally to the other person's needs, then you have no personality! You both were too available, you both were connecting with one need instead of a lot of need. Find ways of *not* finding ways to finish the emotional work. If your needs can be fulfilled, there's no scene.

Find what you touch back to as the center of your world and then go back to it every other moment. Go back, touch it, and then come up with the lines. Touch it again and then go back to the lines. "I need you, let's do this," "I need you, let's drink." "I need you, why are you going?" "I need you, I want some tea." If you see everything in relationship to that center, then you are okay. If you don't, then you seem to move randomly over the territory of the play. And the fact that you constantly change your work from one moment to the next shows that you don't depend on anything. And therefore you have no right to act, because you're *creating* your own acting rather than the acting *emerging* subconsciously out of your needs, needs which cannot be completely justified, clarified, fulfilled in your own way or someone else's. A constant adaptation to the stimulus of the play without a center makes you lose your life, your personality, your needs, and makes the work a kind of social statement, rather than a real one.

There is a great sense of frivolity to this scene. Life catches up

272

with you and you ridicule yourself. You have to allow yourself to go very high and very low. These are people who take their feelings and elevate them and manipulate them but finally the feelings catch up with them and take them to unexpected places. And then, allow the distractions to come in, the distractions of life, deal with what life brings you in the middle of all that's going on inside. It's as if Chekhov brings something almost Chaplinesque to this! It requires the emotional ability to drop one thing and pick up another and go any which way – but, underneath, your great need is still there. Break the parts of each scene up and rehearse them separately and you'll find that.

NSA

* * * * * * * * * * * * * * * * *

Notes on Act IV, a scene between Lopakhin and Trofimov

"The last act will be joyful, just as the entire play is happy and frivolous."

Chekhov (Letters)

Synopsis of scene:

This scene in Act IV takes place on the day that the family prepares for their final departure from the estate. Lopahkin, who has bought the house and orchard, and the student, Trofimov, say good-bye to each other, and attempt to express how they feel about each other. Lopahkin tries to give Trofimov money, which he doesn't accept. Trofimov makes a lofty speech about the future of mankind and in the distance there is the sound of an ax striking a tree in the cherry orchard.

NIKOS The emotional promise in Chekhov is always greater than the text. In this scene there is a lack of fulfillment, so don't fulfill your tasks as actors. Look for the things that aren't said. You both played the logical conversation between the two of them rather than all that is unsaid.

Think of things, as actors, to try that the play will never let you get to, but nonetheless your heart or your imagination compels you to try, rather than making choices that will succeed because of the inevitablity of what is in the scene itself. If you succeed too easily in realizing the scene as written, then we get a scene that feels like it's been spelled out with alphabet blocks.

All the short scenes Chekhov writes are really fourteen little scenes rather than one. At the end of this scene these characters make

273

a great effort to communicate, but the maladjustment is that they are unable to reach a relationship. The scene is about the inability to communicate on a simple level because you want to deal with the person on another level, a deeper level. So the acting springs out of little moments but then gets smothered. Work for the sense of the inner conflict: "my mind is so much against my soul," or "my intellect gets in my way." Select four of the ten or twenty things you want to be dealing with and let them play. The primary circumstance of the scene – that it is a departure – colors all your choices.

* * * * * * * * * * * * * * * * * *

Olympia Dukakis on Playing Lyuba Ranevskaya

"No, I never wanted to make Ranevskaya into someone who had calmed down. Death alone can calm such a woman... It is not difficult to act Ranevskaya. All you've got to do is to strike the right note from the outset; think up a smile and a manner of laughing and know how to dress."

Chekhov, letter to Olga Knipper
Oct. 25, 1903

JEAN A lot of these women are emotionally reckless aren't they? Lyuba, Arkadina –

OLYMPIA Yes. Lyuba Ranevskaya is trying not to be reckless, until that moment where she says, "I love him." She gets reckless. This recklessness is like a motor inside, it's a danger motor, it's going to create danger for people around them and for themselves.

JEAN In the scene in Act III between Lyuba and Petya, she says "You should be making love." She finds his vulnerability and uses it against him. And Arkadina does the same thing to her son in *The Sea Gull*. They say the dangerous things that come out when we lose control with people who are very close to us.

OLYMPIA Well, we want to hurt them.

JEAN Again, there's a reckless lashing out that both of these women do.

OLYMPIA Well, what's great about it is that it's *part* of it. Chekhov
274

doesn't say, that's only what the person is. In other plays a character would have that one trait, that lashing out, let's say, and they would be only that. Here, they have that, and so much else. The fact is that Lyuba's name means "love"! That's it! The woman is that.

JEAN I didn't see you in *The Cherry Orchard*, but I was in the production with Colleen Dewhurst. And I remember one moment, that actually Colleen didn't want to do. It was in the Act I scene when Lyuba sees Trofimov, her dead son's tutor, for the first time in many years. And Nikos directed her to go to him when she first saw him and slap him in the face. Was that something you did when you did the role?

OLYMPIA No, I didn't do that. That's very interesting, though. That is very interesting! What's interesting about that is that Petya is one of the people who was responsible for her son – if I ever play it again, I'm going to try that. It's so unreasonable! That's what so great, it's so – contradictory. It's so hard for that woman to be unkind, so doing that for her would be extraordinary. And would she pay for that! She would pay for having done that. Which would be great because that would really feed the scene between the two of them in Act III. Already, just hearing you tell me that, it's very exciting! What I did was – I played that I – I recognized him and the feeling about my son came up right away and I went away from him. I didn't want that. Then Anya came and said, "It's Petya, Petya." And I didn't want to go to him. But there may have been anger, too. I didn't want to go to him, but then I permitted myself to go, and then I rejected him.

JEAN Here's Ranevskaya's monologue in the second act – read through it, and then, if you will, tell me what it brings up for you.

OLYMPIA [As Ranevskaya]
Oh, my sins, my sins – I've always thrown money around like a lunatic, recklessly, and I married a man who had a genius for debt. My husband drank himself to death on champagne – he was always drunk – and then, to my misfortune, I fell in love with another man. We had an affair and just at that time, it came – it was my first punishment – a blow straight to my heart. Right here in this river my son Grisha, my beautiful little boy, was drowned – I ran away and went abroad – never to return, never to see this river again – I just shut my eyes and ran away in a frenzy of grief. But he – he followed me – mercilessly, brutally. I bought a

275

villa near Mentone because he fell ill there, you see, and for three years I had to nurse him and knew no rest day or night. The sick man exhausted me, my soul dried up. And last year, when the villa had to be sold to pay our debts, I fled to Paris and there he robbed me, and left me for another woman. I tried to poison myself – it was all so stupid, so shameful – And then suddenly I was seized with a longing for Russia, for my own country, for my little girl – Lord, Lord, have mercy on me, forgive my sins! Don't punish me anymore! I got a telegram today from Paris, he asks my forgiveness, begs my return...do I hear music somewhere?

What I realized the last time I did that part – hopefully I'll get to do it again – is how funny that scene is, as well as touching.

That whole scene, the three of them, Lyuba, her brother Gayev and Lopakhin, are walking together and Lopahkin's trying to get her to pay attention to what's going on with her estate. The first time I played it I was trying to avoid him, and then the second time I realized, no, no she loves him! He would talk and she would listen, and say, "Yes, yes," And he would say, "What are you going to do?" and she'd just throw her arms up! She doesn't ignore him, she takes him in and enjoys him, almost. She's never rude to him, never unkind. This is a woman who is never unkind. If she's not downright loving, she's kind. She'd never hurt a single person's feelings – which is part of her problem, that she and her brother are so refined.

Pishchik comes in and asks for money at the end, and she has nothing, but if she could get her hands on money she'd give him money! So in this Act II scene, basically, she knows Lopahkin is trying to help her. His solutions are gauche, but he is trying to help her. She actually thinks about his solution to her financial problems and she realizes she'd be betraying her family to do what he wants. So she keeps thinking something else will come, some other solution will happen, they'll think of something. Something always did. Somebody always took care of it. Something always happened.*

JEAN And this time it just doesn't.

OLYMPIA No. The clock is ticking, that clock is ticking. And the place where she really needs to live, which is with her lover, is in her heart. But here she is, roaming around, coping with the loss of her child. And in that monologue, she goes back to that place, that moment, when it all changed. Somehow if that hadn't happened, her

*Reprinted by permission of the Nikos Psacharopoulos estate.

life would've been different. So the line, "Oh, my sins, my sins." is not only about the son. To think of that as her having a reverie and mourning for the son isn't active enough. I think she sees it in a context, that's the moment when it all turned, if only that hadn't happened. "If only, somehow, I'd been there, or fate had been different, or I'd been able to stop that, everything that followed that would've been different."

JEAN So she's trying to make sense of it?

OLYMPIA This is what's so great about Chekhov. At that moment she talks about her son, but it is in the context of her life. You cannot just make it about the son, you have to bring the whole context. The moment has to exist in the context. It seems like that's complicated, why isn't it just about what she's saying? Because that's not the situation she's in. The situation she's in is that she's been talking all day long and thinking about how to solve the problem about the estate. They've been out for a long lunch, they've been talking and talking and the only thing they can come up with is that she has to sell the land, and she can't bring herself to do it. There should be, I think, a moment or two when you think she might bring herself to do it. Because otherwise, why would Lopakhin stay there? He's got to feel that someplace she's tempted. You've got to feel that.

The person who has really turned off, in regard to his ability to manage life, is her brother, Gayev. She sees that. She's different from her brother, she sees she has to do something. And she also sees that her brother is getting upset and she has to handle that too. That's what's so wonderful. If you go in with just one thing, you stop the fabric. You've got to always weave into all of this fabric that's there. The situation has all these elements that are woven into it, and at certain points one thread emerges and then the other. At certain moments she wants to forget about it, and at other moments she wants to deal with it. And other moments she sees what her brother is doing and recognizes that they can't do it that way, time is running out, and that's exactly what happens in Act II. Someone comes in and says, "My friends, the sun is setting." And then you hear that strange vibration, that noise, of something ominous. And time is running out – that's not the whole scene; the whole scene is not about her awareness of time, but there are moments when that bombs in! So you have to play all of that, it rips like that. Themes come in and down and back and accommodate and adjust. It's incredible to play it, it's like doing jazz. It's got to be what it's like to play jazz.

Entire company of "The Three Sisters", 1987

Notes on
THE THREE SISTERS

"Describe at least one rehearsal of "Three Sisters" for me. Isn't there anything which needs adding or subtracting? Are you acting well, my darling? But watch out now! Don't pull a sad face in the first act. Serious, yes, but not sad. People who had long carried a grief within themselves and have become accustomed to it only whistle and frequently withdraw into themselves. So you can often be thoughtfully withdrawn on stage during conversations. Do you see?"

Chekhov, letter to Olga Knipper,
Jan. 2, 1901

Notes on Act II, a scene between Masha and Vershinin

Synopsis of scene:
   This short scene in Act II between Masha and Vershinin takes place in the early evening on the night of the Carnival. They enter the room in mid-conversation, each of them expressing in general terms their own personal dissatisfaction with their marriages and their lives. At the end of the scene, Vershinin confesses to Masha that he loves her.

NIKOS   In the first act, Masha reads a book and whistles and doesn't talk. In the second act she's talking. The fact that she's talking is more important than what she's saying. In the third act, what she *says* is important. And in the fourth act, she goes back to not talking. As with all of Chekhov, the lines need one strong thing happening underneath. One strong need. Practice putting all the lines in the scene together in the form of a monologue, so that you find your emotional through line, so that the life underneath bubbles up.
   Don't set up the scene as if it is a difficult task for them to talk to each other – those lines become easy for them to say. Vershinin and Masha want to talk to each other, want to be with each other. When you want to talk, you don't worry about what you're saying! Don't protect yourself. When the inspiration does not come you use the

279

craft by prolonging the words or slowing down.

Find within yourself something in the scene that you're dying to be involved with. From the love of conversation comes the love of acting, the love of acting really comes out of the love of of being involved. Find the one thing you're dying to be involved with that goes underneath and then you'll no longer worry *how* to do the scene.

BLYTHE DANNER   I remember this scene very well. Nikos told me to come in and play the grand dame. He said, "you're just putting it on ever so slightly. And it's part little girl and part grand dame." He wanted me to be very colorful in the scene. I remember using my hands very expressively, and sort of curling up and being coy and hitting all those notes you go for when you're infatuated with someone. That kind breathiness and that sort of titillation of being turned on by somebody. And before that, in Act I, we only see Masha being very brooding and sad. I remember being afraid that what I was doing in this scene wouldn't be real because it was so different from the Masha we see in the first Act, the one that's so enshackled, and unhappy. But then it becomes clear that because this man is so attractive to her, he just brings out everything that bespeaks life in her. Things that have been dormant or maybe things that have never been there before at all!

I was very self-conscious at first because I thought I was being excessive! With Masha, I worked on deepening my voice and getting down to a register I'd never used, but when I got to this scene I think my voice was trilling, musical. And I knew that Vershinin liked me and that my body moved in ways he liked. Nikos had us sitting on a chaise, so that was sort of smart too. You didn't see Masha going from a very settled, somber kind of stance in the scene before to someone who was flying around the stage. He kept me bound to something solid like the chaise. I think I even lay down on it. Nikos told me to use the chaise, to make love to it – in an evasive kind of way, to make love to Vershinin through that. A coiling, uncoiling kind of thing. To touch the chaise in the ways I subconsciously wanted to touch him.

In her first speech in this scene, you see that the pattern of her speech is not linear. She's obviously excited and not talking quite logically. That's why Chekhov's so brilliant, it's right there in the words. She confesses her entire life very personally to this man, and then she says, "Of course, I'm not talking about my husband." Another line that was humorous that you wouldn't necessarily think

280

humorous – the line "but with civilians there's such a lot of coarse, vulgar, unpleasant and offensive people." Nikos had me do that as, you know, "Let them eat cake!" It was very Marie Antoinette. It had nothing to do with an honest, dour reflection. It was very funny.

I was talking to my best and oldest friend who's been to Russia a lot, she's a Quaker who's done a lot of work with Russians. And she says what's incredible about the Russians, is that they talk about the soul and about suffering in ways that are so charming and so funny, with so many colors. They can talk about these things quite easily, in a way that Americans can't.

Like this line which is so wonderful – "Do you hear the noise in the chimney?" It's just so human and real. That in the middle of a deep conversation, someone's confessing something to someone else, and then: [Whispers.] "Just listen to that noise in the chimney!" See, this was the wonderful thing about Nikos, he understood these moments. A lot of people might direct this with a pause, an awkward pause, not knowing what to say.

JEAN You're talking about the moment before the line, "Just listen to the chimney noise."

BLYTHE Yes. I mean Vershinin's being so intimate, and he's almost made a confession to her, he says, "I have nobody to talk to but you." And she says, "Just listen to the chimney noise. Just before father died the wind howled in the chimney." There. Just like that. Nikos didn't want me to make a transition before that. It wasn't like, "Oh my Gosh, what do I say to this?" And I don't know what to say, pause, pause, pause: "Just listen to the chimney noise." And that would be the expected thing to do, because directors try to make it logical. But it's not a logical moment! I think it was just that Masha might be ready to come back with, "Isn't that funny, I feel the same thing about you." But because it's so powerful, she can't say that. So she just sort of jumps in with something else.

JEAN I did this scene in class, and I had no idea what to do with that line. And Nikos said something like, "Look, it's very simple. The last time that something really big happened to her, when her father died, the wind howled in the chimney. And now it's happening again!" And that makes so much sense because Vershinin's next line is: "Are you superstitious?"

BLYTHE Yes, and it's funny! I think this line always got a laugh, too, "It's lighter here." I mean it's certainly all there in the writing and yet because he is such a brilliant playwright he leaves so much

281

open to interpretation. A lesser playwright would've filled in the spaces. Then, that's great, Masha has the line, "Somehow I can't help laughing," because the way we did it there was laughter from the beginning of the scene almost. She's intoxicated, with a feeling she's never felt before. None of it was pre-planned, it all just came out like a wellspring. This whole scene was just effortless to play because it was two people who had all this emotion pent up and it came out in giddiness. It's a giddy scene, at least on Masha's part.

* * * * * * * * * * * * * * * * * *

Notes on Act III, a scene between Olga, Masha and Irina

"My darling girl, Masha's confession in Act III is not in the least confession-like, but only a frank conversation. Deliver it nervously, but not despairingly. Don't shout, smile from time to time, but most importantly deliver it so as to convey a sense of the night's fatigue. Also to convey a feeling that you're more intelligent than your sisters, or at least you consider yourself so."

Chekhov, letter to Olga Knipper,
Jan. 21,1901

Synopsis of scene:
This scene takes place in the middle of the night, in Olga and Irina's bedroom. Somewhere nearby a fire has been blazing and Olga is sorting through clothes to give to the victims, many of whom are now at the sisters' home. The chain of circumstances that leads up to the scene between the three of them includes their sister-in-law Natasha abusing Anfisa, their beloved nanny; the long-sober doctor becoming drunk and confessing to killing a patient, and the realization that their brother, Andrei, has mortgaged the house to cover his gambling debts. Irina breaks down and cries to Olga that she now believes they will never achieve their dream of going to Moscow; Olga tries to comfort her and convince her to marry Tusenbach, at the same time confessing the loss of her own dream of happiness. In the midst of this, Natasha crosses through the room with a candle prompting Masha to break her silence and confess to her sisters that she loves Vershinin.

282

NIKOS In Russian plays nobody is trying to take over someone else's feelings, no one is trying to question or doubt those feelings. It's a very American response to diminish or doubt someone's feelings – in the Russian plays feelings are encouraged. Masha's confession here is in response to Irina and Olga's emotion. She wants to get in on it. Natasha crosses with the candle and this makes it possible for Masha to open up, Natasha is the outsider who brings the three of them closer.

Chekhov is not the place to do all the acting between lines. The speech liberates something for Masha, and you must use the speech to let loose, don't put your acting in the moments in between.

I always think that nobody should sit in the third act of *Three Sisters*. Of course, people do sit from time to time, but it should feel like nobody ever sits."

BLYTHE DANNER I remember hating this scene because I thought everybody had an aria and mine was the last one to come and I always waited for it with dread. I think there was something in the staging, it was the only place that I really disagreed with Nikos. We were in some kind of a tableau. It was like we were under a spotlight and I felt like an opera singer. And I know he wanted us all to be facing out towards the audience – well, maybe they weren't, but I was. And we were in this tableau, this picture he had in his mind. We never experimented with this one much. And you know, he could be autocratic at times, and maybe I didn't have the guts to say, "let this one fly." Maybe because everyone else felt content with it and I didn't like to make waves, contrary to what people say! But every so often it seemed like Nikos would just have an image in mind, maybe from the last production or whatever, but here I felt that he didn't want to explore an alternative. But probably I wasn't thinking about it right, I wasn't thinking of it as a scene, I was thinking of it as an aria. Irina and Olga were the duet and I came in as the cello at the end.

JEAN Would you read it through for me?

BLYTHE [As Masha.]
   "...I want to confess, my dear sisters, I feel so terribly depressed. There is something I want to get off my chest. I'll tell you everything, and after that I'll never breathe a word of it again, not to anyone. It's my secret, but you share it. I

283

can't keep it to myself any longer. I love, I love that man. You saw him here just now. Well there it is. In a word, I love Vershinin...

"...But what can I do? At first I found him strange, then I started feeling sorry for him, and finally I began to love him, his voice, his words, his misfortunes, his two little girls...

"...Oh, Olga, you are the silly one. If I love him, it is because it is my fate to do so. That's my lot in life – and he loves me too. Frightening isn't it? Wrong? Oh my dear, we live through our lives somehow, but what will become of us? When we read a novel, it all seems so stale and obvious, but then we fall in love ourselves, and we begin to see that nobody knows anything, and each one of us has to make up his own mind. My darlings, my sisters, I've told you everything and now I'll be silent like Gogol's madman. Silence, silence..." *

He insisted that this speech be big, that it build and climax, maybe that's why I think of it as an aria. In other words, he didn't want any kind of method stuff kind of going here, where you're sort of going to it and then backing off a bit. And I felt insecure about exploring it because this was one he heard in a certain way. Or I never could prove to him that an alternative was acceptable. I think probably in the context of the whole play, he was right about this being the climax – but that's the only time we ever really had blow-ups; The same thing happened when we did the Gorky, *Children of the Sun*, when he would insist on something being almost operatic, you know: very, very large. And if we couldn't fill it we would just sort of be hanging there, we would be the ones having the egg on our faces because we couldn't fill what he wanted. I think the only time I ever really screamed at him was then.

Reprinted by permission of the Nikos Psacharopoulos estate.

Blythe Danner (Nina), Frank Langella (Treplev) in "The Sea Gull," 1974

Notes on
THE SEA GULL

"Well, sir, I have finished my play. I began it forte and wound it up pianissimo – contrary to all the precepts of dramatic art. The end product was a novella. I am more dissatisfied than satisfied and, while reading my new-born play, I became convinced once more that I am no dramatist..."

Chekhov

The following are excerpts from an article called *The Experience of Directing* by Jem Winer for *The New Journal* (New Haven), February 14, 1975.

NJ How did this production for television come about?

NIKOS *The Sea Gull*...was a good choice for me, because Chekhov adapts to television well; he never writes about something or someone you can't see. You just need an exterior and an interior set. Can you imagine *Our Town* on television? It wouldn't work. With *The Sea Gull* I didn't have to keep it a play or make it a movie but could just make it be Chekhov on TV.

NJ How did you go about casting it?

NIKOS I cast the people I like, and I cast them for the Williamstown stage, not for television. Emotional range is primary, since they're all professionals, you assume the vocal and physical range.

NJ How was the actual stage performance?

NIKOS There were some problems. We only rehearsed about two weeks and four days. It's never enough, though people exaggerate how much time you need. Lee Grant had difficulties getting an idea of her aura, the characterization of Arkadina in Moscow. There were also a lot of battles. Lee had thought she was going to relax, enjoy a vacation and her art, and then 37 reviewers came up...

NJ Did the film version change any of the performances?

NIKOS Lee was better on TV than she was on stage where she was too undisciplined. All the others were more or less the same.

NJ Were there any difficulties in the actual filming?

NIKOS We only had five and a half days...the last day we worked twenty-five hours straight. At least the last three hours were pure hell...We ended up relighting the entire play and added special effects. For example, when I had a close-up of Blythe at the beginning we colored the film just a shade pink.

NJ Did you re-shoot many scenes?

NIKOS We shot one line of Blythe's fourteen times to get the right effect. But Act IV was done in one take. We used three cameras most of the time. Usually, when you're selecting shots from the truck, a red light goes on in the camera that is filming. So the actor ends up knowing which of the three cameras is taking his picture. I asked the camera men, "Is there any way that they won't know?" They said, "Yes, if you put the cameras in isolation." Which we did, leaving me to work on it later, taking the time in the editing room. It's not the best way.

NJ Why?

NIKOS It drives you bananas. Especially with tape. I did learn a lot about the medium, when to use close-ups...the rhythm of editing... But the real work was done with the actors.

NJ Were you unhappy with any of the performances?

NIKOS I could not do what I wanted with Trigorin, so often I would cut back to Nina. I tried to get Trigorin to have more urgency on camera... But his characterization was bland, too mushy. He had done it before and never moved away from his earlier performance.

NJ How do you go about directing a play?

NIKOS I read it, then I put it away for a while. I think about it, let it happen to me in my mind. Then I form my ideas...

ND',

NJ Do you tell your actors how you want to do a play?

NIKOS I just let them act. I don't say anything until they say something. It's much better to let the actors develop. You guide them; it's anthologizing, putting them in the right direction.

NJ Have you seen any productions you have especially liked or disliked in the past few years?

NIKOS I really loved Olivier's *Uncle Vanya* in England. It was beautiful. It found what was contemporary in the material. And also Peter Brook's *A Midsummer Night's Dream*, which was most inventive. The worst thing modern directors do is impose things on material...to invent, before you take the time to discover, is dangerous. You don't mix up chemical ingredients unless you first identify them and discover their properties.

* * * * * * * * * * * * * * * * * *

Notes on Act III, a scene between Arkadina and Treplev

"Can you imagine, I'm writing a play which I'll probably not complete before the end of November. I'm writing it not without pleasure, although I offend dreadfully against stage conventions. It's a comedy with three female and six male roles, four acts, a landscape (view of a lake), lots of talk about literature, little action and 180 lbs. of love."
                                        Chekhov, letter to A.S. Suvorin,
                                                        Oct. 21, 1895

Synopsis of scene:
    Treplev, because of his jealousy of his mother's lover, Trigorin, has made a half-hearted attempt at suicide – he tried to shoot himself, but the bullet merely grazed his temple. In this scene he asks his mother to change his bandage. While she does so, he relates to her lovingly, bringing up remembrances of the past, but soon the talk turns back into a heated argument about Trigorin.

NIKOS This is a scene where you don't want to quarrel but eventually quarrel. They are asking things of each other. A side of her wants to change the bandage but the other side doesn't. Very often in Chekhov there is this tension between the contradictory inner aims of the characters. She's not saying to him, "Please be

289

okay, because I love you." She is saying to him, "I have to continue my life, so please be okay."

It's amazing the way it really happens in life – if someone starts doing something, you get upset, you say, "wait, wait, wait" or you get elated, or whatever. That is because you have a blueprint of life within you which the other person doesn't know. So if they connect with the magic word, something happens to you and if they don't connect with the magic word, something does not. I felt you both were missing a sense of how much we react in life to those magic words.

The trick of this scene is the length of the bandage. You have to practice physical things over and over in order for them to work. Chekhov scenes can be so easy if they are fully explored in terms of reality. Props have to be consciously worked out with the lines.

* * * * * * * * * * * * * * * * * * *

Notes on Act IV, a scene between Nina and Treplev

Synopsis of scene:
Act IV takes place two years later than the first three acts, on a cool autumn evening. Dorn, the doctor, has summoned Arkadina back to the estate because of her brother's illness. Treplev, who has begun to achieve some success as a writer, his uncle and several others wait for Arkadina and Trigorin to arrive. We learn that Nina, too, has recently come home, and that the past two years have not been kind to her. Her affair with Trigorin ended disastrously, a child she bore has died, and as an actress she's achieved only marginal success. Arkadina and Trigorin arrive; Treplev and Trigorin agree to forget the past, but Treplev shuns his family when they go into dinner and stays at his desk, trying to write. At this moment Nina appears, distraught. Treplev, still desperately in love with her, tries to convince her to stay with him. Nina, unstable, and realizing that Trigorin is in the next room, struggles to find her strength, and identifies herself as "a seagull." At the end of the scene, Treplev tears up his work, goes out of the room and shoots himself.

NIKOS   If Treplev can free himself by crying, he'll never kill himself. Focus on her, deal with her emotions. Treplev keeps making attempts to solve certain things for Nina in the scene and never succeeds. The scene is really about when we try to do something for someone but everything we try to do is so silly and so

290

inadequate.

Nina comes in with fifteen myths which are temporary realities for her and she relishes each one. Play against the text – Blythe's best moments were when she tried to smile – "If you give me water, everything's going to be okay." But it's not okay. "If we talk about acting I won't cry," – but it doesn't work, she starts to cry anyway. Nina tries to solve her problem by saying things like, "Come and see me when I'm a great actress," but none of these things work. She comes in with a great tiredness, but it's like the tiredness at a tech rehearsal – you're so tired that you have a certain kind of energy to avoid the problems.

This one scene is actually 16 different scenes. It involves Nina both having an image of him, of what she wants him to be, and an image of the way she wants the scene with him to go. These are the circumstances: she has totally changed from what she was, she's been running through the woods, it's raining, the room she comes into is totally changed. She was an innocent that last time she was in this house and now perhaps she's slept with many different people, she's lost her illusions about acting. And before she comes in, she thinks, "I don't want to get emotional," or "I don't want to think about Trigorin or the baby." And everything goes against the plan. "I've rehearsed this just the way I want it to go," – but things just keep coming up, reminders, life, takes her away from her plan.

Nina wants to rewrite the emotional fabric of the scene. You have to come in like you're ready to play the kind of scene you can't play. This makes it much more exciting. She tries to *remember* throughout the scene, remember the things that will shore her, that will help her, she keeps *trying* to remember, but it's – "I can't remember, this doesn't work, that doesn't work, none of these things work for me anymore."

It's a selfish scene about two people needing something that the other can't possibly deliver. She wants help and, again and again, he's not the one who can give it. Rehearse the scene as two monologues, instead of servicing each other as actors. It doesn't matter what you say in the scene or in which order you say it because they are both in their own worlds.   *technique*

Make demands on yourself and your partner, find things that the other person cannot possibly come through with. Set your tasks as actors and then don't worry about how it comes out. Don't worry about the *shape* of your emotional expression. Just trust that it's going to work, and the emotion will come.

Christopher Walken (Ivanov), Laila Robins (Sasha) in "Ivanov," 1983

Notes on
IVANOV

"Contemporary dramatists stuff their plays with angels, scoundrels and fools exclusively – try and find these elements in the whole of Russia! You may find some but not in the extreme forms which dramatists seem to find necessary. I wanted to be original and not bring on a single villain, or a single angel (although I couldn't keep out the fools)..."

Chekhov, letter to his brother Alexander,
October 23, 1887

In the critique of this scene, Nikos explores the moment-to-moment acting work necessary for playing Chekhov as well as the importance of filtering the acting choices through a need that is central to the character.

Synopsis of scene:
Throughout the first two acts of the play, Ivanov feels depressed and despondent with his life and with his marriage without really knowing why. In Act III – just as his wife's doctor is accusing him of killing his wife, Anna, with his blatant, adulterous behavior – Sasha, the young neighbor he has become infatuated with, arrives at his house. It has been two weeks since Anna stumbled on Sasha and Ivanov embracing. Since he hasn't responded to her letters, Sasha decides to seek him out. In the course of the scene she tries to relieve him of his guilt about his dying wife as well as convince him of the possibility of a happier future. He calls himself a failure and wonders why she loves him; she tells him that any girl prefers to love a man who is a failure than one who is a success because then the love is "active."

NIKOS I think the whole problem, because of the specificity of a play like *Ivanov*, is that your moment to moment work didn't make sense. You both did not go back between moments to your original impulse, your original need, and then start from there all over again.

293

So the different things you did were almost denying each other.

For example, [Ivanov], you decided, for no apparent reason, to clear the table, to deal with the bread crumbs, but there was so much that you were doing that did not connect you with something that the material is saying about him being a failure. He says, "I'm a kind of failure, I no longer feel anything." You didn't use that as the character's emotional center and your own emotional center as the blocks that everything else builds from.

[Sasha], sometimes you went towards him and dealt with love, and sometimes you dealt with understanding, and sometimes you dealt with him with annoyance, as when you said, "You haven't come to see us," and sometimes you dealt with trying to manufacture a certain amount of energy with him. But there was really no emotional point of view. There was no possibility for inevitablity in your acting because you had not decided that she has come in to woo him, let's say, or take him away from his wife or to seduce him, or whatever. Whatever was hitting you, you were doing! So it was very interesting and very alive, but it was like doing two steps forward and one step back, three to the right, two to the left, etcetera.

The same thing with you [Ivanov]. Basically you were not dealing with Ivanov as a man who wants desperately to feel certain things, but he doesn't really feel anything. [Nikos acts out the ✶ following.] He is upset and he meanders and he drinks the wine in a certain way, the same way that he opens the book, the same way that he moves away from her, the same way that he goes and opens the windows – and by "the same way," I mean behavior that is always based on a certain, similar kind of need. Instead of having that need which informs everything you do, you on the other hand were – indiscriminate! Sometimes you were very active, sometimes you were very lethargic, you were leaving her to go and drink wine, you were going to break the bottle capriciously rather than saying, [Frustrated, upset.] "Okay, because you tell me to break something I will try to break it, I will try to break it! – No I better not break it, leave me alone, I can't even get up from my chair, [Elongated, loud.] – Please!"

Now it was almost like every moment was so different from every other moment, that you were not allowing the acting instrument to pile up each piece of information and make some kind of sense. Touch base. If you feel that the material is as colorful as that, touch base between lines. Touch base back to the main things that make you do the scene, with the main thread that is there. It is not that you obliterate the differences in the scene, but it's that they all are fed through the same kind of source.

You see, [Sasha], when you kept going and kneeling to him it seemed interesting, but when you knelt you only dealt with the love. You have to filter that love through the lack of patience that you have as well, your impatience with somebody like him. The same thing with you, [Ivanov]. There is no reason for you, every time you say one thing to her, to forget the fact that your other lines are "There is nothing I can do, please leave me alone." When you have a line like, "This is the dog, it's painted from life," it's not exclusively about how the picture was painted, you know! Everything you pick up, everything you do, comes out of the same needs which, in the end, spell something. In the scene I just saw, you, [Sasha], became Ivanov many times, and you [Ivanov] became Sasha. I did not know who was who! I did not know who was dragging and who was being dragged, I did not know who was pushing and who was being pushed.

Look at the circumstances of the material. She keeps trying to make you change, right? That presupposes that there is something sick about you, right? Now, it doesn't matter how you interpret it, you might interpret it that you're just a very lethargic person, you might interpret it that you're so confused and so messed up, but she's the one who keeps saying, "Come on, do it, change!" So obviously, in listening to all these lines, it should give you a clue of the character's emotional impotence, and because of that, a clue about the way the character has of dealing with life. But you kept changing, both of you, and you kept changing, not because the playwright gave you a way to change, and not because your partner was changing. One didn't relate to the other. There were all these interesting things you were doing but it was graffiti time, for both of you, rather than designing time, or planning time. I suggest that you think of the scene as much less horizontal – and much more vertical – in terms of – [Nikos acts it out, vocally building one thing on top of another.] "I'm going to deal with the fact that I'm so upset, and so concerned and I just don't have the energy to be dealing with that woman!"

So, I think that moment-to-moment acting in a scene does not necessarily mean that each moment has to be so different from the others, all it means is that the adaptations are different, but the center of the material is the same. If you find the center of your acting, the acting becomes easy and inevitable, and then, of course, it *appears* inevitable which is great, which is what we all want. And the acting also appears accidental. But if you do not find that point of view, that center, then it's almost like everything that comes into the scene

295

grabs you in a different way – not further on the road toward wherever the scene is going, but as a distraction. You were both very distracted in terms of what you were dealing with in the scene, because I think that you did not have the strong reference, point of reference in terms of the needs of your characters.

In Greece, you know, people bring pine cones to weddings, why I don't know! But there's an expression, "Don't leave the wedding to look for the pine cones." You know? I mean, Chekhov says it, it's the doctor's line from *The Sea Gull*. About not going down the picturesque road. [Dorn, in Act I of *The Sea Gull* says: "In a work of art there must be a clear definite idea. You must know what your object is in writing, for if you follow that picturesque road without a definite aim, you will go astray and your talent will be your ruin."]

You have to do moment-to-moment acting in Chekhov, but it's not *picturesque* moment-to-moment. It's moment-to-moment that is informed by a consistent emotional need.

Nikos, directing.

A COMMON PASSION
Afterword by Steve Lawson

No one who ever knew Nikos Psacharopoulos would claim he was temperamentally akin to Anton Chekhov. "When I know what I want," Nikos once told an interviewer, "I'm very definite about it, and then it's a monologue rather than a dialogue... If I have to be a tyrant, I will be a tyrant." (John Guare, two of whose plays were produced in Williamstown, once mused that the place struck him as a democratic empire, except that it wasn't so much a kingdom as a baroque mini-series.) Given the historical portrait of Chekhov the man – reticent, self-effacing, without apparent ego – the surface contrast with WTF's founding spirit is considerable.

And yet. Having watched Nikos in action for twenty years, I was always fascinated that someone of his fiery Hellenic heritage felt (and showed) such kinship with the major plays of the Russian master. I'm not sure if he knew the line, but I suspect Nikos would have liked a sentence of Chekhov's: "Dissatisfaction with oneself is one of the foundation stones of every real talent." In his work at WTF, above all with the playwrights he adored, such as Chekhov or Tennessee Williams – Nikos was restless, never content to rest on laurels achieved.   N + C

It's always seemed right to me that *The Sea Gull* – so intimately concerned with trying to live a life in art, with the creative self coexisting with the everyday – was the first Chekhov play Nikos directed. The then-Williamstown Summer Theatre had survived seven seasons, some by the skin of its teeth, and the prospect of Chekhov made many observers uneasy. But in a subsequent poll, audiences named *The Sea Gull* as the season's best production.

That response, so warm and unexpected, seems to have galvanized Nikos. A flood of Chekhov productions followed in the next twenty-five years – fifteen in all, plus half a dozen versions of Gorky and Turgenev, all but four directed by Nikos. Almost as if the urge to work, the yearning for change and growth so central to Chekhov's art, had communicated itself to Nikos as an informal credo for his theater.   N + C

In the last act of *The Sea Gull*, Nina confides to Treplev what drives her existence as a struggling actress, that "what matters isn't the fame, it isn't the glory...it's how to endure." At the end of *Uncle Vanya*, Sonia tells Vanya that "we must work" – a line echoed in Tusenbach's paeans to the future in *The Three Sisters* and Trofimov's and Lopakhin's speeches in *The Cherry Orchard*.

Soldiering on, facing an uncertain tomorrow: the leitmotif sounds again and again. In his superb chapter on Chekhov in *The Making of Modern Drama*, Richard Gilman makes a shrewd observation on the playwright's career:

> *"In a manner for which there is scarcely any parallel among the important modern dramatists, Chekhov's plays, particularly the last three – and there are only five major ones together – do seem to merge with one another to form a long, unbroken work."*

We may be in Perm, buried in the country, on an estate; the characters may be officers or caretakers or perpetual students. But Astrov and Arkadina, Varya and Vershinin are offshoots of one extraordinary tree, and the rewards of constant exposure to these plays can be great...as I and many others at Williamstown discovered.

If Chekhov lies in the details, then it's anecdotes that come to mind from the nine Chekhov productions I saw at WTF. My first experience was the 1969 version of *The Cherry Orchard*, three aspects of which have lingered in memory. First, Santo Loquasto's magnificent set, which solved the perennial problem of the Act III ballroom by placing the action on a balcony overlooking the (unseen) dancing below. Second, the late William Hansen's mysteriously beautiful incarnation of old Firs – as it turned out, his last performance at Williamstown. Third, my brief career as a sound board operator. Hit by opening-night nerves, I neglected to switch speakers from the twittering balalaikas at intermission. So, when Act III began, the "distant" martial band came crashing out into the auditorium, deafening the audience and rendering the actors inaudible. Most reviews the next morning mentioned this gaffe, often before analyzing the performances, and that same day I was taken off sound, never to return. In its tragic/pratfall way, a very Chekhovian experience.

The 1974 *Sea Gull* triumphed over a heat wave, a gas crisis, and the need to film the play for "Theatre in America" in a few short days. On the strength of a period of expansion, the theater was now referred to as the Williamstown Festival, and expectations were high. But Mel Gussow's laudatory *New York Times* review began, "Many of the finest actors and actresses in America have appeared in many of the world's finest plays at the Williamstown Theatre Festival," and *The Sea Gull* flew. This was the show which brought Blythe Danner up to portray Nina – her first Williamstown role, and the first of several Chekhovian parts she would play here in years to come.

Watching Blythe, Lee Grant, and Frank Langella film *The Sea Gull* almost made up for my being tapped as an extra, in which capacity I was required to swim bare-assed in a freezing mountain pond and haul heavy trunks and furniture around. In the throes of his TV directing debut, Nikos was in his glory. He especially enjoyed the chance to issue commands over the speaker system from the command trailer, crackling orders like an Athenian Wizard of Oz: "Stephen, move the chair four inches to the left"..."Stephen, the chair"..."*Did you move the chair?*" I kept yelling back (to the air) that I *had* moved the damn chair, but he was happily oblivious.

Then there was the high-culture moment when several production assistant/extras were sprawled around in a stupor, humming snatches of song to stay awake. (This being PBS, it was two a.m.). Fresh as a daisy and ready to shoot the big Act IV Nina-Treplev scene, Nikos was passing through the room and abruptly whirled toward us. "*What was that?*" he demanded. We all looked blank. "That song you were singing, it's *beautiful*! We'll use it for underscoring when Blythe comes running across the field..."

Somehow, I found my voice. "Nikos," I managed to say, "that was the theme song from *I Love Lucy*." He stared at us, intoned "Oh," and left. (Credit where credit is due: Arthur B. Rubinstein ultimately composed a fine score for the teleplay.)

And there was the high-powered *Cherry Orchard* of 1980. As if it weren't enough to have Colleen Dewhurst (Ranevskaya), Maria Tucci (Varya), Austin Pendleton (Trofimov), Kate Burton (Anya), Celeste Holm (Charlotte), Tom Atkins (Lopahkin), George Morfogen (Gayev), and John Glover (Epihodov) on hand, two of the smallest roles – Dunyasha and Yasha – were played respectively by Blythe Danner and Christopher Reeve. As that local critic wrote, this was probably the first *Cherry Orchard* on record where the maid and butler got entrance applause.

In terms of sheer achievement, I'd single out Nikos' 1976 *Three Sisters* – along with the RSC's 1979 version of the play, the best Chekhov I've ever seen. Performances, directorial nuance, design: all coalesced into a remarkable whole. (More than one interview in this book cites this production.) The final, unforgettable image of the three sisters spinning in an exultant dance while the doctor, played by the great William Swetland, sat nearby in impotent self-pity. Or the moment when Blythe Danner's incandescent Masha literally hurled herself through the air at the departing Vershinin. Vignettes such as these illuminated the text: they made me *see*. And see why

Gilman rightly called this "one of the greatest of all plays, a drama as inexhaustible in its way as *Oedipus Rex* and *Hamlet* and *Lear* are in theirs."

Yet the prevailing mood of this production was comic, which shocked some of the more academic-minded reviewers. *The Three Sisters*? That lugubrious play in which nobody ever gets to Moscow? What such a sanctifying, tunnel-vision approach ignores is that Chekhov is often terribly funny, as any writer would be who sees humanity so clearly. And at Nikos' best, out of an inchoate deep feeling for Chekhov's unique music and his own marvelously tangled syntax ("If I don't want them to hear what I am saying, I will not."), he proved to be a match for the work.

That word again! Eulogizing Nikos in a 1989 *New York Times* article, I ended by saying: "He had a life in art; what always mattered was the work." More than once, he vowed that his happiest times were never on opening nights or after great notices, but in rehearsal or the classroom. Go through the "Acting Notebook," the second half of this volume, and as his students take their first halting, uncertain stabs at scenes from Chekhov, Nikos' intensely empathic relationship with these young men and women burns through. And the esteem and affection of the professional actors he worked with color all the interviews.

These interviews move me deeply. Yes, they're with an ensemble of thinking, articulate people. But even more, they exude a feeling of *communion* in the best sense, not some facile, pseudo-mystical, touchy-feeley process. When you read and reread these comments and recollections – overlapping, cross-fertilizing, even contradictory (very Chekhovian!) – you immerse yourself in the tumult of fine artists *at work*. At work with a director/producer who they trusted...to guide them into the heart of a playwright they loved.

Steve Lawson

* * * * * * * * * * * * * * * * * * * *

Steve Lawson marks his 25th year with WTF in 1993. He started there at age 19, served as the theater's first dramaturg, and later became co-associate artistic director. Recipient of degrees from Williams College (1971) and Yale School of Drama (1976), he has been a journalist, playwright and director. Steve's writing credits for television include The Elephant Man, L.A. Law, St. Elsewhere, and the PBS special Broadway's Dreamers: The Legacy of the Group Theater, which won a 1990 Emmy Award and garnered him a nomination for writing.

CHEKHOV CHRONOLOGY
AT WILLIAMSTOWN

Chronology of Williamstown Theatre Festival
Chekhov Productions

"...a play gives you really not a concept;
a concept is an intellectual thing which is
all wrong for the theater.
Theater is like a vision, a dream,
a nightmare or an image -
I refer to plays in terms of color really..."

Nikos Psacharopoulos

THE THREE SISTERS *1987*
Directed by Nikos Psacharopoulos
Setting by John Conklin
Costumes by Jess Goldstein
Lighting by Pat Collins

Olga	Roberta Maxwell
Masha	Amy Irving
Irina	Kate Burton
Andrei	Stephen Collins
Natasha	Amy Van Nostrand
Kulygin	John Heard
Anfisa	Anne Pitoniak
Ferapont	Frank Hamilton
Vershinin	Christopher Walken
Tusenbach	Rob Lowe
Solyony	Daniel Davis
Chebutykin	Louis Zorich
Fedotik	Marcus Giamatti
Rode	Michael Unger

UNCLE VANYA *1984*
Directed by Jeff Bleckner
Settings by Andrew Jackness
Costumes by Jess Goldstein
Lighting by Paul Gallo

Nanny	Katherine Squire
Astrov	Edward Herrmann
Vanya	Austin Pendleton
Serebryakov	Tom Brennan
Sonya	Diane Wiest
Telyegin	Louis Beachner
Yelena	Blythe Danner
Mrs. Voinitsky	Mary Fogarty
Workers	Tony Goldwyn, Mark Wade

IVANOV *1983*
Directed by John Madden
Setting by Kevin Rupnik
Costumes by Dunya Ramicova
Lighting by Paul Gallo

Ivanov	Christopher Walken
Borkin	Clarence Felder
Anna Petrovna	Diane Wiest
County Shabelsky	George Morfogen
Lvov	Christian Clemenson
Lebedev	Tom Brennan
Zinaeeda	Barbara Orson
Sasha	Laila Robins
Babakina	Chris Weatherhead
Avdoyta	Ruth Maynard

THE CHERRY ORCHARD *1969*

Directed by Nikos Psacharopoulos
Settings and Costumes by Santo Loquasto
Lighting by Richard Devin

Dunyasha..Barbette Tweed
Lopakhin...Lee Wallace
Epihodov ....Stan Wiklinski
Firs...William Hansen
Ranevskaya...Olympia Dukakis
Anya ....Laurie Kennedy
Varya ....Joyce Ebert
Gayev...Charles Siebert
Charlotta...Sloane Shelton
Pishchik..Stephen Mendillo
Yasha..David Ackroyd
Trofimov...Austin Pendleton

THE SEA GULL *1968*

Directed by Nikos Psacharopoulos
Settings by Will Steven Armstrong
Costumes by John Conklin and Linda Fisher
Lighting by Peter Hunt

Irina Arkadina..Carolyn Coates
Treplev...David Ackroyd
Sorin ....William Hansen
Nina ....Joyce Ebert
Shamrayev ....Philip Polito
Paulina...Olympia Dukakis
Masha ....Janet Sarno
Trigorin..Maury Cooper
Dorn...Louis Zorich
Medvedenko ....Tom Brennan

THE THREE SISTERS *1965*

Directed by Nikos Psacharopoulos
Settings by D. Atwood Jenkins
Costumes by D. Hudson Sheffield
Lighting by Peter Hunt

Olga ....Carolyn Coates
Masha ....Joyce Ebert
Irina ....Laurie Kennedy
Natasha...Janet Sarno
Andrei...Tom Brennan
Chebutykin ....William Hansen
Tusenbach...Michael Ebert
Solyony...Frank Langella
Anfisa ....Margaret Barker
Ferapont..Paul Barstow
Vershinin ....James Noble
Kulygin...Tony Capodilupo

THE SEA GULL *1974*
Directed by Nikos Psacharopoulos
Setting by Robert Darling
Costumes by Linda Fisher
Lighting by Peter Hunt

Medvedenko ....David Clennon
Masha ....Marian Mercer
Sorin ....William Swetland
Treplev ....Frank Langella
Nina..Blythe Danner
Paulina..Olympia Dukakis
Dorn..Louis Zorich
Shamrayev...George Ede
Arkadina...Lee Grant
Trigorin...Kevin McCarthy

UNCLE VANYA *1972*
Directed by Austin Pendleton
Settings by Santo Loquasto
Costumes by Linda Fisher
Lighting by Roger Meeker

Marina ....Joan Pape
Astrov ....Charles Siebert
Vanya..Lee Wallace
Serebryakov...Emery Battis
Sonya..Laurie Kennedy
Telyegin ....Richard Massur
Yelena...Maria Tucci
Mrs. Voinitsky...Ellene Winn

THE THREE SISTERS *1970*
Directed by Nikos Psacharopoulos
Settings and Costumes by Steven Rubin
Lighting by Richard Devin

Olga..Olympia Dukakis
Masha ....Joyce Ebert
Irina ....Laurie Kennedy
Natasha...Linda Gulder
Andrei...Tom Atkins
Chebutykin ....Louis Zorich
Tusenbach...Yusef Bulos
Solyony...David Clennon
Anfisa...Frances Chaffee
Ferapont..George Ebeling
Vershinin ....Richard Venture
Kulygin...Stephen Mendillo

THE CHERRY ORCHARD *1980*
Directed by Nikos Psacharopoulos
Settings by Andrew Jackness
Costumes by Dunya Ramicova
Lighting by Roger Meeker

Ranevskaya..Colleen Dewhurst
Anya...Kate Burton
Varya..Maria Tucci
Gayev...George Morfogen
Lopakhin...Tom Atkins
Trofimov...Austin Pendleton
Pishchik...Robert Black
Charlotta...Celeste Holm
Epihodov...John Glover
Dunyasha...Blythe Danner
Firs..Jerome Collamore
Yasha...Christopher Reeve

PLATONOV *1977*
Directed by Nikos Psacharopoulos
Settings by Steven Rubin
Costumes by Dunya Ramicova
Lighting by Roger Meeker

Anna Petrovna..Carrie Nye
Sergei...Richard Kavanaugh
Sofia..Jennifer Harmon
Platonov...Joel Grey
Sasha...Colby Willis
Triletski..Peter Evans
Ivan Triletski...Michael Prince
Glagolyev...Richard Woods
Kiril...John Ellis
Abram..Emery Battis
Maria Efimova..Joan Pape
Ossip...George Morfogen

THE THREE SISTERS *1976*
Directed by Nikos Psacharopoulos
Settings by Tony Straiges
Costumes by Zack Brown
Lighting by Roger Meeker

Olga...Olympia Dukakis
Masha..Blythe Danner
Irina..Laurie Kennedy
Natasha..Barbara Eda-Young
Andrei..Richard Kavanaugh
Chebutykin..William Swetland
Tusenbach...Austin Pendleton
Solyony..John Glover
Anfisa..Grayce Grant
Ferapont...Bernard Frawley
Vershinin..Ken Howard
Kulygin..George Guidall

UNCLE VANYA *1964*

Directed by Tom Brennan
Settings by Leor Curtiss Warner
Costumes by D. Hudson Sheffield
Lighting by Peter Hunt and William Mintzer

Serebryakov..Tom Brennan
Yelena...Margaret O'Neill
Sonya..Dixie Marguis
Vanya..Louis Zorich
Astrov...Shepperd Strudwick
Telyegin..William Hansen
Marina..Belle Boch
Mrs. Voinitsky..Frances Chaffee

THE CHERRY ORCHARD *1963*
Directed by Nikos Psacharopoulos
Settings by John Conklin
Costumes by Jeanne Button
Lighting by Peter Hunt

Dunyasha..Barbara Harrison
Lopakhin...Louis Zorich
Epihodov...James Noble
Firs...William Hansen
Ranevskaya...Carolyn Coates
Anya...Margaret Cowles
Varya..Joyce Ebert
Gayev...George Ebeling
Charlotta...Olympia Dukakis
Pishchik..Anthony Capodilupo
Yasha..Michael Ebert
Trofimov..Tom Brennan

THE SEA GULL *1962*

Directed by Nikos Psacharopoulos
Setting by Robert Darling
Costumes by Lloyd Evans
Lighting by Peter Hunt

Arkadina...Carolyn Coates
Treplev..Michael Ebert
Sorin...William Hansen
Nina..Joyce Ebert
Shamrayev...Robert Mathews
Paulina..Margaret Barker
Masha...Sue Ann Gilfillan
Trigorin...John Cunningham
Dorn..John O'Leary
Medvedenko...Tom Brennan

Jean Hackett

Jean Hackett graduated from NYU and studied acting at Circle in the Square Theater School and at the Royal Academy of Dramatic Art in London. While completing her training she spent four seasons as a member of Williamstown Theatre Festival's non-equity acting company, and returned over the years as a member of the equity company, which she was part of for Nikos Psacharopoulos' last production, *The Legend of Oedipus*. In 1982, along with Steve Lawson and Mr. Psacharopoulos, she was co-adapter *of Tennessee Williams, A Celebration*, a six hour collage of scenes from all the Williams plays with a cast of sixty.

Ms. Hackett has played roles on and off-Broadway, as well as at many of the country's leading regional theaters. She recently moved to Los Angeles where she has done television and stage work; and produced, directed and acted in the literary cabaret, *Rants, Rhymes and Lies*, a show honored by a citation from Mayor Tom Bradley for raising funds to restore the public libraries destroyed in the April, 1992 civil unrest. Ms. Hackett is also at work on a collection of short stories.

Photo Credits

Opposite Introduction	*Christopher Read*
Opposite page 1	*C G Wolfson*
page 18	*C G Wolfson*
page 82	*J. Schuyler*
page 92	*B. Marshak*
page 104	*B. Marshak*
page 116	*B. Marshak*
page 138	*J. Glover*
page 160	*Jan A. Wein*
page 172	*B. Marshak*
page 198	*J. Schuyler*
page 278	*Debra Rubenstein*
page 292	*B. Marshak*

The publisher kindly thanks the Williamstown Theatre Festival for the use of the photos in this book.